The Politics of Imagination

The Politics of Imagination offers a multidisciplinary perspective on the contemporary relationship between politics and the imagination. What role does our capacity to form images play in politics? And can we define politics as a struggle for people's imagination? As a result of the increasingly central place of the media in our lives, the political role of imagination has undergone a massive quantitative and a qualitative change. As such, there has been a revival of interest in the concept of imagination, as the intimate connections between our capacity to form images and politics becomes more and more evident. Bringing together scholars from different disciplines and theoretical outlooks, *The Politics of Imagination* examines how the power of imagination reverberates in the various ambits of social and political life: in law, history, art, gender, economy, religion and the social sciences. It will be of considerable interest to those with contemporary interests in philosophy, political philosophy, political science, legal theory, gender studies, sociology, nationalism, identity studies, cultural studies and media studies.

Chiara Bottici is Assistant Professor of Philosophy at the Department of Philosophy of the New School for Social Research, New York.

Benoît Challand is visiting Associate Professor at the Department of Politics of the New School for Social Research and Lecturer at the University of Bologna.

The Politics of Imagination

Edited by
Chiara Bottici
and Benoît Challand

Birkbeck
LAW PRESS

First published 2011
by Birkbeck Law Press
2 Park Square, Milton Park, Abingdon, Oxon OX14 4RN

Simultaneously published in the USA and Canada
by Birkbeck Law Press
711 Third Avenue, New York, NY 10017

Birkbeck Law Press is an imprint of the Taylor & Francis Group, an informa business

British Library Cataloguing in Publication Data
A catalogue record for this book is available from the British Library

Library of Congress Cataloguing in Publication Data
The politics of imagination / edited by Chiara Bottici and Benoît Challand.
p. cm.
Includes bibliographical references and index.
1. Imagination—Political aspects. 2. Imagery (Psychology)—Political aspects. 3. Visualization—Political aspects. 4. Political science—Philosophy. I. Bottici, Chiara. II. Challand, Benoît, 1972–
JA71.P6428 2011
320.01—dc22 2010047899

ISBN: 978–0–415–60154–2 (hbk)
ISBN: 978–0–203–81609–7 (ebk)

Typeset in Garamond
by Keystroke, Station Road, Codsall, Wolverhampton

MIX
Paper from responsible sources
FSC www.fsc.org FSC® C004839

Printed and bound in Great Britain by
TJI Digital, Padstow, Cornwall

Contents

Acknowledgements

This book has a long story. The idea of a collective work on the politics of imagination owes much to the activities of the 'Collettivo EUI', an interdisciplinary group of European scholars and political activists that was active from 1999 until 2005 at the European University Institute in Florence (Italy). In particular, it was during the discussions that accompanied the preparation of the first European Social Forum in Florence in November 2002 that the project took shape. In the first place, we wish therefore to thank all regular members of the Collettivo EUI, who, through their actions as well as their ideas, contributed to plant the seeds of our struggle for imagination. Although the original idea to consider politics as a struggle for people's imagination stemmed from a discussion between the two editors, we feel very much indebted to this political experience. With its multinational and variegated composition, the Collettivo EUI proved to be an ideal place in which to challenge established ways of thinking and thus putting imagination to work.

The project then developed in the following years. In 2007 it was thanks to the generous support of Bo Stråth that we were able to convene a workshop entitled 'Politics as Struggle for People's Imagination' (25–26 January 2007). It is on that occasion that most of the papers gathered in this book were first presented and discussed. Our deepest thanks go to therefore Bo Stråth both for his support and his indefatigable constructive feedback throughout the years. We are also grateful to the European University Institute, in particular the History Department, for hosting the event as well as to all those who participated in the discussions that animated those two days for their comments on earlier drafts of this book.

In the course of the preparation of this book, other people have joined the project, adding their specific competencies to our project so as to give rise to a truly multidisciplinary perspective. We wish to thank them for believing in this project and lending us their invaluable competencies. This has also enabled us to benefit from an intergenerational exchange where the experience gained in different historical moments of reactivation of political imagination (in particular 1968 and the new global movement of the beginning of this millennium) have been compared and put in dialogue with one another.

We want to thank the anonymous reviewers for their useful comments. Other scholars have shared with us their comments and ideas on politics and imagination, either during personal exchanges or at international conferences such as the annual Prague meeting on philosophy and social sciences, where some of the following chapters were first presented and discussed. We would therefore like to express our gratitude to Amy Allen, Irene Becci, Hakim Boulhares, Rainer Forst, Nathalie Karagiannis, Angela Kuehner, Christian Marazzi, Elena Pulcini, Jean Terrier, Camil Ungureanu and Peter Wagner for their comments and feedback. We also thank all contributors for their patience in the different stages of the production. Susan Buck-Morss' contribution has been published elsewhere previously and we therefore thank the editors of *Papers of Surrealism* for their permission to reproduce 'Visual studies and global imagination' (Issue 2 summer 2004).

Furthermore, Benoît Challand would like to acknowledge a generous grant from the European Commission (Marie Curie Intra-European Fellowship, Grant No. 041674) that allowed him to work on, among others, the issues of Islam, imagination and politics.

Finally, for hosting our 'Politics of imagination' in his series as well as providing invaluable support in a number of ways, we wish to thank Costas Douzinas and the staff at Birkbeck Law Press. Without him, this book would not have been possible.

Notes on contributors

Laura Bazzicalupo is Professor of Political Philosophy at the University of Salerno, where she is also the Director of Department of Theory and History of Law and Politics. She has written *Superbia. La passione dell'essere* (Il Mulino 2008), *Il governo delle vite. Biopolitica e economia* (Laterza 2006) and *Politica identità potere* (Torino 2004). She has contributed to various journals such as *Diacritics*, *Filosofia politica*, *Ragion pratica* and *Storia contemporanea* with works on biopolitics, representation and the constitution of political subjectivity.

Chiara Bottici is Assistant Professor of Philosophy at the Department of Philosophy of the New School for Social Research. Her recent publications include *A Philosophy of Political Myth* (Cambridge University Press 2007) and *Uomini e stati. Percorsi di un'analogia,* (ETS 2004; English translation *Men and States*, Palgrave 2009). Also with Benoît Challand, she has written a book entitled *The Myth of the Clash between Civilisations* (Routledge 2010). She has contributed to various international journals such as *Journal of Political Philosophy*, *European Journal of Social Theory*, *European Journal of Political Theory*, *Philosophy and Social Criticism*, *Iride* and *Thesis Eleven*.

Susan Buck-Morss is Professor of Political Philosophy and Social Theory at Cornell University. She is the author of *The Origin of Negative Dialectics: Theodor W. Adorno, Walter Benjamin, and the Frankfurt Institute* (Macmillan 1977), the *Dialectics of Seeing: Walter Benjamin and the Arcades Project* (MIT 1989), *Dreamwork and Catastrophe: the Passing of Mass Utopia in East and West* (MIT 2000), *Thinking Past Terror* (Verso 2003) and *Hegel, Haiti and Universal History* (University of Pittsburgh Press 2008). Her work has been translated into, French, German, Greek, Hebrew, Italian, Japanese, Korean, Portuguese, Serbian, Spanish and Turkish.

Adriano Bugliani, philosopher and psychologist, is Senior Lecturer of Philosophy at the University of Florence. His chief area of interest is continental philosophy and theories of psychoanalysis. He is the author of *La storia della coscienza in Fichte* (Guerini 1998), *La discrezione dello spirito. La psicanalisi e Hegel* (Mimesis 2004) and *Contro di sè. Potere e misconoscimento*

(Mimesis 2009). He has published many essays on German idealism, Husserl's phenomenology, psychology and psychoanalysis, contributing to such journals as *Rethinking History*, *Atque. Materiali tra filosofia e psicoterapia*, *Epoché*, *Filosofia Politica*, *Giornale critico della filosofia italiana*, *Intersezioni* and *Rivista di storia della filosofia and Studi sulla formazione*. He is member of the editorial board of *Iride. Filosofia e discussione pubblica*.

Benoît Challand is visiting Associate Professor at the Department of Politics of the New School for Social Research and Lecturer at the University of Bologna. His major publications include *La Ligue Marxiste Révolutionaire (1969–1980)* (Fribourg University Press 2000) and *Palestinian Civil Society and Foreign Donors: the Power to Promote and to Exclude* (Routledge 2009). He has contributed to the *European Journal of Social Theory*, *Middle Eastern Studies*, *International Journal of Middle Eastern Studies* and *Religion, State and Society*. His work has been translated into Arabic, French, Italian and Japanese.

Alessandro Ferrara is Professor of Political Philosophy at the University of Rome 'Tor Vergata' and President of the Italian Association of Political Philosophy. He is the author of *The Force of the Example. Explorations in the Paradigm of Judgment* (Columbia University Press 2008), *Modernity and Authenticity. A Study of the Social and Ethical Thought of Jean-Jacques Rousseau* (State University of New York Press 1993), *Reflective Authenticity. Rethinking the Project of Modernity* (Routledge 1998) and *Justice and Judgment. The Rise and the Prospect of the Judgment Model in Contemporary Political Philosophy* (Sage 1999). He is on the editorial board of the series *New Directions in Critical Theory* at Columbia University Press and of the journals *Constellations*, *Philosophy and Social Criticism*, *European Journal of Philosophy*.

Thomas Hippler is Lecturer at the Institut d'Études Politiques de Lyon. He has been Research Fellow of the École normale supérieure de lettres et sciences humaines in Lyon, of the Deutsche Forschungsgemeinschaft and of Oxford University. His research interests include the European Enlightenment, the French Revolution and its aftermath in Europe, continental philosophy and political theory. He has published *Soldats et Citoyens* (Presses Universitaires de France 2006; English translation under contract at Routledge) and contributed, among others, to *European Review of History*, *Annales Historiques de la Révolution Française* and *Studia Spinozana*.

Alana Lentin is a social and political theorist, working on the critical theorisation of race, racism and anti-racism. She is Lecturer in Sociology at Sussex University and member of the Centre for Social and Political Thought and the Sussex Centre for Cultural Studies. She is the author of *Racism and Anti-Racism in Europe* (Pluto Press 2004) and *Racism: a Beginner's Guide* (OneWorld 2008). She is also co-editor of *Race and State* (with Ronit Lentin, 2006). She has published articles in *European Journal of Social Theory* and *Patterns of Prejudice* among other journals.

María Pía Lara teaches Moral and Political Philosophy at the Universidad Autónoma Metropolitana in Mexico City. She has published on the subjects of critical theory, feminism, moral philosophy and politics. She is the author of *La Democracia como Proyecto de Identidad Etica* (Anthropos 1992), *Moral Textures. Feminist Narratives in the Public Sphere* (University of California Press/Polity Press 1998) and *Narrating Evil: A Postmetaphysical Theory of Reflective Judgment* (University of Columbia Press 2007). She is also the editor of *Rethinking Evil: Contemporary Perspectives* (University of California Press 2001). Her work has been translated into Czech, Italian, Spanish and Swedish. She is also on the editorial boards of *Constellations*, *La Casa del Tiempo*, *Revista Internacional de Filosofia Politica*, *Signos* and *Thesis Eleven*.

Armando Salvatore is a sociologist of culture and communication who investigates various dimensions of religious traditions and secular formations in historical and comparative perspective. He teaches at the University of Naples 'L'Orientale', Dept. of Social Sciences, and runs a research project on sovereignty and solidarity at the Humboldt Center for Social and Political Research, Berlin. His latest book is *The Public Sphere: Liberal Modernity, Catholicism, Islam* (Palgrave 2007, pb 2010).

Meili Steele is Professor of Comparative Literature at the University of South Carolina. His research interests include literary theory, political theory and the intertwinement between philosophy and literature. He is the author of *Hiding from History: Politics and Public Imagination* (Cornell University Press 2005), *Theorizing Textual Subject: Agency and Oppression* (Cambridge University Press 1997), *Critical Confrontation: Literary Theories in Dialogue* (University of South Carolina Press 1997) and *Realism and the Drama of Reference* (Pennsylvania State University Press 1988).

Hayden White is University Professor at the University of California, Santa Cruz, and Professor of Comparative Literature at Stanford University. His books have had a profound influence on the practice and conceptualization of all the humanities disciplines and include, among others, *Metahistory: The Historical Imagination in Nineteenth-century Europe* (Johns Hopkins University Press 1973), *Tropics of Discourse* (Johns Hopkins University Press 1978), *The Content of the Form* (Johns Hopkins University Press 1987) and *Figural Realism* (Johns Hopkins University Press 1997). His work has been translated into numerous foreign languages.

Introduction

Chiara Bottici and Benoît Challand

We often hear people saying that our politicians lack imagination. In the world of global governance, politics seems to have become simple administration within a general neoliberal consensus and with very little variation in the political options actually available. No much space is left for imagination understood as the radical capacity to envisage things differently and construct alternative political projects. Those who argue that 'another world is possible' – to quote the slogan of the new global movements – are easily labelled as unrealistic, if not as fanatical.[1] As a consequence, they are easily expunged from the spectrum of viable political options.

Yet the political world we live in is a world full of images. One only has to think of the role of the media in our political life. If we compare what politics was a few centuries ago and what it has become now, we cannot but perceive a fundamental change. Politics was once the activity that concerned a few people (the rulers), with whom most ordinary people had almost no visual contact in the course of their life. Today, by way of contrast, rulers are constantly in front of us: their images dominate our screens, nourish, solicit and perhaps even saturate our imagination. Democratisation and the mediatisation of politics has brought about a deep revolution in the nature of politics itself, so much so that politics has become inseparable from the herd of images that daily enters the houses of billions of spectators around the globe.

Perhaps in no other phenomenon is this as clear as in the current resurgence of religion and the politics of identity on the global scene. If the emergence of new social movements for an alternative globalisation was an attempt to

1 I use the more correct term 'new global movement' rather than the 'no global movement' to point to the fact that the new social movements that lined up under the slogan 'another world is possible' are actually movements in favour of globalisation and not against it. The reason why corporate media used the label 'no global' is that they took the perspective of neoliberal ideology according to which to criticise the neoliberal dogmas of free trade and deregulations amounts to a critique of globalisation itself. As an accurate analysis of programme and ideas that circulate among them shows, this is far from being the case. On the content of the critique to neoliberalism of the new global movements, see Graeber 2002.

rekindle political imagination, 9/11 has made it explode, so to speak. All of a sudden terrifying new political scenarios counterpoising 'us' and the 'others' have appeared. While the myth of a clash between civilisation unfolded, a new struggle for people's imagination started: terrorists have been imagined everywhere, thus justifying restrictions to fundamental civic liberties and military enterprises. In turn, the exportation of the 'war on terror' abroad, with all the innocent casualties it has brought about, has further fomented negative representations of the 'west' with their corollary of hate and fanaticism. All this has not simply increased the power of images, but is substantial to it as images became weapons in themselves. We live in a globalising society which eliminates geographical distance only to reap it internally in the form of a spectacular clash between 'us' and 'them' (Bottici and Challand 2010).

Paradoxically, in the epoch of the global village created by the diffusion of the media on a global scale, we often lack the most relevant information about others and even about ourselves. To paraphrase Buck-Morss, we constitute a 'media-saturated but still information-starved public' (2003: 3). Global images are selected by the golden rule of the audience. It is only what makes news by capturing people's attention that is circulated. The result is that the spectacle prevails over the content. We are inundated by images that play with the register of emotions and move imagination, but often do not convey the most relevant information. Debord's prophecy of a society of spectacle (Debord 1994) has been fulfilled. The world is no longer just an immense collection of commodities. It has become a collection of spectacles.

Globalisation seems to have even brought this process to a further stage, so that the need emerges to further reconsider some of Debord's assumptions. Today society of spectacle is *global* not just because it has annihilated geographical distance, but also because it is increasingly difficult to counterpoise it to the reality of facts. Virtual images are not only commodities which can be reproduced on an industrial scale.[2] They are ongoing processes of perpetual maintenance. It is not only their authenticity that has got lost. It is the very possibility of determining a status of truth whatsoever that has vanished. We are now so used to such a condition that it does not come as a surprise to hear that soon after 9/11 videotapes went on sale in China showing the horrific highlights sliced together with scenes from Hollywood disaster movies (Buruma and Margalit 2004: 13). The real thing – two flaming skyscrapers collapsing on thousands of people – was not enough: only Hollywood imagination could capture the flavour of such a catastrophe. The status of truth of the images thus assembled did not matter. We needed a global spectacle adapted to the catastrophe and only Hollywood could offer it.

2 On this point, together with Debord 1994, see also the classic, Benjamin 2002. For a discussion of Benjamin's analysis of the status of images in the age of their technological reproducibility, as well as of its limits, see Bottici's and Buck-Morss' contributions to this volume.

How to account for the paradox of such a world full of images but deprived of imagination? Have images themselves saturated our political imagination? What has politics become after such a revolution? Is it not first and foremost a struggle for people's imagination? The aim of this book is to address those questions by rethinking the nexus of politics and imagination in a multi-disciplinary perspective. In doing so, the contributors to this volume do not start from a pre-given view of both politics (or the political) and imagination, but rather try to explore the different ways to conceptualise both them and their intertwinement.

Yet they all share the idea that we should go beyond the restricted view of imagination as mere fantasy. The idea that imagination is the faculty to represent what does not exist, the unreal, and is therefore only relevant to the ambit of aesthetics, although widespread, is a very limited one. It had its moment around the 18th century, when, as a consequence of the triumph of modern science, imagination was seen as a potential threat for the methodical work of reason and was thus more comfortably placed within the newly constituted ambit of the aesthetic (Friese 2001: 7197; Vattimo 1999: 529). It is still an influential view, not least because it is conveyed by common usage, as in expressions such as 'this is the fruit of your imagination'.

But within the history of western philosophy itself, there is also a broader view going back as far as Aristotle that has recently been recovered from different sides. In this view, imagination is more than mere fantasy: it is the capacity to produce images in the most general sense of the term, independently of the fact of whether what they represent actually exists or not. Imagination in this view also includes the capacity to represent what does not exist but it is not limited to it. It is a much more radical view, in that it includes the production of images of both existing and non-existing objects. To put it in Castoriadis' terms, it is the radical faculty to produce images in the sense of *Bilder*, that is, images without which there would not be any thought at all and which, therefore, precede any thought (Castoriadis 1994).

No other author has stressed the radical character of imagination more systematically than Castoriadis. In his view, imagination is radical, in the double sense that without it there could be no reality as such and that it can always potentially question its objects by disclosing possible alternatives (Castoriadis 1987, 1994). It is a view that thus recovers the fundamental Kantian insight that imagination is the transcendental faculty of synthesis *par excellence* in that it is able to unify the manifold into a single image, but it is also a view that goes beyond Kant. Not only because Kant retreats from this discovery that he makes in the first edition of his *Critique of Pure Reason* and later then relegates imagination to a more intermediary role between intuition and intellect (Arnason 1994; Rundell 1994). Castoriadis goes further than Kant in that, in contrast to him, he does not conceive of imagination merely as an individual faculty. Picking up the thread of psychoanalysis, which has shown that the individual is created through a process of socialisation to the imaginary significations of every society, Castoriadis argued that we are immersed in the social imaginary in which we have grown up. By emphasising the importance of the social context in shaping the free imagination of individuals, Castoriadis overcomes the limits of the Kantian approach and the philosophy of the subject that it presupposes.

Although the different contributors to this volume do not share a common view of imagination, they all accept the assumption that we should go beyond the first and restricted meaning described here. In preparing this collection, we have asked the contributors to discuss the role of imagination understood as the capacity to produce image plays in politics and thus also the possibility to define the latter in terms of the former. In their contributions, some of them tackled the issue from the point of view of imagination as primarily an individual faculty, while others preferred to take the perspective of the social imaginary understood as the social and psychological context that determines the production of images. Others have explored the potentiality of the concept of imaginal, which emphasises the production of images rather than that of the faculty that produced them. The latter is a concept that has recently been recovered from the Muslim Sufi philosophical tradition (Corbin 1979) and developed particularly in the French debate as a third possibility between theories of imagination as an individual faculty and the alternative theories of the imaginary (Fleury 2006). In sum, imagination, imaginary, imaginal are three different perspectives to explore the same issue, namely the role that our capacity to produce images plays in politics.

The reason why such an enterprise is crucial today is twofold. On the one hand, as already suggested, our capacity to form images is playing an increasing (albeit ambivalent) role in contemporary politics. As a consequence of the key position it has acquired in the new economy and the media industry, its incorporation in both the processes of production and consumption of commodities and visual culture, imagination is given unprecedented chances to influence social life and political landscapes and hence also politics. On the other hand, we are still ill equipped in facing this new challenge. In the first place, on a philosophical level, the amount of work done on the concept of imagination is still minimal if compared with the work done on that of reason. For instance there are very few philosophical works dealing with what we could call 'public imagination', whereas studies on 'public reason' abound. There are thus reasons to suspect that particularly today, in the conditions of a global society of spectacle, a more vigorous engagement with the problem of the conditions for 'public imagination' would be particularly welcomed.

Not enough work has been done to systematically explore the nexus of politics and imagination and, even less so, on the theoretical possibility to define politics itself as a struggle for people's imagination. Among the philosophers who recovered the Kantian view of imagination and explored its political role, one should in the first place remember Hannah Arendt. In her *Lectures on Kant's Political Philosophy*, she tried to show the crucial role that imagination plays in politics, in particular for its capacity to strip ourselves of our particularities and thus put ourselves in the others' shoes (Arendt 1982). Yet, her project remained unfinished due to her death and we are left with a few suggestions in this direction rather than a fully fledged theory. Furthermore, her reliance on Kant makes us suspect that she was not fully aware of the ambivalence of imagination, the fact that, as Slavoj Žižek argued, imagination is not only the faculty of synthesis, of putting things together, but also that of madness, of tearing apart pieces of the whole (Žižek 1999: 28–38).

Together with the ambivalence of imagination, it is also its social nature that Arendt tends to overcome. Theories inspired by psychoanalysis have pointed out that there is not an autonomous, pre-given subject, since this is the result of a long process of socialisation that begins very early, with the first encounters with language. In their connubial of psychoanalysis and Marxism towards a critique of ideology, different authors of the Frankfurt School have pointed to the political role of imagination by emphasising the role that society as a whole exercises in the creation of compliant subjects. Yet, most of them remained linked to the Freudian view of imagination as fantasy. As Castoriadis pointed out, although fundamental insights can be derived from Freud's psychoanalysis as to the nature of imagination, it is a fact that he almost never uses the term imagination (*Einbildungskraft*) preferring to it the somehow misleading term 'fantasy' (*Phantasie*) (Castoriadis 1997: 292). As a consequence, in his system, imagination, as the capacity to produce images in the most general sense of the term, is occulted by fantasy understood as the representation of what is not immediately present. And this conflation still permeates many of the authors who have been directly inspired by his work.

This is, for instance, the case of Herbert Marcuse's revaluation of imagination. He thought that in late capitalistic societies, which create compliant one-dimensional human beings through the manipulation of their needs, it is only the aesthetic imagination that conserves the freedom to call the things with their proper name (Marcuse 1991: Chapter 10). Not by chance, then, Marcuse, who remains strongly linked to the Freudian vocabulary, uses imagination and fantasy interchangeably as if they were one and the same thing (Marcuse 1974: 141). Imagination is here mainly the faculty to represent what does not exist and is therefore also systematically associated with utopia (Marcuse 1974: 141–158). But Castoriadis' notion of imagination as the faculty to produce images in the most general sense of the term comes before both the concept of ideology and that of utopia. Without the production of images, there could be no ideology in the sense of false consciousness – but also no utopias. Both the preservation of the status quo through ideology and its subversion through utopias presuppose a world that is given in images and therefore imagination as the radical faculty described by Castoriadis.

On the French side, it is particularly Jacques Lacan that developed the insights of Freud and psychoanalysis. With his emphasis on language and the importance of society in the socialisation of individuals, Lacan went far beyond the idea of imagination as an individual faculty, as it is signalled by the new role that the concept of imaginary plays in his theory. In Lacan's view, the imaginary domain, together with the real and the symbolic, constitutes one of the three fundamental orders of structure. The imaginary is the domain that has its roots in the mirror phase when the infant recognises himself in the specular image in front of him, but also perceives the discrepancy between his fragmented body (over which he has no command) and the unitary image in which he indentifies himself. But such an identification with the specular image is not only a child experience: the ego itself is formed through the identification with such a specular image so that the imaginary, together with the real and the symbolic, comes to be constitutive of the human psyche as such. While in the imaginary the subject is permanently caught by his own image, the symbolic order presents itself to the subject as the big Other, the Law, which is counterpoised to the real – the latter being then a sort of limit concept for what cannot be symbolised and is therefore outside language.[3]

In both Lacan and Žižek, who is the author who has most systematically recovered and developed Lacan's psychoanalysis in contemporary debate, the imaginary is by definition the place of alienation.[4] Although this does not mean that the imaginary is simply illusory (Lacan 1999, vol. 1: 348), it remains by definition the locus of alienation and is therefore counterpoised to the real. In this perspective, the imaginary is therefore once again limited to the ambit of the unreal, although with a much more refined understanding of the real and the imaginary respectively. But if the imaginary is by definition the place of alienation and the unreal, it becomes difficult to account for the free imagination of individuals let alone for the possibility that the imaginary is itself constitutive of the real.

In the contemporary world of virtual reality, it can be problematic to counterpoise the real and the imaginary, because the latter may well have become what is most real. Hence the need to take also a third perspective, that of the imaginal, which looks at the role of images themselves rather than the faculty that constitutes them. As mentioned earlier, Cynthia Fleury has recently introduced the concept in the French debate, but in her usage the concept only points to the fact that between the world of sensibility and that of the intellect there is a third possibility, that of the imaginal. Although her perspective is helpful to point out that there is a *tertium* between imagination and the imaginary, she does not fully explore the consequences of such a view,[5] its political implications in particular, which are at the centre of interest of our analysis.

3 See, for instance, Lacan 1999, both volumes I and II. The distinction between the three orders, imaginary, real and symbolic returns in different places of the text. For a mapping of these, see Lacan 1999, vol. 1: 541.

4 See, for instance, Žižek 1999 and 2006.

5 On this point, see Bottici's contribution to this volume.

The aim of this collection is indeed to rethink the nexus of politics and imagination by drawing from the intellectual traditions mentioned earlier, but also by possibly going beyond them. Furthermore, none of the above mentioned works tackled the intertwinement of politics and imagination in a truly multidisciplinary perspective. Disciplines drawn together in this volume include philosophy, psychoanalysis, sociology, critical race theory, economics, history, literature, critical law theory, media and gender studies. Such a multi-disciplinary approach is crucial today in order to understand the transformations of the nature of images and of the faculty that produces them. To offer but one example: how to understand the impact of computer technology on imagination without a joint effort on the part of a multiplicity of disciplines? The media revolution is at the same time the result of an economic, technological, sociological, cultural and even artistic process which reverberates in various ambits of social life. The introduction of such technologies cannot be fully grasped without considering the crucial role of imagination in the new economy: having become central not only to the consumption process but also to the production of both commodities and labour force, imagination has acquired a new role within cognitive capitalism. Today it is the use value of the labour force as a commodity (and not just the commodities produced) that incorporates this imaginary dimension.[6] As a consequence, there is no escape from the colonisation of desire, because we are colonised not merely as consumers, but also as producers.

This, however, explains only partially the nature of the transformation of imagination and the way in which this influences its relationship with politics. In order to critically conceptualise such a nexus, we also need to discuss both the psychological and the sociological roots of the contemporary intertwinement of politics and imagination. If politics has become a struggle for people's imagination this is, in the first place, due to the fact that such a struggle takes place *within* human beings and not just *among* them. Hence the need to make recourse to the insights of psychoanalysis, which the contributors to this volume do according to their different theoretical orientations (from Freud and Jung to Lacan and Castoriadis).

This does not mean that the social context is or has become irrelevant. On the contrary. Race, tradition, religion and law are the sources from which politics has traditionally tried to derive its (imaginary) legitimacy. Hence the importance of relying on disciplines such as sociology and critical theory of law and race, in order to disentangle such strategies of legitimisation and explore their nexus with our capacity to produce images. Are images a new opium of the people or something that, by illuminating new realities, can also open new spaces for a radical political action? Does representation enable or hinder the possibility of revolution? Imagination produces images, but it is

6 On this point, see Marazzi 1994 and Bazzicalupo's contribution to this volume.

representation that makes them appear as present. Representation is a category that has been crucial to very different disciplines. Together with philosophy, disciplines as diverse as critical theory of history, political theory and literary studies, gender and visual studies have recently been highlighting the power of representation. Hence, the need for philosophy to engage in a dialogue with such disciplines in order to explore the nexus of politics and imagination.

To move on to the delineation of the structure of the volume, the first series of contributions reconstructs the different ways in which our capacity to imagine, on the one hand, and politics, on the other, can be conceptualised, but also why they have today become so entangled with one another that we can formulate the hypothesis that politics has become, more than ever, a form of struggle for people's imagination. In particular, it does so through a double movement: from imagination to politics (Bottici) and from politics to imagination (Ferrara). By raising the question of what constitutes imagination in the first place, Bottici briefly traces the genealogy of this concept, showing that it has been conceived both as a faculty endowed with a positive cognitive and motivational power as well as the source of errors and deceit due to its power to present things that are absent as if they were present. The ambivalences of imagination are exacerbated in social and psychological theory of the imaginary. After a move from the concept of 'imagination' as an individual faculty to that of 'imaginary' understood as a social and psychological context, she argues that we need to take a further step towards the concept of 'imaginal'. In contrast to 'imaginary' as an adjective, which fundamentally means 'fictitious, unreal', the concept of 'imaginal' simply denotes what is made of images, be they real images or not. Furthermore, in contrast to 'imagination' and 'imaginary' as substantives, 'imaginal' can be both the product of a social context and of the free imagination of individuals.

Politics, Bottici argues, depends on the imaginal thus understood, because no public can ever exist without being imagined. Both big and small political communities are 'imaginal beings', because their members need to imagine 'a public' in order to perceive it out of a simple collection of bodies. But politics depends on the imaginal also if we take the more restricted definition of political power as that particular kind of power that can ultimately have recourse to legitimate physical coercion. Indeed, what distinguishes the latter from mere violence is the belief in its imaginal legitimacy. This leads us to the ambivalences of 'imaginal politics', which is particularly evident today in an epoch characterised by the paradox of an apparent lack of imagination and the concomitant excess of it. In conclusion, this is ultimately due to the fact that the imaginal can be both a source of liberation and a source of oppression (Chapter 1).

In contrast to the first contribution which starts with a discussion of 'what is imagination' and emphasises its centrality in the definition of politics, Ferrara's contribution moves the other way around. Starting with a discussion of the definition of politics and its constitutive moments (discourse, judgement, recognition, gift), Ferrara concludes that politics at its best is the promotion of certain ends on the basis of good reasons that move the imagination. Through the concepts of judgement and example, the author argues that there exists a link between good reasons and imagination. Politics depend on imagination because judgement, as Arendt has shown, depends on imagination. And no concrete politics without judgement can ever exist. Without such a capacity to stimulate imagination, good reasons are powerless accountancy of what 'should be', whereas political imagination without good reasons is (as history has shown) the source of disasters and human catastrophes. Through a parallel with Kant's notion of genius, as it is developed in his *Critique of Judgement*, Ferrara argues that good reasons that move the imagination are to politics what the products of artistic genius are to art. Good reasons that move the imagination are the product of the political genius like the works of art are that of the artistic genius. In contrast, manneristical works of art are *geistlos*, without spirit, as uninspiring as political reasons that are unable to stimulate imagination (Chapter 2).

Having explored the conceptual nexus between politics and imagination in both directions (from imagination to politics and from politics to imagination), the next contribution shows that the two movements have been conceptualised relatively early in modernity, despite being subsequently ignored by mainstream political philosophy. It is in Spinoza that we find the first clear conceptualisation of the 'politics of imagination'. Precisely for having combined his theory of political imagination with a radical theory of democracy, Spinoza's thinking can be considered the origin of a genuinely *critical* approach to this topic. Starting with a discussion of the concept of imagination in Spinoza's works, Hippler argues that social life, according to Spinoza, is imaginary in its very essence, because the human world of life (*Lebenswelt*), with its corollaries of intentionality, meaning and objectivity, is structured by the imaginative faculty of the mind.

Subsequently, Hippler applies these findings to the realm of politics by showing that Spinoza analyses the imaginary character of social life according to some of its hegemonic forms of organisation: holy texts, religious and political rituals and civic practices. In this, Spinoza went beyond the modern and the Kantian view of imagination as an individual faculty. This does not mean that imagination is only a means for political oppression. Rather, in terms of ethics, i.e. of the maximal deployment of one's own power (*potentia*), Spinoza believes that a 'powerful' organisation of the social imaginary constitutes the supreme object of politics (Chapter 3).

Having set up the more general framework for the discussion of the politics of imagination, the second set of chapters tries to disentangle it. What are its sources and pitfalls? Bugliani argues that politics is a struggle for people's imagination because such a struggle occurs in the first place *within* human beings rather than *among* them. By focusing on the relationship between psychology and political imagination, he shows that recent psychology operated a reduction of the complexity of the human soul which is functional to modern politics. As Adorno pointed out, the soul, by which Bugliani means the human spirit in its widest meaning, is 'politically incorrect', because it is boundless, inscrutable and cannot therefore be predicted and controlled. Hence the passage from 'soul' to 'mind', which is the superficial, simplest, and thus most predictable portion of the spirit.

Politics needs to repress the soul, because politics needs stability, trends, statistics. What if everyone simply followed its stream of images? What if the power of these images was set free? Even before politics starts, human beings are frightened by the ambivalence of images and imagination. Power is an answer to the terror human beings feel when faced with the abyss of their soul. Power is everywhere because it is a force human beings exert against themselves in the first place, as individuals and as a group. Before I exert power on others, I exert power on *myself*. And I exert power on others *because* I first exert it on myself and cannot therefore tolerate in them the freedom that I do not allow myself. This is the reason why power in general, and political power in particular, is largely unconscious (Chapter 4).

In contrast to Bugliani, Bazzicalupo argues that, if politics is a struggle for people's imagination, this is because such a struggle passes through the new economic machine which operates as a matrix for social relations both at the material and the symbolic level. Referring to Lacan's theory of imaginary, which is not reducible to the symbolic order, and a Derridean lecture of the real as spectrality and foreclosing of representation, Bazzicalupo explores the evolution in the role of imagination within capitalism from its inception up to the current bioeconomic turn of cognitive capitalism. The most recent version of post-Fordist cognitive capitalism came to incorporate directly the space of imagination and therefore also individuals themselves in their daily lives, to an extent that has never before been the case. Capitalist commodities have always had their fetishism, but what is new today is that it is the use value of the labour force as a commodity that incorporates this imaginary dimension. The image of *homo oeconomicus* as human capital drives social imagination in an ambiguous way: *within* the empire of signs and images, but potentially also *against* it. Whereas the image reiterated as commodity becomes empty, the simulacra and *the virtual* claim a non-passive and non-foreseeable role (Chapter 5).

Like Bazzicalupo, Lentin argues that politics is a form of struggle for people's imagination because it is in the first place a question of social and political structures that create the conditions for such a struggle. In particular, her contribution focuses on the construction of race, as a means for the conceptual organisation of humanity, and on racism, as the consequence of the racialisation of those seen as 'inferior' and shows that both are fundamental to an understanding of the political, social and economic structures of modernity. However, the significance of race to state, particularly in the democratic west, is highly contested and conceded to by only a minority of scholars. Why is this so? Race had the double task of categorising human beings into distinguishable groups and of creating a racial hierarchy that scientifically legitimised white supremacy in an age of imperialist domination abroad and bourgeois hegemony at home, but since the end of the Second World War, the west has been involved in 'unproving' race – the central organising principle on which political and social relations had been predicated since the late 19th century. This rapid expunging of race from official, state-endorsed discourses has created a lacuna in western political imagination, which lies at the heart of the contemporary struggle over notions of integration and social cohesion.

What has followed, what we are presently living, is a continual search for a means of conceptualising difference that discursively sidesteps the taboo of race. Why is there a need to order and define 'difference' in some way and why indeed is difference so problematically conceived is at the heart of the question of the western political and sociological imagination. By continually adding new layers of description of human difference that cover over rather than confront race, the west has been involved in a consensual imagining of itself as uniquely different and nonetheless potentially universalist. Building a politics of resistance to the persistence of racism is hindered by the duplicity of the political imaginary at the core of contemporary western self-representation. Constructed on the myth of a 'postracial' society, resistance to racism remains always promised but never quite fulfilled (Chapter 6).

Together with economics and race, religion has been another crucial source of the modern politics of imagination. By focusing on the Messianic imagination that unites the three great monotheisms in a common political theology, Salvatore explores the politics of religious imagination in a *longue durée* perspective (Chapter 7), while Challand concentrates on the novelties brought about by the contemporary post-secularisation setting (Chapter 8). In particular, Salvatore connects the genealogy of Messianic imagination to the tensions unsolved by the order of the so-called Axial Age (c. 800 BC–200 BC) but also shows why they have had an enduring historical impact well into and for modern political phenomena. By recovering Taubes' remarks on Schmitt and Benjamin, he argues that Messianism both helps out the constitution of the modern agent of political order, the so-called state, as the administrator of the profane realm of immanence before the procrastinated second coming of the Christ or even as the agent that 'holds down' (the Greek *katechon*) evil and hinders the coming of the Antichrist (that necessarily precedes Christ's second coming). This also coagulates the neo-Messianic frustrations of diasporic Judaism. The latter became the object of persecution and genocide in the context of modern European state building – that which, in turn, opened the way to the specific political Messianism of Zionism.

The final price of Messianism decried by Taubes is the potential of violence incorporated both in the katechontical nature of the powerful European state and in its replica via Zionism. Yet Taubes also reveals a different price, which might be paid more eagerly by modern individuals. This price comes close to the 'end of history' of global society and its ultimate nihilism described by Benjamin's *Theologico-Political Fragment*. Such a scenario exalts the sovereignty of the self and the liquidity of the imagination. It nourishes human happiness in the immanent order of the world based on the consciousness that the Messiah is not coming, but is absorbed in the process of erosion and 'liquidation' of the order of the world (Chapter 8).

Challand focuses instead on the role of Islam in the contemporary transformations of the politics of imagination. By concentrating on the historical evolutions of Islamism and on the sociological conditions that have turned Islam, the faith, into Islamism, a political ideology, he argues that imagination has played a very important role in this transformation, not only because it enables the creation of the image of a Muslim community, but also because the imposition of the categories of 'modernity' and 'secularity' in the political imaginary was deeply resented by Muslim majority societies. A reaction to these categories has reinforced the perceived need to express resistance in terms of an imagined cultural or religious authenticity, obscuring the fact that problems between Muslim societies and the 'west' are political. This exemplifies the extent to which religions are an emblematic case of the struggle for people's imagination in the contemporary conditions of a globalising world. As a system of beliefs, religion needs to be able to impose its image of the world to gain support. As an aggregation of followers, it must be able to convey the sense of a united community by making people imagine it. As a doctrine, it often resorts to imagining threats in order to survive the challenges of our epoch.

Still, as the analysis of contemporary Islamism shows, former categories for the critique of religion, such as that of alienation and heteronomy, are inadequate when used in a post-secularisation setting. Challand proposes instead a focus on two new categories: externalisation of religion and double heteronomy. In a post-secular setting, that is in a condition where the common social imaginary is confronted with the experience of secularisation, the appropriation of religion by lay institutions and governing regimes cannot but appear as a form of externalisation from their previous places of worship. In turn, this creates a condition of a potential 'double heteronomy', that is a situation where religion is so intermingled with the political responses to the imagined cultural anomie that a critique of religion becomes impossible because it would amount to a refusal of the entire political setting (Chapter 8).

The last set of chapters continues to explore the politics of imagination by focusing on the conceptual couple of representation and revolution. If imagination is the faculty to produce images in the most general sense of the term, representation is what makes images 'present'. Representation is therefore one of the crucial ways in which the struggle for people's imagination takes place, as the last four chapters will argue. In particular, White shows why historical representation has been and still is a crucial place for the politics of imagination, while Steele focuses on the role of literature. By recovering parts of Althusser's concept of 'ideological state apparatuses' and Freud's theories of drives, White criticises the concept of imagination as a mental faculty. In his view, imagination is best understood as a zone of transition between the conscious and the unconscious, where thinking in image and rebus-like combinations are subjected to the repressive and sublimative operations of the censorship. One of the social functions of historical discourse, in both its scholarly and popular forms, is to address and assuage certain existential anxieties rooted in doubts arising in individuals and groups about identity, origin, descent and the like. It is here that the politics of imagination proliferates (Chapter 9).

In contrast to White, Steele looks at the role of literature in the struggle for people's imagination. According to Steele, literature is a means of arguing through the social imaginary. Unlike the philosophical discourse of modernity, literary modernity, as inaugurated by Don Quixote, has not been trying to find a way to reduce the discourses of the social imaginary in order to find a path toward normative and epistemological clarity; rather, it has been parodying, deflating, revising and elevating these languages. Following the insights provided on this point by Ellison and through the analysis of literary examples, Steele argues that race is the site of a political struggle for people's imaginations and he engages in this struggle by taking on the discourses of law, sociology, philosophy and film. The procedures of the antidiscrimination approach to race, the statistics of the anti-domination approach and the norms of public reason can never fully address the site of this political struggle: public imagination (Chapter 10).

By concentrating on gender and visual studies, Lara and Buck-Morss further explore the potential for a revolution of the contemporary politics of imagination. Imagination has played a crucial role in the secular subjection of women. Nonetheless, it also discloses a revolutionary potential. Lara focuses on how feminism can transform (and to a certain extent has already transformed) societies' self-representation and self-understanding using the tools of imagination. The new possibilities are opened by the enlargement of the social imaginary through social practices and habits, the reinterpretation of sources of knowledge and through social and political critique. In her view, feminism connects aesthetic critique with social critique and by doing so it can trigger the transformation of society's self-understanding (Chapter 11).

Finally, Buck-Morss looks at the recent transformation of the nature of images and imagination in a globalised world through the prism of visual studies and argues that this field provides the opportunity of a transformation of thought on a global level. The global artworld is a contradictory space which suggests to us that 'reorientation' rather than 'rejection' of global imagination is the best political strategy.

By reconstructing the transformations of imagination as a consequence of both economic (the information revolution) and artistic processes (contemporary art practices), Buck-Morss shows that images maintain their ambivalent nature in the contemporary world. They can be both the new opium of the people (Kristeva) and the means to motivate the will in the mind (Benjamin), the inhibitor and the enabler of human agency. But it is this very promiscuity of the images that allows for leaks. As the new aesthetics emerging from contemporary art practices teaches us, images can intensify experience, illuminating realities that otherwise go unnoticed. Images can therefore flow outside the bubble of imposed meanings into an aesthetic field not contained by the official narration of power. The crucial question is, therefore, how can theory learn from such practices engaged in stretching the thin membrane of images, providing depth of field, slowing the tempo of perception and allowing thus images to expose a space of common political action (Chapter 12).

This book is an attempt to answer such a challenge. The following contributions do more than highlight problems or deconstruct given categories or narratives. They try to suggest and explore new paths and new concepts along with a reinterpretation or readaptation of older ones in order to frame the space for an emancipative political action. The latter cannot start by eradicating the ambivalences of the contemporary politics of imagination. But, perhaps, we do not even need to do that as it is this very ambiguity of images themselves that opens up new spaces.

References

Arendt, H. 1982, *Lectures on Kant's Political Philosophy*, Brighton, Harvester.

Arnason, J.P. 1994, 'Reason, imagination, interpretation', in Robinson, G. and Rundell, J. (eds) *Rethinking Imagination: Culture and Creativity*, London, Routledge, pp. 155–170.

Benjamin, W. 2002, 'The work of art in the age of its technological reproducibility', in *Selected Writings*, vol. 3, 1935–1938, Cambridge, MA, Belknap Press.

Bottici, C. 2007, *Philosophy of Political Myth*, Cambridge, Cambridge University Press.

Bottici, C. and Challand B. 2010, *The Myth of the Clash of Civilizations*, London, Routledge.

Buck-Morss, S. 2003, *Thinking Past Terror: Islam and Critical Theory on the Left*, London, Verso.

Buruma, I. and Margalit, A. 2004, *Occidentalism. The West on the Eyes of its Enemies*, New York, Penguin.

Castoriadis, C. 1987, *The Imaginary Institution of Society*, Cambridge, Polity Press.

—— 1994, 'Radical imagination and the social instituting imaginary', in *The Castoriadis Reader*, Oxford, Blackwell, pp. 319–338.

—— 1997, *Fait et à faire. Les carrefours du labyrinthe 5*, Paris, Éditions du Seuil.

Corbin, H. 1979, *Corps spirituel et terre céleste*, Paris, Buchet-Castel.

Debord, G. 1994, *The Society of the Spectacle*, New York, Zone Books.

Fleury, C. (ed.) 2006, *Imagination, Imaginaire, Imaginal*, Paris, PUF.

Friese, H. 2001, 'Imagination: history of the concept', in Smelser, N.J. and Baltes, P.B. (eds) *International Encyclopedia of Social & Behavioural Science*, vol. 11, Amsterdam, Elsevier, pp. 7197–7201.

Graeber, D. 2002, 'The new anarchists', *New Left Review*, 13, January–February, pp. 61–73.

Lacan, J. 1999, *Écrits*, Paris, Éditions du Seuil.

Marazzi, C. 1994, *Il posto dei calzini. La svolta linguistica dell'economia*, Turin, Bollati Boringhieri.

Marcuse, H. 1974, *Eros and Civilization: A Philosophical Inquiry into Freud*, Boston, MA, Beacon Press.

—— 1991, *One-dimensional Man: Studies in the Ideology of Advanced Industrial Society*, Boston, MA, Beacon Press.

Robinson, G. and Rundell, J. (eds) 1994, *Rethinking Imagination: Culture and Creativity*, London, Routledge.

Rundell, J. 1994, 'Creativity and judgment: Kant on reason and imagination' in Robinson, G. and Rundell, J. (eds) *Rethinking Imagination: Culture and Creativity*, London, Routledge, pp. 87–117.

Vattimo, A. 1999, 'Immaginazione', in *Enciclopedia di filosofia*, Milano, Garzanti, pp. 528–530.

Žižek, S. 1999, *Enjoy your Symptom! Jacques Lacan in Hollywood and Out*, New York, Routledge.

—— 2006, *How to Read Lacan*, London, Granta Books.

Chapter 1

From imagination to the imaginary and beyond

Towards a theory of imaginal politics

Chiara Bottici

We live in an epoch characterised by the paradox of an excess of imagination and a concomitant lack of it. We often hear people saying that our politicians lack imagination, but the political spectacle put on stage on our screens every day points to an *excess* of imagination. The aim of this contribution is to address such a paradox by discussing the possible ways of conceptualising the nexus of politics and imagination. While Ferrara's contribution to this volume starts with a discussion of the concept of politics and then moves on to show why it depends on that of imagination, I will proceed in the opposite way: from the concept of imagination to that of politics.

To answer the question 'what is imagination?', there are two basic roads. One is analytical and consists in analysing the concept as it is commonly used. Taking this road, one risks being entrapped in the epoch, with no historical depth. The second road is historical and consists in reconstructing the history of the different ways in which the concept has been used over time. This road is equally precarious because one risks ending up in a collection of different meanings juxtaposed one next to the other, in a temporal sequence – without mentioning the fact that an historical reconstruction is always, in its turn, done from the standpoint of the present. Assuming the impossibility to jump out of our epoch, I will take a road in between the two. By adopting a genealogical approach in the sense of Nietzsche (section 1), I will be looking for ruptures rather than for continuity in the history of the concept. This will also throw light on the values that were at stake in such ruptures and therefore set up the ground for a critique of imagination. This brief genealogy will provide the basis for the subsequent step, which consists in an attempt to show the power of imagination, why this is so important in our lives and how we can best conceptualise it (section 2). By distinguishing between 'imagination' and 'imaginary', I will propose to adopt the concept of 'imaginal' as a tool better equipped to account for the political role of our capacity to produce images (section 3). This will lead us into the ambivalences of today's politics of imagination, the fact that, as I will try to argue, it can be a source both of liberation and of oppression (section 4).

1. Two concepts of imagination: a genealogical approach

If we look at the uses of the concept of imagination, it is not difficult to perceive two quite different semantic areas. The first, which goes back to the Greek term *phantasia*, is associated with the production of images (*phantasmata*) that play a decisive role in both cognition and action. Aristotle defined *phantasia* as 'a movement (*kynesis*) produced by a sensation actively operating' and associated it to the root 'light' (*phaos*), by arguing that without light it is impossible to see (*De Anima*: 429a). *Phantasia* is recognised as an important element in the formation of a unitary imagine of objects out of an otherwise unrelated set of data (see, in particular, *De Anima*: 428b 18–30). It is only thanks to this faculty that a collection of forms, colours, movements, etc. is perceived as a table. But Aristotle also recognises that no action is possible without *phantasia* because *phantasia* is at the basis of appetite, which is a form of movement (*De Anima*: 433b 29).

Thus, Aristotle roots *phantasia* in sensation, which is also what ultimately guarantees its cognitive value, but he also recognises the important role that it plays in other ambits of the life of the mind. In particular, he emphasises that we are overwhelmed by sensation when this is actually taking place, so that we do not clearly perceive the role of *phantasia*; but its activity also reverberates when the sensation is no longer operating. This happens, for instance, in memory, when we remember something that has taken place, and in sleep, through the visions that we have in dreams (*Parva naturalia*: 461a ff). *Phantasia*, we can therefore conclude, is for Aristotle a form of light that reverberates in different ambits of our life.

Plato had already associated *phantasia* with the ambit of light. In his view, the site of *phantasia* is the liver because this is a lucid organ, able to reflect images (*Timaeus*: 71ff). Images can come either from senses or from God, as in divination. For Plato, thus, *phantasia* is not always rooted in sensation, as it is for Aristotle. In this way, he inaugurates a view of imagination which sees it as also (but not necessarily) independent from sensuous experience – a view that, together with the Aristotelian one, will be very influential in western philosophy. If Plato sees imagination as potentially independent from senses, this does not mean that he sees in it a source of errors. Indeed, he also associates it with the enlightenment of knowledge, be that either sensitive or divine.

It is with the modern epoch that the concept of imagination starts to be associated with quite a different semantic area. Far from being a source of light, imagination is now seen as a source of darkness, of perturbation of the methodical work of reason. A split is thus established between knowledge, on the one hand, which is guaranteed by the enlightenment of pure reason, and imagination, as the faculty to produce all sorts of illegal marriages and divorces, on the other. Bacon defines imagination as the faculty that 'commonly exceeds the measure of nature, joining at pleasure things which in nature would never have come together, and introducing things which in nature would never have come to pass' (Bacon 1986, II, 1: 292; 1963, II, 1: 494). If imagination has no role in cognition, it can still offer something to human beings: poetry. Imagination, together with memory and reason, is one of the three faculties of the mind, to which the three main divisions of human learning correspond: poesy, history and philosophy (Bacon 1986, II, 1: 292).

In the course of the 17th century, the great century of rationalism, the critique of imagination becomes a sort of commonplace of philosophy, a *passage obligé* for the definition of the scientific method (Guenancia 2006: 43 ff). Like Bacon, Galilei also defines the new scientific method precisely by juxtaposing it to what he calls 'mere imagination'. In *Il saggiatore*, he argues that the 'new philosophy' he is proposing is not a mere 'fruit of imagination' such as the Iliad, precisely because it is written in the vast book of universe that 'stands in front of our eyes' and 'its characters are triangle, circles, and other geometrical figures without which it is impossible to understand a word', without which science would be 'wandering around a dark labyrinth in vain' (Galilei 1996, section 6: 631; trans. mine). Thus, a clear separation is established between the 'new philosophy' with its mathematical language, on the one hand (what we would call 'science'), and poetry, the products of human phantasy such as the Iliad and Odyssey (*le fantasie d'uomo come L'Iliade e l'Odissea*), on the other.

Perhaps in no other author is the critique of imagination as clear as in Pascal. In his fragment on imagination, Pascal describes this faculty as a source of errors and falsity (*maîtresse d'erreur et fausseté*), as a powerful enemy of reason which can control and, at times, even entirely dominate it (see Fragment 44/82, Pascal 1963: 504). If reason never completely surmounts imagination, the contrary is quite the rule. This is ultimately due to the corrupted nature of human beings, who, as a consequence of the original sin, are 'full of natural mistakes, which cannot be eliminated without divine grace' (Pascal 1963: 505; trans. mine). Imagination, more than any other human faculty, is the sign of the irremediably corrupted nature of human beings, of the fact that they cannot always follow the two sources of truth (reason and senses).[7]

This passage from a positive view of imagination which associates it with the sphere of *light* (the Greek *phantasia*) to a negative one, which sees in it a sign of the *dark* side of human nature, resulted in a striking semantic break. The outcome of the great 17th-century critiques of the concept of imagination is the fact that, by the 18th century, the term '*phantasia*' was moved to the sphere of the unreal – as is still the case for the corresponding English term

7 Maguire criticises this reading of Pascal by saying that he has a much more positive view of imagination (Maguire 2006: 17–59). Still, it can hardly be denied that what emerges in this fragment is a rather negative view of imagination. Among the supporters of such a reading, see Cocking 1994: 265 and Robinson and Rundell 1994: 120.

'fantasy'. Fantasy, indeed, came to be associated with the ambit of the unreal and the newly constituted sphere of aesthetics (Friese 2001: 7197; Vattimo 1999b: 529).

The values that are at stake in this process are those of the project of modernity and, therefore, in the first place, that of the autonomy of the individual. Within this project, imagination has a crucial role to play in the newly constituted ambit of aesthetics. If imagination is a source of errors from the point of view of the methodical work of pure reason, it still has something to offer to human beings. This is the capacity to make all sorts of marriages and divorces which, illegal from the point of view of pure reason, find their proper function in the ambit of art. The concept of art as an autonomous domain grounded on the notion of taste is a creature of modernity and one that presupposes its own specific faculty (Vattimo 1999a: 340).[8] The exclusion of imagination from the ambit of knowledge, therefore, goes hand in hand with a process of subjectification of aesthetics (Gadamer 1988: I, II). If science is the domain of reason and understanding where only an *objective* knowledge of the world can be attained, imagination has a function in the sphere of aesthetics, precisely because of its capricious, unpredictable, *subjective* character.[9]

From this point of view, Kant's *Critique of the Power of Judgment*, which appeared in 1790, was a turning point. In the preface of this book, Kant labelled as 'aesthetical' the judgement concerning the beautiful and the sublime (Kant 2000: pref.).[10] The judgment of taste is defined by a contraposition with cognitive judgment: while the latter operates by subsuming the particular into a general rule, the former is the kind of judgement in which a universal is sought in the particular. Even if these judgements rest on a spontaneous agreement with a subjective sentiment of pleasure–displeasure and, at the same time, are expected to have some kind of universality because they are linked to a sort of 'aesthetical common sense' (Kant 2000: 22), they do not contribute to the advancement of knowledge.

Kant's philosophy represents a watershed also from another point of view. In the first edition of his *Critique of Pure Reason* of 1781 – almost 10 years before the *Critique of the Power of Judgement* – he put forward quite a different concept of imagination, which at least partially recovers the Aristotelian tradition. Kant

8 Before modern times, the term art (*ars*) covered a very wide meaning, including everything that had to do with the application of general principles to a certain domain. For instance, in the Middle Ages, *artes* included the dialectic (i.e., philosophy itself) together with grammar, rhetoric, arithmetic, geometry, astronomy and music. Subsequently, the meaning of the term has been restricted to that of the fine arts.

9 The most important exception to his view is Vico's concept of 'universali fantastici' (Vico 1999). Vico recognised the cognitive function of imagination, in its nexus with poetry, but this view remained marginal at least until Romanticism. For a discussion of the modern authors who recognise the cognitive role of imagination, see Maguire 2006.

10 A sign of the earlier usage of the term 'aesthetical' can still be found in his *Critique of Pure Reason* (Kant 1998).

sustained that imagination has a central role for the possibility of knowledge itself (Kant 1998: A101). Imagination appears here as the only faculty that can guarantee a 'pure transcendental synthesis', i.e. the fact that a set of otherwise unrelated sensitive impressions can be perceived as a single image. In a crucial passage from the first edition, imagination, as the active capacity for the synthesis of the manifold, is said to be the condition for bringing the plurality of intuitions into single images and thus also the transcendental condition of all knowledge (Kant 1998: A101).

However, if here Kant comes close to admitting a sort of primacy of imagination (Arnason 1994: 160), in the second edition of his *Critique of Pure Reason*, which appeared in 1787, he retreats from this discovery and relegates imagination to a more subordinated and intermediary role between intellect and intuition. Section A95-A130 is replaced by a new section (B129-B169). Here Kant distinguishes between what he now calls the figurative synthesis of imagination from its intellectual counterpart, the transcendental schematism, which today remains one of the most obscure concepts in the *Critique*, but still has taken the primary place of imagination (Kant 1998: B 152, B 181).[11]

By reducing his previous claim over the formative power of the imagination and its crucial role in the process of knowledge, Kant restates a more conventional division between reason and imagination, science and art. Critique is set apart from creativity and collapses into cognitivism, while the imagination is treated either mediately, for its secondary role, or aesthetically, as source of those free marriages, which are illegal from the point of view of pure reason, but legitimate in the field of art (Rundell 1994a, 1994b).

I shall not dwell on this point here.[12] Let me just point out that, with respect to this view, Romanticism will attempt to revaluate the central role of imagination. Early Romanticism, in particular, denied the primacy of intellect for the attainment of knowledge and revaluated imagination as what can guarantee the autonomy of the aesthetic sphere. Novalis, for instance, sees in it a power that can liberate from the senses and understanding: while the latter are mechanical and oppressive, imagination is a source of freedom. As he openly put it, 'imagination is this wonderful sense that can replace all senses for us – and that already stand under the power of our will. The outward-oriented senses appear to be entirely governed by mechanical laws – imagination, in contrast, is evidently not tied to the presence and touch of external stimuli' (Novalis 1977: II, 650; trans. mine). Art, as the domain created by the freedom of imagination, can therefore bring together what has been separated by Enlightenment.

11 Castoriadis 1997 and Rundell 1994a, 1994b.

12 I have further developed this genealogy of imagination in Bottici 2011: Chapter 1.

2. Beyond imagination: from the imaginary to the imaginal

The emphasis on the productive side of imagination will have a great impact on the Romantics' effort to revaluate imagination. However, such an attempt appears more as a restoration of what has been criticised by Enlightenment, rather than as a radical questioning of the premises of Enlightenment itself. For instance, in Novalis' quotation we find the same opposition between imagination and understanding that is one of the premises of the Enlightenment. Romanticism fully remains within and, at times, even hypertrophied the metaphysics of the subject that sustained the Enlightenment. As Adorno and Horkheimer (among others) pointed out, the modern dualism that presents the subject as a punctual ego facing a reality that is given is one of the very premises of Enlightenment itself (Adorno and Horkheimer 1997).

This is patent in the Cartesian distinction between the ego understood as thinking (*res cogitans*) and the external world understood as an amalgam of matter and movement (*res extensa*) or, again, in Galilei's concept of nature as a book that is given before our eyes. The world for Galilei is something that is a given in front of us, like a book, so that all what we have to do to understand it is to learn its mathematical quantitative language, which only can be done by depriving ourselves of all that has to do with qualities, that is of all that is merely *subjective*. As he provocatively puts it, 'once we remove ears, tongues and noses, there remain figures, numbers and movements' (Galilei 1996: section 48, 780; trans. mine).

In the face of such a dualism, the subject with her nose and mouth, on the one hand, and the objective world with its mathematical language, on the other, the response of Romanticism has been a new form of metaphysics of the subject. Be it the absolutism of an ego that encompasses the external world in itself (Fichte) or the metaphysics of a philosophy of art (Schelling and Schlegel), the Cartesian subject is in all these cases reinterpreted, expanded, hypertrophied, but not radically questioned.[13] The task of this section is to stress the need for a further step, one that consists in vindicating the power of imagination, at the same time avoiding the traps of a philosophy of the subject. We are not pure subjects who simply contemplate a world that is 'given', but neither are we subjects who encapsulate the world within our consciousness. We are something in between the two. The problem is to understand what we are as 'imagining' beings.

As it has been observed, a great deal of philosophical work has been done in order to move away from a concept of reason encapsulated in a philosophy of the subject – as it is signalled, terminologically speaking, by the passage from the term 'reason' to the more context-oriented concept of 'rationality' (Arnason

13 For this critique of Romanticism, see Bottici 2007: Chapter 3.

1994). While a lot of work has been done on the concept of rationality and its possible contribution to the project of autonomy, nothing similar has been done on the concept of imagination. In comparison to reason, imagination has remained a marginal topic in recent philosophical debates. However, just as the move from a philosophy of subject to a new emphasis on context has led from a theory of 'reason' to one of 'rationality', we have assisted the beginning of a parallel development from a theory of 'imagination' to a theory of the 'imaginary'.

Psychoanalysis and structuralism both contributed to this development – the former with a new emphasis on the complexity of psychic life and the latter with a new attention to the products of imagination. Myths, fables, fairy tales, rituals, totemic practises, all have been analysed as part of the social imaginary – one just has to think of Freud's and Jung's contributions in this direction or, more recently, of the structuralist analyses inspired by Lévi-Strauss. And this certainly contributed to a deeper understanding of the concept of imaginary. The most important result is perhaps the move away from a view of the self as a mere sum of separated faculties.

The risk, however, in putting too much emphasis on contexts is that of exchanging a problematic metaphysics of the subject for an equally problematic metaphysics of the context. The point is to find a way to keep the balance between the context and the subject, on the one hand, and between the different subjects and different contexts, on the other. Two risks must be avoided. The first is the temptation to encompass the context into subject, even if this is understood in a more complex way. For instance, this may happen by considering the different products of the social imaginary as mere results of universal features of the human mind, be they universal complexes (Freud) or universal linguistic structures (Lévi-Strauss). The problem here is to subsume the context in a metaphysics of the subject that even if it is understood in a more complex way (as encompassing both a conscious and an unconscious life) is still a subject conceived of as separated from the reality that he or she is facing.[14]

The second risk is to recompose the subject into the context(s). For instance, in many conceptions that have been inspired by Romanticism or by Wittgenstein's philosophy of language the subject is dissolved into single, self-enclosed forms of life. These, as a consequence, are then often seen as reciprocally incommunicable contexts (Coulter 1999; von Savigny 1991). The basic argument is that if meanings derive from language games and if these are basically encapsulated in forms of life that are separated from one another, then no communication is possible among them.[15] The problem, however, is that such a view reifies contexts, as if they were self-enclosed units and therefore

14 This clearly emerges in Freud's and Lévi-Strauss' treatments of myth (Bottici 2007: Chapter 5).

15 In fact, as I have argued elsewhere, Wittgenstein is very ambiguous on the concept of forms of life (Bottici 2007: 94–97).

ultimately exchanges the point of view of a philosophy of the subject for a metaphysic of the context, that is, for a form of solipsism on a larger scale.

Part of the problem is linked to the fact that the amount of philosophical work done on the concept of imagination and imaginary is still minimal if compared with the work done on that of reason/rationality. Emblematically one of the potentially most powerful philosophical theories of imagination remained unwritten. Hannah Arendt's project in the last years of her life was that of a theory of judgement based on the concept of imagination, but she died before she could fully develop her theory. Instead of a fully fledged theory that could have represented the ripest fruit of the heritage of phenomenology, we are left with a few fragments of a possible theory.[16]

By recovering Kant's intuitions, in particular as they are developed in the first edition of his *Critique of Pure Reason*, Arendt emphasised the power of imagination for both cognition and action. Imagination is the faculty that mediates between universal and particular by providing both schemata for cognition and exemplars for action (Arendt 1982: 72 ff, 79–85). As Kant has already argued in order to explain how is it possible that a series of sense data can be recognised as a unitary object – a table, say – we need to possess a mental image of what a table must be like. This, Arendt argues:

> [C]an be conceived of as a Platonic idea or Kantian schema; that is, one has before the eyes of one's mind a schematic or merely *formal table* shape to which every table somehow must conform. Or one proceeds, conversely, from the many tables one has seen in one's life, strips them of all secondary qualities, and the remainder is a table-in-general, containing the minimum properties common to all tables: the *abstract table*. One more possibility is left, and this enters into judgements that are not cognitions: one may encounter or think of some table that one judges to be the best possible table and take this table as the example of how tables actually should be: the *exemplary table* ('example' comes from *eximere*, 'to single out some particular'). This exemplar is and remains a particular that in its very particularity reveals the generality that otherwise could not be defined. Courage is like Achilles etc.
>
> (Arendt 1982: 76–77)[17]

Examples are thus fundamental not just in cognition, but also for action. This is because, as she openly puts it by recovering a Kantian expression 'examples

16 On the French side, Husserl's phenomenological intuitions on the role of imagination have been developed by Sartre. In both his writings on the topic, however, Sartre remains linked to the concept of imagination as faculty to represent what does not exist, which is still an enlightened approach to imagination (Sartre 1936, 1940).

17 On the importance of the notion of 'example', see Ferrara 2008. Ferrara, however, criticises Arendt's analogy between examples and cognitive schemata.

are the go-cart of judgements', they are what sustain us when we formulate judgments. 'The example is the particular that contains in itself, or is supposed to contain, a concept or a general rule' (Arendt 1982: 84). How is one able to judge an act as courageous? If one were an ancient Greek, Arendt argues, one would have in the depths of one's mind the example of Achilles. Imagination is central here because it makes present to our mind what is not in front of us. If we say somebody is good, we are probably thinking of examples such as St Francis or Jesus or some other archetype of goodness (Arendt 1982: 84).

However, imagination, as Arendt argues elsewhere, is also central to human life from another point of view. As the faculty to make present what is potentially absent it is at the very basis of the possibility of action. As she points out at the beginning of *Lying in Politics*, a characteristic of human action is that it always begins something new in the world – and this does not mean that it starts *ex nihilo*, but simply that it adds something. This capacity to begin something new depends, in its turn, on our capacity to mentally remove ourselves from where we are physically located and imagine that things might as well be different from what they actually are (Arendt 1972: 5). This capacity to change facts, or to act, therefore fundamentally depends on imagination. But, as Arendt observes, from the same faculty also depends the capacity, so often met in politics, to deny factual truth (Arendt 1972: 5). Hence the ambivalence of imagination, the fact that it can be a means for emancipation and thus critique of what is given, but also for the subjection to it. Otherwise put, imagination can be a source of both freedom and domination.

Among the authors who systematically explored the relationship between imagination and the modern project of autonomy, Castoriadis certainly played a crucial role. Furthermore he also contributed to the passage from a theory of imagination (as it still seems to be the one that Arendt would have developed) to one of the imaginary. Castoriadis' starting point is not the separated individual but social life itself. In his view, all acts, both individual and collective, without which no society could survive – labour, consumption, love, war, etc. – are impossible outside a symbolic network, even though they are not always directly symbols themselves (Castoriadis 1987: 117). All functions performed within any society are, in fact, 'functions of something', i.e. they are functions only in as far as their ends can be defined. These ends, which vary from society to society as well as from one epoch to the other, can only be defined at the level of those social significations without which no social function or need could ever be defined: this is the level at which the 'social imaginary' operates. Any society continually defines and redefines its needs and no society can ever survive outside the imaginary significations that constitute it and are constituted by it. The institution of a society presupposes the institution of imaginary significations that must, in principle, be able to provide meaning to whatever presents itself.

The limits derived from the fact that the work of the social imaginary must always start from the material that it finds already there (nature, history, etc.)

(Castoriadis 1987: 125) notwithstanding, social imaginary has a capacity for virtual universal covering, so that any irruption of the raw world can immediately be treated as a sign of something, that is, it can be interpreted away and thus exorcised. Even that which collides with this order can be subject to a symbolic processing: transgression of social rule can become an 'illness' and completely alien societies that are fundamentally at odds with a given social imaginary can become 'strangers', 'savages' or even 'impious' (Castoriadis 1991).

At the same time, however, the major threat to the instituted society is its own creativity. The merit of Castoriadis' concept of radical social imaginary is to point out that the *instituting* social imaginary is always at the same time *instituted*. No society could ever exist if individuals created by the society itself had not created it. Society can exist concretely only through the fragmentary and complementary incarnation and incorporation of its institution and its imaginary significations in the living, talking and acting individuals of that society. Athenian society is nothing but the Athenians, Castoriadis observes; without them, it is only remnants of a transformed landscape, the debris of marble and vases, indecipherable inscriptions and worn statues fished out of the Mediterranean. But Athenians are Athenians only by means of the *nomos* of the *polis*. It is in this relationship between an instituted society, on the one hand – which infinitely transcends the totality of the individuals that 'compose' it, but can actually exist only by being 'realised' in the individuals that it produces – and these individuals, on the other, that we experience an unprecedented type of relationship that cannot be thought of under the categories of the whole and its parts, the set and its elements and, even less, the universal and the particular (Castoriadis 1991: 145).

However, Castoriadis seems to contradict this view when he speaks of an 'absolute scission' between the two poles of the instituted and instituting social imaginary: the social-historical, on the one hand, and what he calls the 'psyche' or 'psychical monad', on the other (see, for instance, Castoriadis 1987: 204ff). The psyche is said to be monadic because it is 'pure representational/affective/intentional flux', indeterminate and, in principle, unmasterable. Drawing inspiration from the theory but also his own experience as psychoanalyst, Castoriadis argues that it is only through an always incomplete violent and forceful process of socialisation that a social individual can be produced. This happens through a process of schooling that starts with the very first encounter with language (in the first place, the language of the mother). Through socialisation, the psyche is forced to give up its initial objects and to invest in (*cathecting*) socially instituted objects, rules and the world. It is through the internalisation of the worlds and the imaginary significations created by society that an 'individual', properly speaking, is created out of a 'screaming monster' (Castoriadis 1991: 148).

As has been observed, Castoriadis' thesis about the monadic isolation and the fundamental 'hetereogeneity' between the psyche and society seems to lead to a highly problematic, and thus untenable, metaphysical opposition (Habermas 1987: 327). Once we find ourselves within the monadic isolation of the unconscious, it becomes difficult even to explain how communication is possible in the first place (Whitebook 1989).[18] However, we can recover Castoriadis' insights on the role of the instituting and instituted social imaginary without relying on such metaphysical assumptions. In particular, even within a view of the self inspired by psychoanalysis there is no need to conceive of the psyche in terms of monadic isolation. Rather, it could be argued that our basic instinct when we enter the world is to *relate* to the other – in particular to the figure of the mother to look for nourishment. We are not monadic selves that become dependent on one another through a violent socialisation. On the contrary, we are from the very beginning *dependent* beings, monadic drives notwithstanding.

Yet, Castoriadis' theory contains very important intuitions as to the power of imagination, as well as to what we can call the 'politics of imagination'. Castoriadis' work has deeply contributed to the recent rediscovery of the importance of images and imagination in our social and political life, as well as to the development of a much more complex view of political imagination. Three aspects of his theory are particularly relevant: first the idea of a *radical* imagination, second, the emphasis on the idea of the *imaginary* and, finally, the relationship between the *instituting* and *instituted* side of the imaginary institution of a society.

With regards to the first, the term 'radical' has the function of stressing that, as Aristotle asserted, together with an imitative and reproductive or combinatory '*phantasia*', there is also what can be called a primary imagination. This consists in the faculty of producing 'images in the largest possible sense (that of 'forms', '*Bilder*'), that is images without which there would not be any thought at all and which, therefore, precede any thought' (Castoriadis 1997). Imagination does not imply therefore in the first place the non-existence of the objects of imagination, even though we can also have images that do not correspond to anything in the external world. Images are our way to be in the world, so that one could even say that no world is given for us that is not imagined.

The reason why imagination came to be associated with the idea of fictitiousness is that it can create *ex nihilo* – not *in nihilo* or *cum nihilo*. The western ensemble logic, which is based on the identity assumption *ex nihilo nihil*, could not, as a consequence, but conceive of imagination as essentially non-existence. To this identity and set logic, which could never account for

18 In fact, Habermas is in no better situation. Castoriadis starts with the monadic isolation and then the problem becomes to establish how communication is possible; Habermas starts with the fact of communication but then the problem is how this relates to the unconscious. On this point, see Whitebook, 1989.

the fact that when 'x = x' it is always 'x = non x', Castoriadis counterpoises the logic of magmas. The concept of magma points to the fact that significations are not 'determinate beings' but webs of reference (*faisceaux de renvois*). These are certainly always determinable but they never are completely determinate (Castoriadis 1987: 221).

To sum up, the expression 'radical imagination' has the function of conveying two ideas. In the first place 'radical' points to the link with the project of autonomy (Castoriadis 1987, 1991). In Castoriadis' view, imagination can always potentially question it own products and can, therefore, be a means for the critique. And critique is the condition of autonomy understood as the possibility to give oneself one's law. In the second place, *radical* points to the connection with the concept of creation, with the fact that imagination comes before the distinction between 'real' and 'fictitious'. In other words, it is because radical imagination exists that 'reality' exists for us – and, therefore, one can add, it exists *tout court* (Castoriadis 1997).

This is also emphasised by the idea of social *imaginary*, which is the second point that is relevant for us. The concept of social imaginary points out that there is not a subject, on the one hand, and the reality, on the other. As we have already noted, the passage from the concept of *imagination* to that of *imaginary* reflects a change from a *subject*-oriented approach to a *context*-oriented one (Arnason 1994). Castoriadis' concept of the social imaginary also has the function of underlining the idea that the definition of 'reality' itself depends on the instituting and instituted social imaginary and *not* vice versa (Castoriadis 1991: 147). The fact that the word 'reality' has been conceived in so many different ways shows that all societies have somehow constituted their 'reality'.[19]

Otherwise put, the definition of the 'real' is the result of the dialectics between the instituted and the instituting side of the social imaginary. Behind this idea there is a complex view of the relationship between individuals, who cannot but exist within imaginary significations, and a social imaginary, which cannot but exist in and through individuals themselves. This complexity, which, as Castoriadis himself points out, cannot be reduced to simple relationships such as that between whole and part, the general and the particular, stands at odds with Castoriadis' own idea of a complete heterogeneity between the monadic psyche and society. Again the problem is that of how to conceive of the relationship between subjects and contexts.

As we have seen, the concept of imagination stands within a philosophy of the subject, whereas that of imaginary signals a new distance from such a view. The danger, however, is to fall into an equally problematic metaphysics

19 Suffice here to say that during the Middle Ages the world *realitas* meant 'perfection' so that the most real being was God and the less real our sense perceptions that are never perfect, whereas with the modern epoch the term came to assume the opposite meaning. I have reconstructed this passage in Bottici 2007: Chapters 2, 3.

of contexts. There seems to be no way out of this difficulty: if one starts with 'imagination' conceived of as an individual faculty, the problem is how to conceive of the relationship between individual imagination and the social context. If we begin with the concept of the social imaginary, the problem becomes how to reconcile it with the free imagination of individuals. The problem seems unsolvable and Castoriadis' metaphysical opposition between society and the monadic psyche is the sign that there is no easy way out from it.

Again, this is also due to the relatively limited amount of work that has been done on the topic, if compared with the work done on the concept of reason/rationality. A first direction of research is to begin with a radical questioning of the very starting points: 'imagination' as an individual faculty and 'imaginary' as a social product. If we conceive of human beings as the always problematic result of a tension between the two poles, as beings equally dependent and independent, social and monadic, as, indeed, I think we should, we need a new concept. After a passage from 'imagination' to 'imaginary', we need to take a further step and focus on what we can call the 'imaginal'. If imagination is an individual faculty and the imaginary a social context, 'imaginal' is simply what is made out of images, an adjective denoting something that can be the product of both an individual faculty and a social context. Otherwise put, 'imaginal' is simply the quality of a product that stands in between the two.

The term 'imaginal' has been introduced in the current philosophical debate by Corbin, who derived it from Arabic philosophy. Here, the Latin term *mundus imaginalis*, from the Arab *'alam al-mithal*, denotes all that is in between the world of pure intellectual intuitions and that of mere sense perceptions (Corbin 1979). Corbin, like others after him, uses the concept for specific purposes (to recover the intuition of the Persian philosophy), but for us it is sufficient to note that the concept of imaginal points to the fact that between pure intellect and the forms of sensibility, to use a Kantian expression, there is something else which also has a cognitive function and cannot simply be relegated to the ambit of the unreal and the fictitious.

The main purpose of Corbin, and of others who have followed him,[20] has been to distinguish between 'imaginal' (*imaginal*), as that which is simply made of images, from 'imaginary' (*imaginaire*), which means what is purely fictitious, unreal. The same distinction holds in the English language, where 'imaginal', according to the *Oxford English Dictionary*, denotes primarily what pertains to imagination or to mental images, whereas 'imaginary' primarily means what exists only in fancy and has no real existence and, therefore is opposed to 'real', 'actual' (Simpson and Weiner 1989, vol. II: 668).

20 The term has been recovered by Hillman in the context of his project of a renewed Jungian psychology although with a slightly different meaning (Hillman 1972), and more recently by Fleury (2006), who remains closer to Corbin's texts.

To conclude this point, the concept of imaginal points to the fact that the content of our images is not necessarily unreal, although this may also be the case (and here, as we will see, lies the ambivalence of the imaginal). In this sense, 'imaginal' is in the first place opposed to 'imaginary' as an adjective denoting a quality of images. But 'imaginal' is also distinguished from 'imaginary' as a substantive, because as what is simply made of images it can be the product both of a social imaginary and of the individual faculty of imagination.[21]

3. The political and the imaginal

What is the relationship between the imaginal and the political?

If we understand politics in its broadest meaning as whatever pertains to the *polis*, to the decisions concerning the fate of a community, the link is quite clear. In this sense, politics coincides with the public, and therefore also includes all that concerns the social.[22] Politics thus understood depends on the imaginal because it is only by imagining the public that it exists. This holds for large communities such as the modern states, but also for small ones. If the former are patently 'imaginal beings' because it is evident that only by imagining them one can perceive a sense of belonging with fellow strangers, the same holds for the latter: even in small communities, based on face-to-face relationships, you need to imagine a community in order to make it exist out of a simple collection of individuals. Communities exist because we *imagine* they exist. What you see gathered together in Athens' *agora* is a set of bodies, not (yet) a *polis*. I say *imaginal* beings, and not imagined beings, to point out that they are not only the result of an action on the side of the individuals, but always also what shapes the imagination of individuals.[23] To put it in Castoriadis' term, they are always *instituting* and *instituted*.

To sum up, the political is imaginal because it depends on the possibility to imagine commonalities, but also, as we will now see by turning to Arendt, because it depends on the possibility of freeing oneself of one's particularities. In her political reading of Kant's notion of taste, Arendt stressed precisely this point. Imagination, as what mediates between the particular and the universal in judgement, is what enables us to take the point of view of others. As she wrote in commenting on Kant's *Critique of Judgement*:

> an enlarged community is the condition *sine qua non* of right judgement; one's community sense makes it possible to enlarge one's mentality.

21 I have further developed the concept of imaginal in Bottici 2011.

22 For a reconstruction of this concept of politics, which derives from the ancient Greek term *politikos*, see, for instance, Bobbio 1990: 800.

23 The reference here is obviously to Anderson's *Imagined Communities* (Anderson 1991).

> Negatively speaking, this means that one is able to abstract from private conditions and circumstances, which, as far as judgement is concerned, limit and inhibit its exercise. Private conditions condition us; imagination and reflection enable us to liberate ourselves from them and to attain that relative impartiality that is the specific virtue of judgement.
>
> (Arendt 1982: 73)

Thus, the imaginal is what enables us to perceive the being-in-common but also, at the same time, what makes it exist. If we cannot take others' points of view, to put ourselves in their shoes, to assume an enlarged mentality then no political *lato sensu* can exist. However, the imaginal is also central to politics if we understand it in the more restricted sense of an activity characterised by the potential recourse to legitimate coercion.[24] Political power is a specific form of power, where power in general is the capacity to make somebody do what she would otherwise not do. In this sense, political power differs from other forms of power precisely because it has recourse to legitimate physical coercion. But to be perceived of as *legitimate*, political power needs to make sense within the imaginary significations of a society. If it fails to do so, it ceases to be political power and becomes mere violence, physical force. This is ultimately the reason why it rests on the imaginal.

As Castoriadis also notes, political power (he also terms it 'explicit power') is essential to every society. This is so because the fundamental ground power exercised by the instituting dimension of a society can never completely succeed in its attempt to forge compliant subjects. The instituted dimension of the social-historical will always re-emerge, because no society can ever completely subsume individuals in itself. This is the reason why, in Castoriadis' view, there has always been a dimension of the social institution in charge of this essential function: to re-establish order, to ensure the life and operation of society against whatever endangers them (Castoriadis 1991: 154).

Whether such a power is necessary in principle as Castoriadis argues or not, it is undoubtedly that, as far as it exists, it needs to rely on the imaginal. To put it in Castoriadis' words:

> Beneath the monopoly of legitimate violence lies the monopoly of the valid signification. The throne of the Lord of signification stands above the throne of the Lord of violence. The voice of the arms can only begin to be heard amid the crash of the collapsing edifice of institutions. And for violence to manifest itself effectively, the word – the injunctions of the existing power – has to keep its magic over the 'group of armed men' (Engels). The fourth company of the Pavlovsky regiment, guards to His Majesty the Czar, and the Semenovsky regiment, were the strongest pillars

24 For this definition, see for instance, Weber 1978, I: section 17, IV: sections 1, 2.

> of the throne, until those days of the February 26 and 27, 1917 when they fraternized with the crowd and turned their guns against their officers. The mightiest army in the world will not protect you if it is not loyal to you – and the ultimate foundation of its loyalty is its imaginary belief in your imaginary legitimacy.
>
> (Castoriadis 1991: 155–156)

There can be innumerable sources of legitimacy. In this book, we analyse many of them. If we take, for instance, Weber's typology of the bases of legitimacy (tradition, faith, enactment), we see that all of them rely in one way or another on the imaginal (Weber 1978, vol. I: 36–38, 212 ff). In the case of charismatic power, people obey commands because they have a faith in the sacred or heroic image of the person exercising them. But the imaginal is also crucial in traditional power: no tradition can be respected without imagining something that connects the past with the present at the same time. What is a tradition if not an imaginal being? Finally, the imaginal is also crucial for bureaucratic power. In order to believe in the legality of an institution, you need to possess a certain image of what law must be like, an exemplar law, to use Arendt's expression. It comes as no surprise to discover then that even law has always had its politics of images.[25]

If the imaginal is essential to the political, it is so with all the ambivalence that had been noted about imagination long ago. Imagination as the faculty to produce images is radical because it can make present what is absent in the double sense of creating something new, but also of denying facts. As Arendt observed, imagination is central both to our capacity for action, to begin something new in the world, but also to our ability to lie. In both cases, we deny what is given: in the first case, by creating something new, in the second by concealing it.

Hence the necessity to rethink the imaginal in connection with the project of autonomy. It is in the radical capacity of imagination to question its own products that lies the possibility of critique. Nobody pointed this out better that Castoriadis. Also guided by his own reading of the history of the Athenian *polis*, he pushed the argument as far as to postulate a distinction between the concept of the political and that of politics. While 'political' denotes politics as commonly understood (what Castoriadis also called 'explicit power'), politics, such as it was created by the Greeks, amounts to the explicit putting into question of the established institution of society (Castoriadis 1991: 159). Not by chance then he attributed to the Greeks both discoveries of politics and philosophy: Greek thought amounts to the putting into question of the most important dimension of the institution of society, the representations and norms of the tribe and the very notion of truth itself.

25 On this point, see Douzinas and Nead 1999.

Whether the Greeks invented both philosophy and politics in Castoriadis' sense is at least disputable.[26] But even if they did so, we should rather call it democratic politics. The fact that Castoriadis talks about 'true politics' or 'politics properly conceived',[27] that he needs to add those two little words, 'true' and 'properly', is a sign that he is trying to persuade us of something that goes against common understanding. In contrast to Castoriadis, I think one should be allowed to violate the maxim *nomina non sunt multiplicando praeter necessitatem*, if one needs to. But in this case, there is a name for what Castoriadis calls 'true politics' and that is democracy. Let us therefore stick to our previous (and more common) definition of politics.

Yet the point that Castoriadis makes about the need to rethink the link between the imaginal and the political in connection with the project of autonomy should be further discussed. In what conditions can the imaginal be a means to pursue autonomy? The most general answer is when the imaginal is a means for critique, in other words, when the imaginal is able to question its own products. This is not always easy to realise because, as Castoriadis himself noted, every society will attempt to cover up the instituting dimension of society through the imputation of the origin of the institution and of its social significations to an extra-social source (Castoriadis 1991: 153). By 'extrasocial', Castoriadis means 'external to the actual, living society': external in this sense are therefore the gods, but, also, founding ancestors.

More generally we can say that the greatest danger is any attempt at a closure of meaning operated against or through the imaginal itself. Religion, and in particular the three religions of the Book, are a potential example. By attributing to an *other* the source of truth, the religions of the book tend to cover up the instituted dimension of a society. 'So it is written' actually means 'you cannot imagine it otherwise'. Certainly a book can be interpreted, but as Castoriadis again pointed out, 'interpretations' and 'commentaries' are the means employed by world religions in order to process and assimilate the new. Once a closure of meaning has been operated, 'interpretations' become the means through which the new can be subjected to a fictitious, but efficient, *reductio* and a closure of meaning thus perpetuated while apparently accepting the new (Castoriadis 1991: 153).[28]

Innumerable are, however, the means through which such a closure can be operated. Science can be another source. By saying that 'it is scientifically proven' that things are a certain way and therefore cannot be otherwise, the imaginal is closed. If science says that a given population is genetically superior to another, you need other scientific proofs in order to imagine them otherwise.

26 For instance, I have argued elsewhere that the very idea of a Greek's invention of philosophy is rather problematic (Bottici 2007: 20–43).

27 See, for instance, Castoriadis 1991: 160.

28 On this point, see also Bottici 2009 and Challand's contribution to this volume.

Traditions can be another potential source of closure: to say that things have *always* been a certain way and should therefore be preserved amounts to saying 'you should not imagine them otherwise'. But what I want to do in conclusion is to address this point with regards to the ambivalence that the imaginal is generating within contemporary conditions.

4. Contemporary transformations: the global society of the spectacle

On the one hand, contemporary politics is overwhelmed by the imaginal. It depends on images, not only because images mediate our being in the world and are therefore crucial for any sort of communication – political communication being no exception. There seems to be something more, a sort of hypertrophy of the imaginal, in the first place due to the massive diffusion of the media. If we think of what politics used to be before streams of images started to enter our homes through television, it is clear that images are no longer what mediates our doing politics, but have become an end in themselves, which risk doing politics in our stead. One only has to think of the so-called mass marketing of politics and what democracy has become in an age of manufactured images on an industrial scale (Newman 1999).

On the other hand, politics seems to lack imagination in the sense of the capacity to question what is given. In an epoch when politics is reduced to governance, to simple administration within a general neoliberal consensus there is no space to imagine things differently.[29] This apparent paradox is in fact the result of a hypertrophy of the more *passive* side of imagination, which happened at the expense of the more *active* side of it. We are so image saturated that it becomes increasingly difficult to create new images. This is the consequence of a change in both the *quantity* and the *quality* of the images produced in a global epoch. With regard to the first, we cannot but notice a decisive increase in the quantity of images that enter our life. In particular, the quantity of images produced by the media has reached such a proportion as to determine also a qualitative leap: images have become an end in themselves and political spectacle prevails over politics as such.

Many authors have noticed, for instance, the ritual function of elections. By virtue of their mere repetition, elections reinforce a certain model of society by providing it with visible continuity. But today the quantity of images that accompanies elections in most western countries has become such that the spectacle completely prevails over the content. Images are too numerous; they

29 The term governance was coined in the 1980s to denote the politics of the World Bank in a juridical context that denied the World Bank the right to exercise functions of government. Since then, 'governance' became synonymous with a way of doing politics that does not imply government and therefore quite often amounts to mere technique (Bottici 2006).

need to be filtered in some way. It is the dominant rule of the audience that does the job: only those images that can capture people's attention are selected. Hence, the prevalence of the register of the spectacle. However, the battle that is put on the stage of our screens during elections occults that, in fact, no real battle is taking place, because the real clash is not among the official candidates (who most often have very similar programmes), but outside the screens. The real fight is between the political options that are admitted and those that are left out. The decisive distance is not that between candidates to elections, but between those who get a role in the spectacle and those who can only look at it.[30]

In the second place, there has also been an intrinsic *qualitative* change in the nature of images, a change that is likely deeply to affect the link between the political and the imaginal. Behind the virtual revolution there is indeed a deep change in the nature of images: not only have images become commodities, which are therefore subjected to the laws and treatment of all other commodities, but they are now also malleable in a way that has never been the case.[31] Images are not only *reproducible* in series, but they are also *modifiable* up to a point where they can be completely falsified. In other words, images have completely lost their link with the 'here' and the 'now'.

One way to illustrate this point is to start with Benjamin's remarks on the work of art in the age of its technological reproducibility. Benjamin argues that as a consequence of their reproducibility (mainly due to photography and cinema) works of art have lost their 'aura'. The aura is defined as 'a strange tissue of space and time: the unique apparition of a distance, however near it may be' (Benjamin 2002: 104–105). Artistic images have lost their being *hic et nunc*, here and now. A piece of music can be repeated in different spaces and times in a substantially identical form so that we can say that this is precisely that concert, played by X and Y in the moment Z and not any other. Similarly, a photograph can be reproduced *ad infinitum* without its being possible to distinguish between the original and the copies.

With the advent of virtual images, we have reached a further level. Photography and cinema, it can be argued, still had a connection with the *hic et nunc*. A picture needed to be taken before being reproduced and a film needed to be shot in the first place. Even if they could be both cut and assembled in different ways at different times they still had their original here and now, the moment when they were taken, turned, created. All this is overcome by virtuality. There is no *hic et nunc* in a virtual image, and therefore

30 The reason why surveys on the role of the media in elections often fail to catch their real impact is that they often simply assess the extent to which media have influenced preferences for one or another official candidate. In fact, the power of the media comes well before, in making certain political options possible.

31 On the commoditisation of images within contemporary capitalism, see Bazzicalupo's contribution to this volume.

also no original to orient us and thus no authenticity to be preserved. Virtual images are not objects that can be created at once, but on-going processes. There is no original creation, but only a process of perpetual maintenance.

One of the problems connected with this transformation is the fact that images still tend to present themselves as carriers of a *hic et nunc*. Many of the pathologies of the imaginal of our time are linked to the fact that there is no easy way to determine the content of the reality of images. Still, there is also a potential for new forms of democratisation in all this. Everybody has the potential to modify a virtual image. If a film needed expensive equipment to be shot, now a mobile phone seems to suffice.

Perhaps it is too early to grasp fully the implications of such a transformation. There are, however, signs which seem to point to a very different direction from the one taken at the time of Benjamin. Commenting on the possible positive consequences of the transformation he witnessed, Benjamin observed that the technology of reproduction detaches the reproduced object from the sphere of tradition: by replicating the work many times over, it substitutes a mass existence for a unique existence. In his view, the result of this process should be the shattering of every form of tradition. Benjamin's reasoning is quite clear: if tradition depends on the authenticity of things and if mass reproduction destroys authenticity, then it must also destroy tradition.

He thought that this was most evident in film. The social impact of film, particularly in its most positive form, has a 'destructive, cathartic side' namely 'the liquidation of the value of tradition in the cultural heritage' (Benjamin 2002: 104). By commenting on the possible site for such liquidation, he observed as follows:

> This phenomenon is most apparent in the great historical films. It is assimilating ever more advanced positions in its spread. When Abel Gance fervently proclaimed in 1927, 'Shakespeare, Rembrandt, Beethoven will make films . . . All legends, all mythologies, and all myths, all founders of religions, indeed, all religions . . . attend their celluloid resurrections, and the heroes are pressing at the gates' he was inviting the reader, no doubt unawares, to witness a comprehensive liquidation.
>
> (Benjamin 2002: 104)

The sarcastic tone of this passage shows how certain Benjamin was about his prediction. Benjamin wrote this passage between late December 1935 and the beginning of February 1936. Nearly a century later, we can say that he was completely mistaken or that at least the technological developments that have followed have rendered his analysis antiquated. Indeed, not only have we had geniuses such as Beethoven and Rembrandt making films, but, moreover, we are assisting to a resurrection of all sorts of myths and religions in the imaginal (Bottici 2007, 2009). The only difference is that they are not *celluloid*, but *virtual* resurrections.

To conclude, the imaginal seems to have kept and perhaps even exacerbated the ambivalence that accompanied the genealogy of the concept. Particularly in its link to the political, the imaginal displays its potential both for emancipation and for oppression. The imaginal can both open the path for critique, and thus autonomy, but also close it, as easily as it has opened it. Going back to the metaphor used by Plato and Aristotle, we can say that it is both a source of light and a source of darkness.

References

Adorno, T.W. and Horkheimer, M. 1997, *Dialectic of Enlightenment*, London, Verso.
Anderson, B. 1991, *Imagined Communities. Reflections on the Spread of Nationalism*, London, Verso.
Arendt, H. 1972, 'Lying in politics', in *Crises of the Republic*, New York and London, Harvest/HBJ.
—— 1982, *Lectures on Kant's Political Philosophy*, Brighton, Harvester.
Aristotle. 1964, *On the Soul. Parva Naturalia. On Breath* (trans. W.S. Hett), Cambridge, Loeb Classical Library, Harvard University Press.
Arnason, J.P. 1994, 'Reason, imagination, interpretation', in Robinson, G. and Rundell, J. (eds) *Rethinking Imagination: Culture and Creativity*, London, Routledge, pp. 155–170.
Bacon, F. 1963, *De dignitate et augmentis scientiarum*, in *The Works of Francis Bacon*, vol. I, Stuttgart, Fromann, pp. 415–838.
—— 1986, *Of the Dignity and Advancement of Learning*, in *The Works of Francis Bacon*, vol. IV, Stuttgart, Fromann, pp. 275–498.
Benjamin, W. 2002, 'The work of art in the age of its technological reproducibility', in *Selected Writings, Volume 3, 1935–1938*, Cambridge, MA, Belknap Press.
Bobbio, N. 1990, 'Politica', in *Dizionario di politica*, Torino, UTET.
Bottici, C. 2006, 'Guerra e conflitto in un mondo globalizzato: governance o impero?', *Quaderni Forum*, XIX (3): 29–48.
—— 2007, *Philosophy of Political Myth*, Cambridge: Cambridge University Press.
—— 2009, 'The politics of imagination and the public role of religion', *Philosophy and Social Criticism*, 35 (8): 985–1005.
—— 2011, *Imaginal Politics*, forthcoming, Columbia University Press.
Busino, G. (ed.) 1989, *Autonomie et autotransformation de la société. La philosophie militante de Cornelius Castoriadis*, Geneva, Libraire Droz.
Castoriadis, C. 1987, *The Imaginary Institution of Society*, Cambridge, Polity Press.
—— 1991, 'Power, politics, autonomy', in *Philosophy, Politics, Autonomy – Essays in Political Philosophy*, Oxford, Oxford University Press, pp. 143–175.
—— 1997, 'Radical imagination and the social instituting imaginary', in *The Castoriadis Reader*, Oxford, Blackwell, pp. 319–338.
Cocking, J.M. 1994, *Imagination: A Study in the History of Ideas*, London, Routledge.
Corbin, H. 1979, *Corp spirituel et terre céleste*, Paris, Buchet-Chastel.
Coulter, J. 1999, 'Discourse and mind', *Human Studies*, 22: 163–181.
Douzinas, C. and Nead, L. 1999, *Law and Image*, Chicago, University of Chicago Press.
Ferrara, S. 2008, *The Force of the Example. Explorations in the Paradigm of Judgment*, New York, Columbia University Press.
Fleury, C. 2006, *Imagination, imaginaire, imaginal*, Paris, PUF.

Friese, H. 2001, 'Imagination: history of the concept', in Smelser, N.J. and Baltes, P.B. (eds) *International Encyclopedia of Social & Behavioural Sciences*, vol. 11, Amsterdam, Elsevier, pp. 7197–7201.

Gadamer, H.G. 1988, *Truth and Method*, London, Sheed & Ward.

Galilei, G. 1996, 'Il saggiatore', in *Opere. Volume I*, Torino, UTET.

Guenancia, P. 2006, 'La critique cartésienne des critiques de l'imagination', in Fleury, C. (ed.) *Imagination, imaginaire, imaginal*, Paris, PUF, pp. 43–76.

Habermas, J. 1987, *The Philosophical Discourse of Modernity. Twelve Lectures*, Cambridge, Polity Press.

Hillman, J. 1972, *The Myth of the Analysis*, Evanston, IL, Northwestern University Press.

Kant, I. 1998, 'Critique of pure reason' (trans. P. Guyer and A.W. Wood), in *The Cambridge Edition of the Works of Immanuel Kant*, Cambridge, Cambridge University Press.

—— 2000, *Critique of the Power of Judgment* (trans. P. Guyer and E. Matthews), in *The Cambridge Edition of the Works of Immanuel Kant*, Cambridge, Cambridge University Press.

Maguire, M. 2006, *The Conversion of Imagination. From Pascal through Rousseau to Tocqueville*, Cambridge, MA, Harvard University Press.

Newman, B. 1999, *The Mass Marketing of Politics. Democracy in an Age of Manufactured Images*, London, Sage.

Novalis. 1977, 'Schriften', in *Die Werke Friedrich von Hardenbergs*, Stuttgart, Kohlhammer.

Pascal, B. 1963, *Oeuvres complètes*, Paris, Seuil.

Plato. 1989, *The Collected Dialogues* (trans. E. Hamilton and H. Cairns), Princeton, Princeton University Press.

Robinson, G. and Rundell, J. (eds) 1994, *Rethinking Imagination: Culture and Creativity*, London, Routledge.

Rundell, J. 1994a, 'Introduction', in Robinson, G. and Rundell, J. (eds) *Rethinking Imagination: Culture and Creativity*, London, Routledge, pp. 1–11.

—— 1994b, 'Creativity and judgment: Kant on reason and imagination', in Robinson, G. and Rundell, J. (eds) *Rethinking Imagination: Culture and Creativity*, London, Routledge, pp. 87–117.

Sartre, J.P. 1936, *L'imagination*, Paris, PUF.

—— 1940, *L'imaginaire*, Paris, Gallimard.

Simpson, J.A. and Weiner, E.S.C. (eds) 1989, *The Oxford English Dictionary*, Oxford, Clarendon Press.

Vattimo, A. 1999a, 'Estetica', in *Enciclopedia di filosofia*, Milano, Garzanti, pp. 340–345.

—— 1999b, 'Immaginazione', in *Enciclopedia di filosofia*, Milano, Garzanti, pp. 528–530.

Vico, G. 1999, *New Science* (trans. D. Marsh), London, Penguin.

von Savigny, E. 1991, 'Common behavior of many a kind', in Arrington, R.L. and Glock, H.J. (eds) *Wittgenstein's Philosophical Investigations: Text and Context*, London, Routledge, pp. 105–119.

Weber, M. 1978, *Economy and Society*, Berkeley, University of California Press.

Whitebook, J. 1989, 'Intersubjectivity and the monadic core of the psyche: Habermas and Castoriadis on the unconscious', in Busino, G. (ed.) *Autonomie et autotransformation de la société. La philosophie militante de Cornelius Castoriadis*, Geneva, Libraire Droz, pp. 225–245.

Chapter 2

Politics at its best

Reasons that move the imagination

Alessandro Ferrara

1. *L'imagination au pouvoir*

The year 1968 is often said to have changed our sense of what politics is. From the slow boring of hard plankwood that Max Weber was keen on likening it to, suddenly, for hundreds of thousands of young demonstrators in Paris and countless other cities of the west, politics had come to signify a reappropriation of the ability to shape one's life against the strictures of perceived reality: 'Be realistic: ask for the impossible' was another popular slogan. During the four decades that have elapsed since that moment, politics has by and large been more on the side of the slow boring than on that of a tidal wave of the imagination, except perhaps when the Berlin Wall fell in November 1989. In any event, although politics is indeed a recurrent object of our discourse, rarely do we pause to define it.

This is what I would like to do in this chapter: building on a certain understanding of the social I will first try to grapple with the task of offering a definition of politics (section 2); then I look at some constitutive moments of politics in the light of four different philosophical paradigms that can cast light on them: discourse, judgment, recognition and gift (sections 3 and 4). Finally, I'll go back to the relation of politics to the imagination, recasting it from the immediate shortcircuit that has been a starting point in 1968 to a reflective structural relation (section 5). This approach is different from that of Bottici and others in this volume, in that the imagination will be addressed in its meaning as the capacity to represent what is not immediately present and in the role it plays in helping us make sense of politics at its best.

2. Defining politics

To offer a definition of politics without taking sides *in* politics is the challenge that I would like to take up: meeting it means to characterize politics in such a way that no one, regardless of her substantive views, can, as the received formula goes, 'reasonably reject' such view as reductive, parochial, biased.

Motivated by a pragmatist inclination to pay tribute to common sense as the starting point of reflection, I turned to the top level of common sense, the kind of common sense reflected in Webster's dictionary, for a Wittgensteinian dispensable ladder from which to begin our ascent to knowledge. But when I saw politics defined as 'the science and art of political government' and 'the conducting of political affairs', I threw the ladder away in utter desperation and resolved to try to build it on my own.

Let us start from the three most shareable premises that we can imagine. First, no human being exists who does not act and whose action does not fit, albeit only in a merely mental sense, within a larger human collectivity. Second, no action can be envisaged without reference to some notion of ends and means. Third, no preestablished harmony exists between all the ends pursued by human beings and the social unions within which they live. Hence the need for politics: politics sinks its roots in the unavoidable necessity of coordinating the ends of one's own action with those underlying other people's actions when we live in a shared world.

Let us comment briefly on each of these assumptions. Human beings do not live in isolation. This proposition can be agreed to both by those who explain the fact of sociation in terms of a special propensity of the human being qua *zoon politikòn* (Aristotle, Hegel, Marx) and by those who explain sociation in terms of its convenience for beings to various degrees weak, desirous and rational (Hobbes, Locke, Rousseau).

Furthermore, whichever anthropological view and whichever theory of action we subscribe to, no one will deny that every human being, among the many things he or she does, somehow also *acts.* And whenever we speak of action, as opposed to some neurological reflex, inevitably we presuppose the relevance of 'means' and 'ends'. Thus every human being lives her life within a larger human group, whatever this group's size, and acts by using certain means to reach certain ends.

We need not bother to know whether these means and ends are autonomously chosen or tacitly derived from the traditions that prevail in the social union to which the individual considered belongs. More important for the purpose of our discussion is the idea – also uncontroversial – that these means and the respective ends display a certain temporal sequentiality. We are not doomed to pursue just one end at a time. Rather, our being allegedly endowed with a modicum of rationality means, among other things, that usually we can will something for the sake of something else or, in other words, we can envisage certain ends as means to further ends. Consequently, being notoriously finite human beings, we must also accept the idea that in the mind of each individual there exists one or more ends that no longer prelude to further links in the chain – one or more 'ultimate ends'.

Mere logic requires that for every individual member of a given society there exists one or more ends that are not means to any further end – namely, one or more ultimate ends. Borrowing the strong term 'contradiction' from the vocabulary of logic, Parsons argues that it is no less than *contradictory* for us to think that a number of individuals belong in one and the same society, as opposed to the state of nature, and at the same time that their ultimate ends are totally unrelated or, which is the same, in a random relation.[32] This is not to say that the relation among these subjective ultimate ends should be thought of as harmonic – very often it may be an antagonistic relation – but it means that such a relation cannot but be patterned in one way or other or, in other words, *cannot be random*. This frame of reference, elaborated in order to account for the nature of social institutions, as Parsons calls them, or more generally for the nature of the social, enables us at the same time to understand the nature of politics.

In fact, we will not have any difficulty in acknowledging that these ultimate ends pursued by the individuals of a given society, though in some kind of non-random relation to one another, are not likely to be identical. If they are not identical and if – as we will also have no difficulty supposing – the amount of resources altogether available in the social union considered are not unlimited and do not allow the simultaneous pursuit of all the ends striven after by all individuals, there arises the need of *prioritizing* these ends. In this ineludible need sinks its roots that way of relating to the world which we call politics. Only a human form of association to which unlimited resources were available and which could equally satisfy all the ends striven after by all of its members could dispense with politics. The important role of the imagination becomes manifest here: by enabling us to project an image of the world, the imagination allows us to perceive certain ends as deserving more or less priority over others and, more particularly, to envisage new ends. But we will return to this later.

The space of politics, roughly speaking, is thus the space where a priority is assigned to those ends to whose pursuit the not unlimited resources of a given social union are to be allocated. Even the creation of sovereignty, understood by Hobbes as stemming from a unanimous desire to protect the integrity of human life, is not at all the *big bang* of politics. Rather, it is a by-product of an even prior orientation consisting in unanimously prioritizing security over any other end.

To define politics in terms of the ineludible need to select which set of needs deserves to be assigned the limited resources collectively available allows us to create a notion of politics topographically located before the bifurcation, and thus neutral, between the two classically opposed ways of understanding the task of philosophically reflecting on politics – namely, the 'normative' and the 'realistic' understanding of this task. In fact, we can rethink the alternative quality of these two approaches as the alternative between those who think that assigning priority to certain ends can never prescind from a dimension of sheer force and those who instead think that such assignment must take place in the light of reasons which, at least ideally, neutralize all relations of force among the supporters of the various options.

32 Cf. Parsons 1990: 322–323.

Not all forms and processes of prioritization of ends, however, fall within the domain of politics. When I wonder which of my ends deserves priority – when I silently deliberate on whether to accept a certain academic position or to speed up the writing of a new book – I'm obviously not engaging in politics. When I deliberate with other members of my family whether to devolve a given amount of money to purchase a new car or to take an extended visit to a far flung country, obviously we are not faced with political deliberation. Here we encounter another fundamental ingredient of any definition of politics: the distinction of *public and private*.[33] Only that deliberation on the priority of ends is political which – either on account of the nature of the controversy, or on account of the large number of people entitled to participate, or on account of the mode of deliberation, or on account of all or some combination of these elements – produces outcomes which are binding for everybody.

By definition, public is anything that affects the overlap among the individuals' ultimate ends and among the institutional segments of the social union considered: to find out what is and what is not included within this area of overlap – and thus to find out what can truly count as a shared end – is an eminently political task. But public is also what is binding for everybody despite its not being an ultimate end. Politics is, in fact, also the arena where interests and values compete for consent, the arena of contestation between what is favored by some and rejected by others. The political quality of the contest between opposing interests – for example, the contest between supporters and critics of public funding for private schools – rests often not so much on their constituting ultimate ends, but on the impact that the prevailing of one interest or other would have for society as a whole. Thus if the representatives of the association of employers negotiate with the unions on the norms for laying off workers, this is a political controversy, despite its taking place outside state institutions such as parliaments. Also in this case, we are merely anticipating a general idea that specific political philosophers then articulate in their own vocabulary: namely, the idea that what goes on outside political and state institutions proper – within civil society (Hegel), in the sphere of production (Marx) or in the public sphere (Habermas) – may at times possess more political significance and exert a larger impact on society than what takes place within formal institutional contexts.

To sum up then, what is private falls beyond the scope of politics in the sense that its inherent normativity, if any dimension of 'ought' is bound up with it, binds no one else than the actors directly involved in the action. My promise to invite you over for dinner on Saturday is binding only for me and my family. Private is what is located beyond the threshold past which formal political power, namely state institutions, must refrain from exerting influence.

33 On this distinction, see Weintraub 1997. For a feminist critique of the distinction, see Gavison 1992 and Pateman 1983.

Private is that which is at the single individual's or a group of individuals' disposal. But the dividing line between what is private and what is public is itself a fluctuating line and an object of political contestation, as is the case, for example, in every discussion on the application and enforcement of individual rights.

Finally, to conclude this general section on the nature of politics, we should be wary of understanding politics along functionalist lines, merely or mainly as a way of satisfying our more or less shared needs, desires and preferences in light of the more general values that inspire our conduct. Most of all, we should be wary of equating politics with the 'institutional' and the *staatlich*, as the common sense definition offered by Webster's dictionary does. For politics is also the locus in which *new* values and *new* needs are articulated. And it is here that the imagination, as the faculty for disclosing the new by representing what is not immediately present, becomes crucial. In its routine mode, politics coordinates shared values and perceived needs in order to find consensual policies for satisfying those needs, but in its most edifying and elevated moments, politics always entails a redrawing of the map of our values and needs. In other words, politics at its best is the articulation of reasons that move the imagination. But before addressing that topic, the constitutive blocks of politics in our horizon must first be explored.

3. Politics in our horizon

The definition offered thus far, however, is merely a rough approximation that needs more substance added if it is to become a picture in which we recognize the contours of what politics is for us, given our own philosophical horizon and questions. In thickening our notion of politics, we inevitably leave behind the terrain of what goes without saying, but I hope the new territory that we are entering now will, nonetheless, remain characterized by an ample share of reasonable consensus.

To understand what politics is for us, at the beginning of the 21st century, requires that we grasp what it means for it to be *autonomous* and for it to take place within a *global horizon.* Furthermore, it requires that we clarify what its *constitutive moments* are and how each of them is best highlighted by one of the paradigms present within our horizon (section 4). Finally, a complete understanding of what politics is for us also requires that we reconstruct our sense of what politics at its best is and, in this connection, the relation of politics to the imagination will be addressed (section 5).

Ever since Machiavelli's times we have learned to consider politics as an autonomous activity. But our understanding of what such autonomy means has suffered a certain distortion. Only one of the philosophical seeds planted by Machiavelli has come to fruition, whereas the other has fallen on a very inhospitable terrain and has blossomed only recently. For a long time the phrase 'the autonomy of politics' has quintessentially meant 'autonomy from morals' and in turn such 'autonomy from morals' has boiled down to the idea of a 'deontological difference' between the degrees of freedom attributed to the ordinary citizen and those attributed to government officials – a deontological difference on which I will briefly comment when discussing the import of the global horizon for our perception of politics. However, the autonomy of politics from moral principles, from religious commands and from a traditional ethos is far from exhausting the meaning of the phrase 'the autonomy of politics'. Only since the second half of the 20th century, and thanks to the work of two authors as diverse as Hannah Arendt and John Rawls, has the second seed contained in Machiavelli's view of politics begun to blossom. This second seed is the autonomy of politics from what we shall call theory or metaphysics.

For both Arendt and the author of *Political Liberalism*, politics cannot be understood as the 'application' or the 'translation into practice' of principles imported from a non-political sphere, be it a religious sphere or even philosophical reflection as such. Only the Arendtian critique of the roots of totalitarianism and the antiperfectionist 'political' liberalism of the second phase of Rawls's work can lead us to a definitive break with the 'myth of the cave' whose spell has imbued our view of politics for over two millennia.

Modern politics, and even more so democratic politics, cannot consist of bringing into the cave an idea of the Good that we have contemplated outside: the scene of modern politics is the cave itself. Least of all can legitimate rulership be grounded on imposing a solitary vision of the Good onto recalcitrant subjects. Politics so conceived quickly turns into a struggle between factions that try to win the whole world to some general truth. Instead, with a radical departure from this long established tradition, Rawls urges on us that 'the zeal to embody the whole truth in politics is incompatible with an idea of public reason that belongs with democratic citizenship' (Rawls 1999: 133). Public reason is a subspecies of a deliberative reason which neither surrenders to the world of appearance, to *doxa*, to remain within Plato's vocabulary, nor presumes that salvation can originate from without, but instead tries tenaciously to distinguish better and worse, what is more and what is less just, what is more reasonable and what is less so, within the light conditions of the cave. Similarly, for Arendt, politics is the art of defining who we are, of turning us into what we want to be, without responding to the intimations of any other discourse than that of politics.

The autonomy of politics, thus understood, means that the standards for identifying what is worth pursuing together, in concert, are to be found inside politics and not outside it, namely inside the context of a life of freedom in which everybody can search for and testify to her own truth – philosophical, religious, existential truth – and try to convince as many other people as she can through the force of her arguments and of her example, as long as she never tries to support such truth through that coercive power of the state, which is legitimately, as opposed to arbitrarily, used only if it is used in the service of a truth shared by everybody, albeit a somewhat 'limited' truth.

Furthermore, to understand political action, perhaps more than any other type of action, requires that we grasp the nature of and the constraints posed by the context within which it takes place. Political action takes on different features if it occurs in a Greek *polis*, in an empire, in a medieval fiefdom, a free city-state, a Renaissance 'signoria', a nation-state or the globalized world. Our own horizon for political action is the globalized world. The facts of globalization are easily stated: the full unfolding of a world economy from which no country can successfully insulate itself and the rise of a global financial market, where the fluctuations of exchange rates, of currencies and equities overwhelm the steering capacity of any global player, including the Federal Reserve Bank; the rise of environmental risks that are limited by no border; the formation of migratory waves that no nation-state can face and curb on its own; the rise of media of mass communication which stimulate the growth of a global public sphere sometimes activated in terms of indignation, other times in terms of compassion or other emotions; the development of a culture industry which markets its products worldwide and contributes to the rise of a popular culture of global scope.

Much more difficult to grasp is the normative implications of these facts to the nature of politics in our time. The first challenge before us is to free our conception of politics from the fetters of 'methodological nationalism'. Not just the basics of 'international relations', but all the central categories of politics – freedom, justice, equality, peace, legitimation and many others – have to be reconfigured on a scale global from the outset. Freedom secured in one single country could lose its meaning unless freedom is guaranteed in the relation among the countries of the world. Justice could easily become a travesty of justice unless a measure of distributive justice across the various countries of the world can be secured. The equality of the citizens of a single country makes little sense vis-à-vis massive inequalities in the world. Peace in one region of the world is not unaffected by the wars that ravage other parts. What is considered legitimate in one country may very well fail to stand up to the scrutiny of a broader form of consciousness, no longer bound to a parochial locality, and may be rejected by the international community. Such reconfiguration certainly requires an effort of imagination but also has the potential for opening up a new phase of politics at its best.

These are the contours of the new horizon within which the autonomy of politics from morality needs to be rethought. If we interrogate Machiavelli on the grounds that justify the 'deontological difference' or on why the prince is to be allowed an extra degree of freedom in his political conduct and why the principles of morality are less binding on him than they are for those subjected to his rule, the answer that we glean from a reconstruction of his thought is entirely bound up with the horizon of the Westphalian system of states under formation in his times. The 'deontological difference' finds its raison-d'être in the circumstance that while the ordinary citizen can see the torts he may suffer remedied within a functioning rule of law, the prince has no rule of law or judicial procedure to appeal to should his state suffer harm because of his abiding by the principles of morality, of his keeping to his word, of his being loyal to allies and the like. The absence of binding law in the relations among states is the reason why the prince should legitimately be allowed to take the law into his hands at all times, in a way that is precluded to the ordinary citizen and why he should be allowed to disentangle his political conduct from the principles of morality.

However, once we move to a different horizon, where hypothetically the relations among the states of the world respond to a cosmopolitan rule of law, our understanding of the relation between politics and morality cannot remain unaffected. Domestically, all justification for the deontological difference collapses in light of the concrete actionability in international courts of the torts unjustly suffered by a single state. But also at the global level there is no reason for the officials in charge of the cosmopolitan institutions to benefit from the deontological difference in that by definition there is no 'external' moment of world-politics, no tort that the cosmopolis as such can suffer – at least as long as the Earth remains the only arena for politics.

4. The building blocks of politics: discourse, judgment, recognition and the gift

Let me recapitulate. Politics in general then is the activity of *promoting, with outcomes purportedly binding for all, the priority of certain publicly relevant ends over others not simultaneously pursuable, or of promoting new ends and to promote them in full autonomy from both morals and theory within a horizon no longer coextensive with the nation-state*. In section 5, we will see in more detail how in this process of prioritizing ends the imagination, together with reason, plays a crucial role insofar as it discloses what is not immediately in front of us.

We can examine this general notion of politics from the vantage point of a variety of paradigms, each of which can highlight one aspect of the complex practice we term politics.

Let me start with the question: '*How* does politics, relative to other activities, promote the priority of certain public ends relative to others?' Leaving aside those realistic theories that have emphasized the role of force or of the threat of force as the main variable that accounts for success in prioritizing certain ends, let us limit our inquiry to democratic politics only. The competitive conceptions of democracy – Dahl, Downs, Lipset, Schumpeter and others – explain the capacity for politics to promote certain ends relative to others by reference to the fact that the proponents of a given political orientation – candidates and parties competing for popular vote – manage to offer a platform that meets with the preferences of a larger number of citizens than the platform put forward by the proponents of a competing orientation. Political action at its best consists of assembling and successfully marketing a political proposal that satisfies a larger popular demand, where demand is an aggregate of unscrutinized preferences.

Instead, for deliberative conceptions of democracy – Benhabib, Cohen, Habermas, but in a broader sense also Rawls, Laden and many others – the priority of certain ends over others is promoted, when politics operates in a non-distorted way, through the force of reasons. These reasons are exchanged in a public space that different authors name in different ways and then work their way to an institutional forum in which binding decisions, on both the legislative and the executive side, are made. Without this moment of *discourse* – broadly understood as the exchange of reasons under conditions of good faith, equality and reciprocity – politics would be based merely on force and the contingencies of power. Apel and Habermas have provided the most important contribution to our understanding of what it means for a given political practice to get closer to or further away from the ideal standard of an exchange of reasons in the absence of coercion. Discourse as an exchange of reasons is not only an ideal. Its minimal presence (even just a token one) is also a lower threshold of political decency. That minimal presence in the form of a practice of consultation, albeit non-egalitarian, is, for Rawls, what distinguishes decent peoples – peoples who do not adopt a democratic or liberal regime but nonetheless deserve to be part of a peaceful 'society of peoples' – from peoples who do not object to living in an 'outlaw state' and with whom we can only relate on the level of force.[34]

Hence my first thesis concerning the constituents of politics: to pay the discursive moment of politics its dues means that no acceptable form of politics can exist which does not include the exchange of reasons as part and parcel of that more general effort of promoting the priority of certain public ends of which politics as such consists.

At the same time, this thesis about the ineliminability of reason giving and reason assessing from politics must not be confused with the disputable idea that the exchange of reasons exhausts what needs to be said about politics: politics can never be reduced to an exchange of reasons for the purpose of assessing which one is the best. Neither can the assessment of reason be taken as the only regulative ideal relevant for politics – as many neo-Kantian approaches to politics urge on us – without missing several other constitutive moments of politics.[35]

In fact, a political praxis based only on the discursive assessment of the priority of public ends would never come to a 'closure', would never result in

34 See Rawls 1999: 71–72 and 80–81.

35 Up to a given point in Habermas' intellectual trajectory, this inspiration has characterized his discursive approach. Starting from *Between Facts and Norms* (1992), however, Habermas has explicitly included a pragmatic moment within politics and has addressed it in terms of the distinction between 'rational consensus' and 'compromise'. See Habermas 1992: 196–198.

a specific decision, unless at some point a moment of *judgment* did not intervene. Not only are the diverse priorities supported by the various parties based on conflicting reasons in favor or against, but these reasons themselves can have a different and again controversial weight, depending on their salience for larger and more comprehensive conceptions that compete for our consent. Sometimes – and this may be even more unfortunate – the reasons in favor or against a certain prioritization of public ends have roughly the same weight in the eyes of the deliberative body. Then the nightmare of any discursive view of a normativity and politics quickly comes true. That nightmare is a situation of 'tie', namely a situation in which it is incumbent on you and me, as co-deliberating individuals, to make the difference, to break the tie without being able to take refuge in the position of someone who merely registers or takes notice of the greater weight of the reasons put forward by one party relative to the opposing party and then adds her own non-influential consent to an already formed majority. Under those circumstances, the goodness of reason has to be addressed independently of the rationality of a consensus on their goodness, which is not yet formed.

The case of a tie, however, is but a special case that helps us understand the ineliminability of the moment of judgment within politics. To make the point in more general terms, the discursive quality of reason – when we speak of politics – is to be understood as a 'deliberative discursiveness', namely, an exercise of discourse that remains anchored to a practical context and within imagined borders, aims at solving a given problem with material and symbolic resources which are finite and largely (albeit not exclusively) pre-given, and aims at solving it within a temporal horizon which, differently than in the case of speculative reason, cannot be indeterminedly extended.

The judgment moment in politics bridges the gap between the unlimited openness of speculative-critical discourse – our questions on the nature of freedom, of justice, of equality, of *laicité* may *never* receive a conclusive answer as long as the human mind survives – with the finiteness of the context within which a political problem arises and requires a solution within a temporal frame that it is not up to the deliberators to extend at their will. This gap is bridged by judgment not by way of limiting the pluralism of the alternative positions that are assessed in discourse, but by way of harnessing politics to the reasonable, namely to the area of overlap where what is shared can be found. The art of judgment is the art of extending as far as possible this area of overlap while continuing to preserve the ability of what lies within the area of overlapping consensus to exemplarily reflect the superordinate identity which includes the conflicting parties. This exemplary relation between what is overlappingly shared and who we are, which constitutes the only source from which the reasonable draws its distinctive normative force once we distinguish public reason from practical reason, provides the basis for *everyone* – no matter whether concurring or dissenting, majority or minority – to accept the full legitimacy of a politically binding, yet non-unanimous, decision. Once again, the normative force of exemplarity (Ferrara 2008) presupposes the capacity of our imagination to represent what is not immediately in front of us and to foster an enlarged mentality (section 5).

No politics, however, can take place without interlocutors. No discourse can exist without a 'who' of discourse, a partner in our dialogue. Neither can a judgment exist without an addressee of that judgment. And because no politics can exist without society (or better put, without our anticipating mentally the representations, needs and reactions of others like us), there can be no politics without *recognition*. Even Napoleon, when he famously stated that 'France needs no recognition. It simply is there, like the sun', was addressing that statement to *someone*. Now, recognition is relevant to politics in three senses.

First, recognition is constitutive for politics in a quasi-transcendental sense: namely, recognizing the other as a subject, a subject endowed with intentionality as I am, is a condition of the possibility of *social*, and thus also of *political* action. I never perform social actions directed or addressed to animals or things. When I do perform them, in fact, I always address other human subjects by means of affecting animals and things, just like when I replace a flat tire on someone's car. In this quasi-transcendental sense, recognition becomes relevant for politics only when extreme political oppression refuses someone – slaves, inmates of concentration camps, tortured prisoners of Abu Ghraib – recognition as a full human being or, in Margalit's words, when politics falls below the level of decency (Margalit 1996).

In a second sense, recognition is something which, far from being a condition of the possibility of political action, may or may not be attributed to a person or a group. It is the recognition we attribute to newly formed states, to new parties, to older parties that undergo reformation, to 'statesmen', to liberation movements who represent entire peoples, to NGOs qua representatives of certain collective interests. Only in this second sense can we truly speak of a 'politics of recognition', which hinges on the way we use language in order to designate political actors. When Iraqi combatants are called *insurgentes* in the newspaper *El Paìs*, when dissidents become 'freedom fighters', there we discover the power of recognition in politics and we discover as well the extent to which the previous two moments of the assessment of reason and of judgment depend, in fact, on a third constitutive moment: namely, our recognition of who is entitled to have access to the space of reasons and of judgment.

Finally, recognition is relevant for politics also in a third sense. Insofar as politics is something different from a disinterested search for truth – theoretical or practical truth alike – but is rather a segment of deliberative reason, understood as a kind of reason that assesses alternative arguments for the sake of a good tempered by the right, then who raises a claim is as important as the substance of the claim. From this point of view, recognition becomes the term through which we signal the importance of who is saying what. We are not in politics, but in some other practice, if we assume that the meaning of what is being stated bears no relation to the person who is stating it. Thus a reflection on politics and recognition has as a third focus an inquiry into what can be affirmed in general about the relation between utterance and utterer, action and actor.

Finally, constitutive for politics is the moment of the *gift*. This may sound paradoxical, especially considering that politics has often been defined as the practice of rationally pursuing one's own ends. Politics, however, could not even exist if we didn't presuppose the practice of gift giving, understood as the willingness to give priority to something beyond one's own self, individual or collective, and to 'step back' from one's own priorities. Acting in concert, as opposed to solipsistically, presupposes not just that other minds exist within my *cognitive* horizon, but also that I be willing to enter, at least for the time being, a donative relation with someone else, namely a temporarily donative relation that includes a moment of reciprocity.

This point is forcefully made by Plato, at the beginning of our western conversation on justice and politics, when, in the *Republic*, Socrates observes, against Trasymachus, that in order to be able to act and achieve something even a band of robbers and thieves must presuppose a willingness on the part of its members to subordinate their individual greed to the priorities set by the communal project pursued (Plato I, 351b–352a). The same point is emphasized by Montesquieu, when he points out that without a widespread orientation to 'virtue' among the citizens a republic cannot last over time (Montesquieu 1989: Book 3, Chapter 3). We find the same basic idea in Rawls's idea that an actor, individual or collective, can be rational but not reasonable (Rawls 2005: 48–54). We can find it in Arendt's claim that politics blossoms when the preoccupation for individual life is replaced by love for the common world (Arendt 1959: 23–27). We finally find it in the words of great politicians, for example, in the famous inaugural speech by J.F. Kennedy, when he said: 'Do not ask what America can do for you, but what you can do for America.'

It is inaccurate to think that the rise of a modern economy, as a differentiated infrastructure of exchange, has made the donative dimension superfluous in social life. On the contrary, it has purified gift giving of all residues of instrumental functions. Although in one sense modern differentiation has made informal donating an ideally gratuitous act, the structural call for reciprocation remains bound up with it. Modern politics cannot be conceived solely on the basis of discourse, judgment and recognition. Understanding it requires that we grasp the constitutiveness of a dimension of reciprocal donation. From a substantive point of view, the political gift par excellence is *trust*: trust in our representative, trust in our ally, trust in the good faith of our interlocutor, trust in the other person's intention to fulfill her promises and to honor the terms of agreement that she will consent to. Without these forms of trust only conflict exists and the practice of politics as we have hitherto characterized it becomes impossible. Above all, no politics is possible – but only open conflict – if we do not trust that participants in a political space are willing to yield to the priorities of others, should this appear necessary in light of shared reasons – up to the supreme donation, giving one's life, which often politics has requested.

Let me conclude this section on the constituents of politics by addressing the one constituent which thus far has loomed large by its absence: power. How can we discuss the nature of politics and be silent on the relation of power to political action? Implicitly, the point I have tried to convey is that political power – understood with Weber as the capacity to have someone do something which he would not spontaneously do without our input, and moreover to have someone act in such a way out of his belief in our being entitled to ask for his compliance – conceptually comes in only *subsequently*, namely *after* politics as here described has run its course, *after* a given priority of ends has been established. For in a democratic context the legitimacy of orders and of our obligation to obey follows from and does not precede the consensual, albeit perhaps indirect, prioritization of collective ends.

On the other hand, power cannot be reduced to legitimate political power or authority. Power as influence, *Macht*, is also part of the political game and often functions as an intervening variable in our prioritizing certain ends. It concurs and sometimes interferes with good reasons in such process and in a sense is an ineliminable fact of politics, just as crime is an ineliminable component of social action. Crime is deviation from a socially accepted norm, and as such undesirable, but the human imperfection of all our social arrangements makes it so that no crimeless society can exist. Similarly, no political process can take place which is thoroughly shielded from the effects of power as *Macht*. This is a banal factual truth: what is important is the role that we assign to this banal fact in the construction of our concept of politics. And our choice, as it has been implicitly conveyed by what we have said thus far, is to keep this fact at the semantic margins of politics. Power without legitimation, a kind of power that establishes our ends as opposed to deriving from our shared ends, is just background noise that disturbs the political process: it cannot reflect freedom, it only reflects the contingency of arbitrary force.

5. Reasons that move the imagination

Until now I have tried to outline the basic structure of the practice we call politics and to identify some of its constituent moments. But such an outline cannot exhaust the meaning of politics. Let me turn to what politics can be expected to be when it operates *at its best*.

At several junctures of its bimillenary history, the entwinement of politics and myth has been the object of reflections. When it functions at its best politics is not just reasoning or good reasons plus considered judgment as to what is possible. Again, Plato reminds us of this aspect when he warns us to be prepared to resist against three big counter-waves aroused by his egalitarian radicalism and when he understands justice as harmony or congruence among the faculties of the soul. We are reminded of the same thing when Aristotle defines the state as a community (*koinonia*) that strives for *eudaimonia*, when Machiavelli in his *Discourses* elucidates the meaning of *vivere civile* and when Rousseau portrays the legislator as someone who can indicate the common good to us and can move us by appeal to a divine authority (Machiavelli 2008: Book I, Chapter XVII; Rousseau 1967: 42–45). Politics at its best is the weaving of *vision* into the texture of what is possible. Not surprisingly, the term 'art' is as often associated with politics as is the term 'science'.

It has been said that it is typical of artistic excellence to introduce chaos into order, to revolutionize styles and create new ones, to activate the imagination and engage the faculties of the mind in a self-sustaining and never-ending cross-fertilization, to disclose new ways of experiencing the world, to transfigure the commonplace. In so doing, however, the work of art seems to draw on a more fundamental source – exemplarity and its force, which proceeds from the radical self-congruence of an identity and appears to reconcile 'is' and 'ought', 'facts' and 'norms'. This source also nourishes political innovation.

All the important junctures at which something new has emerged in politics and has transformed the world – the idea of natural rights, the idea of the legitimacy of government resting on the 'consensus of the governed', the inalienable right to the 'pursuit of happiness', *liberté, egalité, fraternité*, the abolition of slavery, universal suffrage, human rights, the welfare state, gender equality, the idea of sustainability, the idea of a right of the future generations – were junctures at which what is new never prevailed by virtue of its following logically from what already exists, but rather by virtue of its conveying a new vista on the world we share in common and highlighting some hitherto unnoticed potentialities of it. Like the work of art, so the outstanding political deed arouses a sense of 'enhancement of life', the enriching and enhancement of a life lived in common and commands our consent by virtue of its exemplary ability to reconcile what exists and what we value in a here and now which we can draw on also from elsewhere and a later point in time. When it has operated apart from good reasons – reasons that we can come to share in discourse – the ability possessed by politics to move the imagination has only produced disasters, first and foremost 20th-century totalitarianism, but, by the same token, if disjoined from the force of imagination nourished by exemplarity, good reasons are only mere accountancy of what should be.

Thus politics at its best is *the prioritization of ends in light of good reasons that can move our imagination*. And by setting our imagination in motion, politics at its best induces the feeling of an enhancement, enriching or deepening of the range of possibilities afforded by our life in common or, drawing on a different vocabulary, it *discloses a new political world* for us, in which we recognize the reflection of our freedom.

Let us cursorily highlight a number of junctures at which this intrinsic connection of politics and the imagination becomes apparent. One such juncture is constituted by the phenomenon of *radical evil*. If we are unwilling to define the radicality of radical evil – for example, the radicality of evil on the scale of the Holocaust, the gulag, the Cambodian Killing Fields, the Rwandan genocide of the Tutsi as opposed to the ordinary evil of tax cheating, nepotism or violation of zoning codes – by reference to the violation of some divine, metaphysical or otherwise transcendent principle, we can resort to the idea that radical evil *exemplifies us at our worst* and necessarily changes our image of ourselves.[36] Nazism horrifies us because it occurred in the very midst of one of the most developed and civilized parts of Europe. Ethnic cleansing in former Yugoslavia elicits moral sentiments of horror also in relation to the fact that it is taking place *after* we all thought that the lesson of Auschwitz had been thoroughly metabolized. This fact of our moral life suggests that perhaps our perspective ought to change. The criterion for the radicality of radical evil ought perhaps to be internal to us, the moral community, rather than external, objective. The point is, however, that – as Plato and Kant have argued – no human being and no community deliberately acts in an evil manner. Even the Nazis perpetrated their crimes in the name of an idea of the good, understood as maximizing the chances for survival and flourishing of the German people by means of securing its racial purity. Thus moral communities always discover *afterward* – *ex post facto* – that what was done by their members in pursuit of shared views of the good was indeed radically evil. Crucial is then the role of the imagination in enabling a moral community to take distance from a conception of the good which now appears 'perverse' and from the actions performed in its name. This transition could not be possible – and the perverse conception of the good would undergo infinite immunization – if our imagination, qua capacity to make present in the mind what is not before the senses, would not pierce through the sedimented social constructions and reflect the experience of the victims. Without the work of the imagination no 'enlarged mentality' is possible, but only a cognitive group solipsism. Without an 'enlarged mentality', or the ability to see things with the eyes of another, different from us, nothing can pierce the immunizing armor of our collective representations.

Another significant juncture at which politics requires the activation of the imagination concerns human rights and their justification. The justification of human rights as fundamental limits to state sovereignty cannot follow the familiar liberal path of appealing to the consent of free and equal citizens of a global society, for the simple reason that, as Rawls pointed out in *The Law of Peoples*, we cannot project our liberal understanding of legitimation worldwide without thereby implicitly imposing a western modern scheme – the notion of free and equal individual citizens – onto non-modern and non-western political cultures that proceed from different understandings of legitimacy (Rawls 1999: 64–67). An alternative strategy for justifying human rights

36 On this view of evil, see Ferrara 2008: 80–98.

would appeal to the notion of humanity as the possessor of the one identity, reconstructible via public reason, whose fulfillment requires that we, among other things, enforce respect for human rights. Such notion of the fulfillment of the identity of humanity, which by way of its all-inclusiveness exerts a normative force on all more local identities that are part of it, is obviously a situated identity, a concrete universal whose substantive content varies over time. If the justification of human rights rests then on the thesis that an ideal identity of humanity that includes respect for human rights is capable of bringing humanity to a fulfillment *more complete* than other ethical ideals that do not comprise human rights,[37] then it becomes apparent that the imagination plays a fundamental role in a conception of politics for a just world. More than from general moral principles, the justification of the cogency of human rights for any notion of a politically just world will have to proceed from imagining what form of life the flourishing of humanity could give rise to – for example, the 'world society' envisaged by Shmuel Eisenstadt in his theory of 'multiple modernities'.[38]

A third juncture at which the nexus of politics and the imagination becomes important concerns the reconfiguring of democracy when it operates at a post-national level. Democracy has adaptively survived the loss of the possibility of physically gathering the whole demos in the public square, by becoming *representative* democracy and continuing to refer to the idea of the citizens being the authors of the laws that they obey. Political imagination will be needed in order to envisage what new form this founding notion of authorship of the laws can take on in post-national, whether regional or cosmopolitan, contexts no longer characterized by the conjunction of one nation, one state apparatus, one economy, one culture and one constitution.

Finally, in the context of a reflection on the changing relation of religion and politics in a post-secular society, the Habermasian idea of an 'asymmetrical burden' (Habermas 2006: 9) imposed on citizens of faith by the democratic requirement that legislative, administrative and judicial decisions be justified on the basis of reasons acceptable to all could never have been formulated without the imaginative effort to open up secular reason to a receptivity towards the worldview of believers, not to mention of the creative imagination needed in order to envisage institutions – which never existed throughout history – capable of redressing and compensating this asymmetrical burden.

It is not by chance that in the past, before the religious wars would produce a radical separation of religion and politics, politics in its highest moments was merged with the sacred. Politics back then used to draw on the same source as the sacred, namely on the experience of witnessing the force of the social bond reflected in a symbolic form. Within the horizon we inhabit today, the

37 See Ferrara 2008: 137–139.

38 For an overview, see Eisenstadt 2005: 1–30.

awareness of finitude from which the acceptance of pluralism proceeds has severed the link between politics and the historical manifestations of the sacred, but not the link between politics and the force that generates the sacred. Good reasons convince, but only good reasons that move the imagination can *mobilize* people and in this sense great politics today still preserves a trace of its own past. Its ability to mobilize rests on the promise to inscribe the exemplarity of certain moral intuitions capable of reconciling 'is' and 'ought' – first and foremost the intuition concerning the equal dignity of all human beings, the redressing of humiliation, indignation before injustice – into the form of our communal life.

This is our first approximation to the concept of politics; this is the ladder that we are now ready to throw away.

References

Arendt, H. 1959, *The Human Condition. A Study of the Central Dilemmas Facing Modern Man*, Garden City, NY, Doubleday Anchor.

Eisenstadt, S. (ed.) 2005, *Multiple Modernities*, New Brunswick, NJ, Transaction Publishers.

Ferrara, A. 2008, *The Force of the Example. Explorations in the Paradigm of Judgment*, New York, Columbia University Press.

Gavison, R. 1992, 'Feminism and the private/public distinction', *Stanford Law Review*, 45 (1): 1–45.

Habermas, J. 1992, *Faktizität und Geltung. Beiträge zur Diskurstheorie des Rechts und des demokratischen Rechtsstaat*, Frankfurt, Suhrkamp.

—— 2006, 'Religion in the public sphere', *European Journal of Philosophy*, 14 (1): 1–25.

Machiavelli, N. 2008, *Discourses on Livy* (1521) (trans. J.C. Bondanella and P. Bondanella), Oxford, Oxford University Press.

Margalit, A. 1996, *The Decent Society*, Cambridge, MA, Harvard University Press.

Montesquieu. 1989, *The Spirit of the Laws* (1748) (trans. A.M. Cohler, B.C. Miller and H. Stone), Cambridge Texts in the History of Political Thought, Cambridge, Cambridge University Press.

Parsons, T. 1990, 'Prolegomena to a theory of social institutions' (1935), *American Sociological Review*, 55: 319–333.

Pateman, C. 1983, 'Feminist critiques of the public/private distinction', in Benn, S.I. and Gaus, G.F. (eds) *Public and Private in Social Life*, New York, St. Martin's Press.

Plato. 2007, *The Republic* (360 BC) (trans. D. Lee), Harmondsworth, Penguin.

Rawls, J. 1999, *'The Idea of Public Reason Revisited'*, in *The Law of Peoples, with 'The Idea of Public Reason Revisited'*, Cambridge, MA, Harvard University Press.

—— 2005, *Political Liberalism* (1993) (expanded edn), New York, Columbia University Press.

Rousseau, J.J. 1967, *The Social Contract and Discourse on the Origin of Inequality* (ed. and intro. L.G. Crocker), New York, Simon & Schuster.

Weintraub, J. 1997, 'The theory and politics of the public/private distinction', in Weintraub, J. and Kumar, K. (eds) *Private and Public in Thought and Practice*, Chicago, University of Chicago Press, pp. 1–42.

Chapter 3

The politics of imagination

Spinoza and the origins of critical theory

Thomas Hippler

The problem of imagination is intimately linked to the problem of the Enlightenment. Seventeenth-century rationalism and 18th-century philosophy were keen to distinguish reason from its opposite, imagination. In the realm of politics, the 'Enlightenment project' consisted in the attempts to define 'rational' forms of politics as opposed from religious superstition and the belief in unquestioned authorities. Both sides of the dichotomy – reason and imagination – are ultimately located within the autonomy of the individual. Responsible citizens are defined as reasonable beings and it is this capacity of reasoning that makes them able to peacefully live together in society. The clearest expression of this idea can certainly be found in the Universal Declaration of Human Rights of 1948, the first article stating that '*All human beings* are born free and equal in dignity and rights. They *are endowed with reason* and conscience and should act towards one another in a spirit of brotherhood' (emphasis mine). Reason and conscience is what defines the humanity of a person in the political realm. Inversely, from Kant's *Critique of the Power of Judgement* onwards and at least late into the 20th century, the realm of aesthetics relies foremost on the core category of the 'genius', i.e. of an autonomous individual endowed with an exceptionally developed faculty of productive imagination. 'Enlightenment' can therefore be seen as the source of the divide between reason and imagination and of the subsequent location of both terms within an autonomous individual.

It may be argued that we live in a fully 'enlightened' world to the extent in which politics has become fully 'rational' – i.e. it 'is reduced to governance, to simple administration within a general neoliberal consensus [where] there is no space to imagine things differently'.[39] Unfortunately, this kind of rational politics of global governance does not leave any space for human agency. As a consequence of this, the 'autonomous individual', which is at the root of enlightened politics, is deprived of any positive meaning and the autonomy of reason has turned into its contrary. Consequently, any attempts to re-appropriate

39 See Bottici's contribution to this book.

agency are, of necessity, driven by 'imagination' – be it the slogan 'another world is possible' of new social movements, or 19 religious fanatics, driven by their 'excess of imagination' and challenging the most powerful nation in the world. Enlightenment is thus taken into a 'negative dialectic' in which reason and autonomy turn into fanaticism and heteronomy.

In this chapter, I want to argue that this vision of things is highly problematic and that it is in Spinoza that an alternative critical and radical view can be found. The problem starts with the concept of 'Enlightenment' itself. As Jonathan Israel has convincingly shown, there is not just one Enlightenment, but several different strands of Enlightenment thought. The 'radical Enlightenment' with Spinoza as its central figure 'rejected all compromise with the past and sought to sweep away existing structures entirely, rejecting the Creation as traditionally understood in Judaeo-Christian civilization, and the intervention of a providential God in human affairs, denying the possibility of miracles, and reward and punishment in an afterlife, scorning all forms of ecclesiastical authority, and refusing to accept that there is any God-ordained social hierarchy' (Israel 2001: 11–12). In front of this radical strand, Leibnizians, Malebranchians and Newtonians are the three branches of the 'moderate Enlightenment' that were looking for compromises between radical rationalism and the established authorities: they thus appear rather as 'intellectual counter-offensives' to the radical challenge. Strangely enough, however, Israel, after having historically mapped the Enlightenment, does not draw the obvious yet puzzling conclusion that 'the Enlightenment' as it is defined and defended by advocates of the 'project of modernity' such as Habermas (see Habermas 1987), is but a myth of intellectual history: Habermas' 'Enlightenment' is indeed nothing but the continuation of the 17th-century intellectual counter-offensive against emancipative claims of the radical Enlightenment. Conversely, the ideas of these 'anti-Enlightenment obscurantists' which are Habermas' main adversaries can without too much difficulty be linked to Spinoza's legacy, i.e., to the most radical strand of the Enlightenment. This is immediately clear for Althusser and Deleuze, but also holds true for Lacan and Foucault. To put it bluntly, we have, on the one hand, the radical Enlightenment tradition from Spinoza to what is labelled 'post-structuralism', and, on the other, the 'moderate Enlightenment' tradition from Newton to Habermas, via Kant.

However, if Spinoza has been the blind spot of the Enlightenment debate – being both the historical starting point of the Enlightenment and the main theoretical reference for contemporary 'Enlightenment criticism' – this is essentially because of his theory of imagination. Spinoza's thought is indeed a 'savage anomaly' (Negri 1991) within 17th-century rationalism inasmuch as 'imagination' is a key concept of his philosophical edifice and at the same time his theory of imagination is completely different from the rationalistic dualism of reason vs. imagination. This is why we can find an 'Enlightenment criticism' *avant la lettre* in Spinoza and why Spinoza is instrumental for avoiding the dialectic of Enlightenment without renouncing to its achievements. Accordingly, Spinoza puts the autonomous individual into question, inviting us to conceive individuality as a process rather than as something that is given.

Spinoza can thus be considered as a forerunner of critical theory in a threefold sense. First, he is linked to critical theory in the narrow sense of the early 'Frankfurt School' inasmuch as his philosophy, in contrast to 'traditional theory', serves essentially practical purposes and seeks human emancipation (see Horkheimer 1982: 244). Second, Spinoza offers us the vision of 'another Enlightenment' that would not be subject to the 'negative dialectics' described by Horkheimer and Adorno (Horkheimer and Adorno 1972). Third, Spinoza's philosophy is also a forerunner of critical theory in the broader sense, including psychoanalysis, post-colonial studies and critical race theory – i.e. theoretical orientations inspired by post-structuralist thought (see Norris 1991). In this last sense, however, there is a fundamental difference between Spinoza-inspired approaches and the second generation of Frankfurt critical theory, inasmuch as this latter is to a great extent characterised by a return to Kant. I want to argue in this chapter that Spinoza offers us a version both of the Enlightenment and of critical theory that differs radically from the Kantian legacy. And this is why we need to have a closer look at Spinoza's texts in order to decipher his theory of imagination and its role for politics.

In section 1 of this chapter, I will thus briefly point out some general features of imagination in Spinoza, including the distinction between imagination and reason. A second section will deal with the role of imagination for the ethical process of liberation. Simultaneously, this section will qualify the distinction between reason and imagination (mentioned earlier), arguing that both are but minimal and maximal degrees of the human *potentia*. The third section will focus on the political implications of these findings. As a conclusion, I try to outline what Spinoza's politics of imagination could look like (section 4).

1. Spinoza's theory of imagination

An outline of Spinoza's theory of imagination can be found in the second part of his *Ethics*.[40] However, the appendix to the first part of this work had already prepared the introduction of the *problematique* of imagination, arguing that 'all men are born ignorant of the causes of things'. As a consequence of this, we all 'rather imagine than understand'. The second part of the *Ethics* deals with the

40 I will cite Spinoza's works in the following way: For the *Ethics*: E, followed by the part, D (=definition), P (=proposition), and 'sc' (=scholium), 'cor' (=corollary) or dem (=demonstration). Example: E2 P40 sc2 stands for second scholium to the 40th proposition of the second part of the *Ethics*. TTP stands for *Theological-Political Treatise*, followed by the number of the chapter. As to the *Political Treatise*, TP is used, followed by the chapter and paragraph. I have used the English edition of Spinoza's works by Elwes, but I have often modified his translations, citing the original Latin wording as often as possible.

'nature and the origin of the mind'. Surprisingly, however, it begins not with a definition of the mind, but of the body. This expresses Spinoza's idea that the mind is nothing other than the idea of the body (E2 P13). However, this does not mean that the mind has an adequate idea of the body (E2 P24). Neither does it imply an adequate perception of exterior objects (E2 P25). Why is this so?

The human body is indeed composed of a 'very great number of individuals' (Postulate 1 after E2 P13) and, as a consequence of this, also the mind is not a 'simple idea, but composed of a very great number of ideas' (E2 P15). This high complexity of the human body and mind has different consequences. On the one hand, it makes the body capable of receiving a very great number of impressions and this, in turn, enables the mind to 'perceive a very great number of things' (E2 P14). In other words, this complexity constitutes an openness to the world, which enables human beings to enhance their *potentia* (which can be translated into 'power' or into 'agency')[41] and thus their virtue – *potentia* and virtue being by definition the same thing (E4 D7).

On the other hand, this complexity has the consequence that the affections of the body and thus the perceptions of the mind are always potentially blurred since they involve multiple perceptions both of the different parts of the human body and of exterior objects (E2 P16). There is no 'elementary degree' of mental life and no originary unity of perception but humans perceive the world *en bloc*, as confused, contradictory and un-analysable. Therefore, the mind is not clear and distinct (E2 P28 sc). Perceiving things after the 'natural order of nature', the human mind has only a confused and fragmentary knowledge of both itself and of the outer reality (E2 P29 cor). Accordingly, the spontaneous perception of reality is potentially hallucinatory: we can perceive objects that are absent as if they were present (E2 P17 cor). We do not perceive things as such but only the 'images of things'. In other words, we imagine:

> [T]o retain the usual phraseology, the modifications of the human body, of which the ideas represent external bodies as present to us *(Corporis humani affectiones, quarum ideae Corpora externa, velut nobis praesentia repraesentant)*, we will call the images of things, though they do not recall the figure of things. When the mind regards bodies in this fashion, we say that it imagines.
>
> (E2 P17 sc)

The wording is important: associating the words 'present' and 'represent' (*praesentia repraesentant*), Spinoza argues that human perception proceeds from

41 It is not possible to find adequate English equivalents for the differentiation between different kinds of power, which Spinoza designs by the concepts of *potentia*, *potestas* and *imperium*. I will therefore cite Spinoza's original Latin concepts. *Potentia*, especially in the syntagma *agendi potentia* which occurs 45 times in the *Ethics*, can also be translated by 'agency' understood as a 'power to act'.

the representation of an object to the conclusion that this object is actually present (Macherey 1997: 182). In other words, objects are only given through our representation of them. Moreover, by this definition of images, Spinoza completely inverts their traditional meaning: as clearly stated, images are not considered as objects of the mental realm but of the corporeal sphere.[42] The passage to the mental sphere is made only in a second step, when these images of things become objects of ideas. And this is precisely the definition of imagination.

Furthermore, Spinoza identifies imagination as the first of three kinds of knowledge (E2 P40 sc2). The second kind of knowledge – labelled 'reason' (*ratio*) – is constituted through *notiones communes*, that is, through characteristics that are common of all things and which, therefore, are conceived adequately, clearly, and distinctly (E2 P38 cor). The third kind of knowledge is labelled 'intuitive science' and it is defined as proceeding 'from an adequate idea of the absolute essence of certain attributes of God to the adequate knowledge of the essence of things' (E2 P40 sc2). This definition appears completely enigmatic, since in contrast to the definitions of the first and the second kind of knowledge – which merely resume previous steps of the reasoning – it had not been prepared or anticipated by the text. Moreover, Spinoza does not come back to the issue until the very end of the *Ethics* from E5 P20 sc onwards.

The difference between imagination, on the one hand, and reason and intuitive science, on the other, is explained in E2 P41. Imagination 'is the unique cause of falsity, whereas the knowledge derived from the latter is necessarily true'. The formulation is interesting because of its asymmetry: the second (reason) and third (intuitive science) kinds provide true knowledge, but the knowledge of the first kind (imagination) is not necessarily false. It is only the cause of falsity. Moreover, the very fact of distinguishing three kinds of knowledge, instead of the traditional distinction between truth and error, indicates that Spinoza indeed qualifies this binary distinction. As to the difference between reason and intuitive science, it consists in the fact that the former is concerned with what is common among different things, whereas the latter is the knowledge of single entities (E5 P36 sc).

Even if imagination is designed as the unique cause of falsity, this does not imply a general rejection of the first kind of knowledge. Spinoza does indeed not consider the inadequate and imaginary perceptions as 'errors'. They are, on the contrary, the necessary results of the human constitution and, as such, they involve even a certain type of 'truth', however not in the sense of an adequate representation of reality but precisely as the truth of the human body itself. Thus, 'imagination' does not necessarily equal 'error':

42 See also, in the same sense, E5 P1 and E5 P14.

> [T]he imaginations of the mind, looked at in themselves, do not contain error. The mind does not err in the mere act of imagining, but only in so far as it is regarded as being without the idea, which excludes the existence of such things as it imagines to be present to it. If the mind, while imagining non-existent things as present to it, is at the same time conscious that they do not really exist, this power of imagination must be set down to the virtue of its nature, and not to a fault, especially if this faculty of imagination depends solely on its own nature – that is [. . .] if this faculty of imagination be free.
>
> (E2 P17 sc)

This paragraph clearly indicates that imagination, despite the falseness it may engender, does not have to be rejected. Moreover, neither does the erroneous affirmation of the reality of the contents of the imaginary representation have to be rejected, for the simple reason that these representations, which necessarily occur, necessarily also imply the affirmation of their object. The 'error' only comes in a second step and it consists in the fact that we do not have a clear knowledge of the imaginary character of these representations. To put it in other words, error is not a consequence of imagination but of the ignorance of the imaginary character of imagination. Hence imagination is not only recognised as necessary. It constitutes, on the contrary, a *potentia* of human nature (see Hippler 2000). It is, as such, an essential starting point for the ethical project of liberation, which is exposed in the first section of the fifth part of the *Ethics*. However, before considering this final ethical perspective and the role of imagination in it, we must insist on some other characteristics that are inextricably linked to the functioning of imagination: the divide between objects and subjects and the social character of imagination.

I have on several occasions talked about 'objects of representation'. However, talking of 'objects' is not fully correct and Spinoza actually employs the term 'external bodies' (E2 P17 sc). There is a precise reason for this. The differentiation between 'subjects' and 'objects' is in itself inseparable from the mechanisms of affectivity and thus of imagination. This is to say they do not reflect the nature of things. This point has been demonstrated at length by other commentators (see in particular Bove 1996: 19–75; Macherey 1995: 127–182) and I will limit myself to a brief summary of their findings. The human mind is incapable of imagining the 'small differences between individuals' (E2 P40 sc) and it is thus necessary to 'unify' the disparate perceptions according to mental schemes that Spinoza designs as *notiones Transcendentales* and *Universales.* These terms are not only entirely 'imaginary' but 'represent ideas in the highest degree confused'. By the same token, the imaginary confusion also indicates a properly human activity of organisation of the disparate perceptions. Perceptive confusion is thus not only to be considered as a sign of the weakness of the human mind, but it is the necessary consequence of an active simplification that enables humans to effectively cope with reality.

In this sense, Spinoza is not so far removed from Kant's conception of transcendental imagination (see Frohschammer 1879) as a faculty of synthesis according to 'schemes' (Kant 1968 III: 189). There is a crucial difference, however. Kant ultimately reduces the multiplicity of our representations to the 'original-synthetical unity of apperception', that is, to self-consciousness (Kant 1968 III: 174). To put it bluntly, for Kant, perception is linked to the identity of the subject via the transcendental function of imagination, whereas Spinoza denies any transcendental value to imagination.[43]

However, this active mastery of reality by processes of imagination is inseparable from yet another dimension, which is not confined to the narrow epistemological realm. The primary mental function – which Spinoza defines as 'the very essence of humans' – is actually desire (according to the first definition of affects in the third part of the *Ethics*) and desire as such does not have an object. Furthermore, it is one of the particularities of the human mind to spontaneously associate affects to the ideas it forms. There are not 'pure' ideas or concepts of the mind, but ideas are necessarily invested with affectivity. Accordingly, 'objects' are necessarily invested with affectivity and this imaginary and affective constitution of objects is what the ulterior philosophical tradition has termed a 'world' and, more precisely, *Lebenswelt*.

The political impact of the imaginary constitution of the *Lebenswelt* follows necessarily from these characteristics. Human beings need to live in society, but since they do not always act reasonably, their passions tend to throw them into opposition (TTP5). Passions, however, 'depend only on inadequate ideas' (E3 P3) and these latter stem from imagination (E2 P41). Imagination and passions are thus intimately linked. For this reason, it is necessary to establish a political power that is able to defend the law and thus contain the antagonistic passions in society. The means by which this pacification can be achieved, however, are still passions, since humans are necessarily subject to passions and thus rarely act reasonably (E4 P35 sc). More precisely, the passions used for social pacification are hope and fear: hope for a better life in the future and fear of punishment. However, since 'human nature will not submit to absolute repression' (TTP5), it is more useful for the political power to rely on hope than fear. It is imagination that provides the link between the social creation of hope and the stability of the state.

2. Imagining reason

The theme of imagination plays a considerable role in the fifth and final part of the *Ethics*, which deals with the power of the intellect and the possibilities of human liberation. This last part of the work is actually quite clearly cut into

43 This also implies that Spinoza renounces any attempt to fix the identity of the subject (see later).

two sections: the first runs from propositions 1 to 20 and the second from 21 to the end (see Macherey 1994). The first section treats the project of human liberation 'if we take account of time' (E5 P7), whereas the second section envisages the problem *sub specie aeternitatis*, 'from a point of view of eternity', and thus without reference to time. This, however, means that the first section deals precisely with the point of view of imagination (see Jaquet 1997), thus discussing the role of imagination for the project of human liberation. Again only in the second and last section does Spinoza treat the issue *sub specie aeternitatis* and thus without reference to time or imagination. The structure of the fifth part of the *Ethics* thus clearly indicates that there are two different ways to achieve liberation, but we shall only consider the first way, where imagination indeed plays a key role.

Most generally put, this first perspective envisages liberation as a process of mental reorganisation of the objects attached to the human passions. As pointed out earlier, human desire imaginarily invests 'things' with affectivity. By this process, the human being constitutes itself as a subject of passions and simultaneously it constitutes the 'objects' of the world. It has to be borne in mind that these are altogether imaginary representations. However, the ethical project does not reject these representations but tries to reorganise the passionate investment of reality in a more 'reasonable' way. An affect can be moderated if it ceases to be linked to the representation of an external cause as its cause. Similarly, the affect ceases to be a passion towards an object (E5 P2–4). This opens the possibility for a 'clear and distinct' knowledge of the affect and, by this, it ceases to be a passion altogether. Knowing one's own passions means detaching them from their contingent relation to an external object. What is at stake here is thus the knowledge and the de-objectivation of passions. In this way Spinoza actually operates a distinction *within* the concept of imagination, which, rather than opposing imagination to reason, will put the emphasis of the connection between them. In other words, the distinction between the different kinds of knowledge is clearly qualified. Rather than a clear-cut distinction, there is indeed a graduation between the three kinds of knowledge: reason, in other words, is not opposed to imagination but both signify two poles within the same continuum. And the same holds true for 'intuitive science', i.e., the third kind of knowledge, which is treated in the second and last section of the fifth part of the *Ethics*. The crucial divide here is not the one between reason and imagination, or between truth and falsity, but the one between *activity* and *passivity*. It has further to be borne in mind, however, that there is no binary opposition between them either. Rather, they indicate maximal and minimal degrees of the human agency (*agendi potentia*). The ethics of imagination consists in imagining more 'powerfully', that is, to enhance one's imaginative agency. It is this reasoning in terms of degrees instead of binary oppositions that constitutes the difference between Spinoza and the ulterior Enlightenment tradition inspired by Kant. By posing binary distinctions 'the Enlightenment' operates *ipso facto* as a series of exclusions and, to the extent to which the positive side is more inclusive, the deeper becomes the exclusion. Thus, once 'humanity' is defined by reason, is becomes logical that the lack of reason is associated to a denial of humanity. In other words, binary distinctions are not just always confronted to the problem of how to cope with the excluded part, but the negative part is already present in the positive part. In contrast to this line of thinking, it is precisely Spinoza's 'monism' that prevents his falling into the 'negative dialectic of Enlightenment' typical of binary oppositions.

How does this differentiation within imagination work and how may imagination become gradually more 'reasonable'? This augmentation of activity and reason is made possible not by a reduction of imagination but, on the contrary, by making imagination most active. Spinoza thus defines a minimal and a maximal degree of imagination, which are designated by the words of *simpliciter . . . imaginamur* (E5 P5) and *distinctiùs, & magis vividè imaginamur* (E5 P6 sc): we thus can imagine either 'simply' or 'more distinctly and vividly'. It is worth noting that Spinoza designs imagination with the characteristic of 'distinction', which traditionally denotes true knowledge, as in Descartes' 'clear and distinct' knowledge. Associating the rational affects produced by reason to the functioning of imagination Spinoza clearly indicates that the remedy against the harmful effects of imagination is not to be found in renouncing imagination, but actually in determining a more reasonable way to imagine. How this is to be achieved is exposed in E5 P11–13, which explains certain characteristics of 'images'. And the solution is precisely found in the fact that affects that are attached to (*refertur*) a multiplicity of things tend to be more powerful. This, however, clearly recalls the definition of reason, i.e. the formation of clear and distinct ideas through the common characteristics of things. The human mind, while imagining, is capable of applying the distinctive features of reason to imagination. Reason is but one of the modalities of imagination.

This leads to the formation of a new affect and the concomitant formation of a new 'object' of passionate investment. This new affect is called 'love towards god' (*amor erga Deum*). The most universal object to which the images produced by the human mind can be attached is the idea of god (E1 P14). On the one hand, this 'idea of god' is clearly a concept produced by imagination, for the simple reason that god in itself is not at all an 'object' of reality – god, indeed, is not an object at all, since it is coextensive with the universal necessity of nature (E1 P15–16). But, on the other hand, this imaginary representation of god as an object also matches some of the characteristics of the rational definition of god, since this 'object' is completely detached from passionate investment. The formation of the imaginary yet rational concept of god in this sense thus leads necessarily to a de-passionate conception of reality. Interestingly, the last proposition of this sequence (E5 P20) abandons the individual perspective of the psychic mechanisms of imagination and discusses its interpersonal, collective, and thus, in the last instance, political dimension. Liberation is thus not envisaged as an individual matter. It is, on the contrary inseparably linked to the association with the greatest possible number of other individuals. This is another crucial divide between Spinoza and the mainstream Enlightenment tradition: whereas this latter conceptualised 'rational' forms of political association as necessarily based on the rationality of autonomous individuals, Spinoza's conception of the individual is in itself 'trans-individual'. Accordingly, political liberty cannot be based on individual autonomy, but political and personal liberation are interrelated processes. However, as Spinoza makes clear, this collective liberation takes place according to the same mechanisms of 'reasonable imagination': society, according to Spinoza, most fundamentally relies on an imaginary configuration of desire.

3. Politics as imagination

These general findings about the theory of imagination in the *Ethics* will now permit us to address its political implications. Very generally put, Spinoza's theoretical standpoint is equally opposed to normative and to purely descriptive claims. On the one hand, he explicitly criticises all attempts to understand politics in terms of morals: there is no such thing as a 'rational model' that would, in a second step, allow comparing the political reality to its model. On the other hand, it would equally be erroneous to consider Spinoza's politics as purely descriptive, since there is clearly an ethical perspective, which is already announced by the very title of the work. As a result, Spinoza's approach to politics can be described as an attempt to individuate objective tendencies in political life and to evaluate them by making use of the hypothetical 'model of the human nature' sketched out in the preface to the fourth part of the *Ethics*. After having shown the theoretical inconsistency of the notions of 'perfection' and of 'good and evil', Spinoza reintroduces these very notions, but restricting their sphere of application: 'inasmuch as we desire to form an idea of man as a type of human nature which we may hold in view, it will be useful for us to retain the terms in question, in the sense I have indicated' (E4 pref). The verb *cupimus* ('we desire') is crucial here, since it clearly indicates the hypothetical nature of the notions of perfection, good and a model of human nature. These notions are indeed denied any meaning per se. They are hypothetical and subordinated to the desire for a good life, which is understood as the most active form of being. Therefore, Spinoza's ethical perspective towards politics excludes binary oppositions typical for approaches in moral terms, like good and evil, allowed and forbidden or code and actions. Human actions and human life are considered within a homogeneous and continuous field that lies between the extremes of activity and passivity. The *exemplar naturae humanae* serves the purpose of defining a maximal degree of the possible deployment of human agency and thus *agendi potentia*, virtue and happiness.

Politics, according to Spinoza, is foremost located in the sphere of passions and thus of imagination. Hence the first characteristic of politics, which can be termed 'contrariety'. Precisely because humans are subject to passions, they are potentially opposed to one another, *contrarii*. Inadequate ideas due to imaginary schemes of perception produce socially harmful passions, inasmuch as they 'alienate' the individuals, placing them under the action of external causes. According to the imaginary mechanisms of object constitution, human beings are thus mutually the objects of their passions. Only if humans 'live under the conduct of reason' do they 'agree' (*conveniunt*) among themselves (E4 P35). As such, humans 'are most useful' to humans, but inadequate ideas and passions prevent them from recognising this fact and from acting accordingly. As a consequence, passions (which are a consequence of imagination) are causes of division, whereas reason is a cause of unity. However, this binary divide needs qualification. To be dominated by passions is indeed the normal human condition and it seems to follow from this that peaceful life in common is impossible. Obviously, this is not the case and humans spontaneously live together, while being passionately opposed to each other. Social life, in other words, is envisaged as obviously possible (since it is real), but nevertheless marked by an intrinsic difficulty and a fundamental instability. This is the point where political power comes in depriving citizens of their natural right and forcing them to live peacefully together.

In other words, imagination and passions are clearly designated as causes of social disharmony. However, it is clear that reason cannot be a remedy against this harmful situation, and therefore the force of a political power is needed. This is one example of Spinoza's 'realism' according to which it would be an illusion to think that peace can be obtained by reasonable behaviour alone. However, there is another explanation why reason is powerless against antagonistic passions. According to E4 P1 'no positive quality possessed by a false idea is removed by the presence of what is true, in virtue of its being true'. The fact of being true does not have a direct impact on affects, but an affect, according to E4 P7 'can only be coerced or destroyed by another affect contrary thereto, and stronger than the affect to be coerced'. Therefore:

> [o]n this law society can be established, so long as it keeps in its own hand the right, possessed by everyone, of avenging injury, and pronouncing on good and evil; and provided it also possesses the power to lay down a general rule of conduct, and to pass laws sanctioned, not by reason, which is powerless in restraining affect, but by threats.

As a result, society and its institutions serve as a substitute for the lack of reason. However, this does not mean that Spinoza considers society as reasonable in itself. Society exists as a matter of fact and it does so in using the laws of natural right in order to modify its consequences. Moreover, it is only because humans do not live under the command of reason that organised forms of society exist in the first place. The consequence of this existence is certainly a greater rationality in the conduct of human affairs, but this does not imply that society has in itself a rational foundation (TP VI, 3). Moreover, the concepts of right and wrong, and of just and unjust, are altogether creations of society and they are defined as a function of the specific interests of this collective entity. This is another important point of divergence between Spinoza and the mainstream Enlightenment tradition: neither society nor the state is reasonable as such and politics is not primarily guided by reason but by passions. Thus imagination and the ethical process consists in organising these passions and this imagination in a more reasonable way.

This theoretical option avoids a number of shortcomings of 'enlightened' political theory, in particular the need to cope with and thus to reintegrate what has previously been excluded. For instance, once we have defined 'politics' as guided by 'reason' we become aware that completely reasonable politics lacks imagination and thus creativity, and we therefore think about ways to inject some 'imagination' into the tedious governance of current affairs in order to make politics 'better'.[44] Then, however, the question arises about how much imagination and creativity 'reasonable' politics can possibly stand, since an 'excess of imagination' will lead to fanaticism, thus undermining the rational bases of politics. We are therefore driven to ask ourselves how to repress these excesses of imagination. In other words, reason is in permanent need of imagination but imagination is always repressed – and what has been repressed always returns.

However, if Spinoza approaches here the problem from the sole point of view of coercion, he qualifies this outlook in other texts. Coercion actually has its limits, since, 'human nature will not submit to absolute repression' (see Balibar 1997). As a consequence, it is not sufficient for a society to rely on fear exclusively: what is needed is also a social organisation of hope. Accordingly, each society is in need of an organisation of the imaginary that is able to link hope to the sake of society. Each society has to find a solution to the problem of a creation of a sense of belonging of its members and in the societies that Spinoza analyses, this is the function of religion, and more precisely of this complex called 'theologico-political': 'This, then, was the object of the ceremonial law, that men should do nothing of their own free will, but should always act under external authority, and should continually confess by their actions and thoughts that they were not their own masters, but were entirely under the control of others' (TTP5). The ceremonial sanctification of everyday life thus provides institutionally a supplement of 'meaning' to individual actions, and this 'meaning' consists in the creation of a sense of belonging. Spinoza's political theory was thus already capable of taking into account these issues which became an object of mainstream political theory only in the second half of the 20th century with thinkers like Arendt or Habermas (Moreau 1994: 459). By the means of bodily signs (Spinoza cites the Jewish practice of circumcision and the Chinese braid), rituals, ceremonies and other social

44 See Ferrara's contribution to this book.

practices which are analysed in some detail in the *Theologico-Political Treatise*, Spinoza provides a description of society as an overall organisation of its members' imagination that bears striking resemblance to 'ideological state-apparatuses' described by Althusser (Althusser 1976) and of *dispositifs* of power/knowledge according to Foucault (Foucault 1975; see also Montag 1995). It is in this sense that Spinoza employs the expression of 'apparatus' in the preface to the *Theologico-Political Treatise*: Society is thus an 'apparatus of consensus' by the means of homogenisation of people's imagination.

If the *civitas* has its origin in the lack of reasonable conduct of the individuals, and thus in the fact that they are subject to imagination, the power relations involved in it contain a large part of imaginary too (Matheron 1986). According to natural right, each one acts according to the necessity of their own nature, which means practically that the individual *potentiae* constantly affront one another. There is thus a constant contrariety between antagonistic *potentiae* with momentary superiorities of some over others. Now, a power relationship exists when it is possible to stabilise temporarily such superiority. However, human force can be physical or mental and Spinoza actually argues that the latter is the more important one:

> He has another under his authority *(potestas)*, who holds him bound, or has taken from him arms and means of defence or escape, or inspired him with fear, or so attached him to himself by past favour, that the man obliged would rather please his benefactor than himself, and live after his mind than after his own. He that has another under authority in the first or second of these ways, holds but his body, not his mind. But in the third or fourth way he has made dependent on himself as well the mind as the body of the other; yet only as long as the fear or hope lasts, for upon the removal of the feeling the other is left independent.

There are thus two kind of power of which the first is purely physical, whereas the second is clearly 'imaginary' in nature – even if the consequences are fully real – because it relies on a manipulation of human passions. And this is precisely the way in which state power works. This latter is obviously not purely coercive and it can even be said that there is a negative proportionality between coercion and force: the stronger the state, the less it needs to actually employ coercive means. It is sufficient to make people imagine that it does have the means to coerce.

But what is the nature and the origin of these means of coercion in the first place? From the brief outline of the foundations of the *civitas* given in the fourth part of the *Ethics*, it immediately becomes clear that the state is not understood as a unity, but as an association of different elements. In this sense, the state has the same ontological status as any other composed body and Spinoza actually applies to it the same analytical framework as the one he applies to human individuals. As to the question of where the power and thus the means of coercion of the state stem from, it is thus clear that their origin must be looked for in the *potentiae* of the individuals whose association forms not only the *civitas*, but indeed also the *imperium*, i.e., political power or, according to Elwes' translation, dominion: 'This right, which is determined by the power of a multitude, is generally called Dominion' (*Hoc ius, quod multitudinis potentia definitur, imperium appellari solet*, TP2, 17).

The power of the state (*imperium*), in other words, stems from a 'confiscation' of the individuals' power (*potentia*) for the sake of the state. Foucault's dictum that 'power comes from below' (Foucault 1976: 124) thus hold true for Spinoza. This 'confiscation' is indeed imaginary to the extent that the *potentiae* of the governed remain theirs. Yet this confiscation is also real to the extent that the governed are actually determined to accept it (Matheron 1986: 114). In other words, there is no opposition between imagination and power, since power is essentially imaginary, yet very real in its effects. However, the resemblance between imagination and power also functions in the opposite direction, inasmuch as imagination also has an effect on power relations themselves. Spinoza develops this point in the preface to the *Theologio-Political Treatise*: the 'phantoms of imagination' (*imaginationis deliria*) like superstition are the best means by which a tyrannical power can keep humans in a state of intellectual and thus political dependence since, Spinoza says, citing Quintius Curtius (4, X), 'to govern a multitude nothing is more efficient than superstition' (*nihil efficacius multitudinem regit, quam superstitio*):

> But if, in a monarchical regime the supreme and essential mystery be to hoodwink the subjects, and to mask the fear which keeps them down, with the specious guard of religion, so that men may fight as bravely for slavery as for safety *(pro servitio, tanquam pro salute pungent)* and count as not shame but highest honour to risk their blood and their lives for the vainglory of a tyrant; yet in a free republic no more mischievous expedient could be planned or attempted.

In this sense, Spinoza's ethical objective is without any doubt to inject 'reason' into the imaginary representations that keep people under domination. However, as already pointed out, this development of reason cannot be achieved at the detriment of imagination but it has necessarily to proceed by a rationalisation of the imaginary beliefs. Reason and the imaginary are not opposed to each other, but the imaginary can be more or less reasonable in the sense that it can be more or less attached to *notiones communes*, to the common characteristics of things.

4. Imaginative agency

It thus seems that Spinoza's understanding of politics is entirely centred on imagination. As a result, politics, according to Spinoza, appears indeed to be a 'struggle for imagination'. Power relations make use of imagination in their functioning. Societies and states cannot exist without an apparatus of imagination. And even resistance to domination is unthinkable without imagination. In order to shed light on this issue, we have to consider a two-sided situation.

On the one hand, resistance to domination is actually necessarily an integral part of politics and there is a simple ontological reason for this. The foundations of the state have been defined as a rational use of passions in order to establish a right that is capable of containing the antagonistic individual rights (E4 P37 sc). This, however, means that the power of the state is in potential contradiction with the passionate desire of each individual. The very existence of society thus necessarily creates anti-social passions (Matheron 1968). And these passions may lead, in certain historical circumstances, to revolts and revolutions. Spinoza discusses this point in the 18th chapter of the *Theologico-Political Treatise* with reference to the contemporary events of the English Revolution:

> I must not, however, omit to state that it is no less dangerous to remove a monarch, though he is on all hands admitted to be a tyrant. For his people are accustomed to royal authority and will obey no other, despising and mocking at any less august control. It is therefore necessary, as the prophets discovered of old, if one king be removed, that he should be replaced by another, who will be a tyrant from necessity rather than choice. [. . .] Hence it comes to pass that peoples have often changed their tyrants, but never removed them or changed the monarchical form of government into any other. The English people furnish us with a terrible example of this fact.

Spinoza thus denies the possibility that revolutions may bring about liberation because revolutions change only specific effects of oppression without changing the causes. Oppression, therefore, is bound to return under different forms. But this does not lead him to condemn revolutions from a moral point of view, since they indeed necessarily occur in society in exactly the same way in which individuals are submitted to passions. However, there is always and necessarily a resistance to oppression and absolute submission to power is theoretically unconceivable (see Balibar 1997).

Furthermore, and this is the second side of a politics of resistance, the preceding paragraph also emphasises another point: if revolutions necessarily fail, this is so because people are accustomed to a certain political organisation. They have their political institutions, laws, customs, as well as their theologico-political 'apparatuses of imagination'. These latter in particular produce and reproduce a certain imaginary configuration of desire, which – by this very fact – are factors to be accounted for. In other words, even if there is a desire for political change (for instance because the tyranny exercised by the king is perceived as unbearable), the fundamental structure of imagination and desire is unaffected by this. Spinoza's case study into this point is the role of prophecy in the first two chapters of the *Theologico-Political Treatise*. Very briefly summarised, Spinoza argues that a prophet is a prophet if, and only if, there is a moral community of which the prophet embodies the norms and values to the highest degree (Laux 1993). The social function of the prophet is to recall these norms into the memories of the members of society.

Prophecy is thus defined as a process of communication between a prophet and a given population on the basis of a common set of values, desires and schemes of imagination. To the extent that Spinoza defines, moreover, the contents of prophecy as 'highly dubious', we have to conclude that prophecy as a social practice constituted indeed an 'imagination on imagination': prophecy consists in a particularly 'vivid imagination' of the prophet, but this vivid imagination echoes the fundamental structure of imagination of a given society. Furthermore, all individual or collective desires are structured, among other factors, through social schemes of imagination. Foucault's term of *dispositif* would perfectly well describe this function, because it involves both a given material apparatus and an imaginary context or, to put it in Foucault's terms, power and knowledge. Accordingly, this structure of collective desire may be understood as forming the 'actual essence' of a given society and, as such, this society necessarily, according to the sixths proposition of the third part of the *Ethics*, 'tries to persevere in its being' (E3 P6 and E3 P7). In other words, the social imaginary, while constructing the schemes of perception of the members of society, is also an object (all objects being by definition imaginary) of their desire (Bove 1996: 230). In the case of an oppressive regime, this means precisely that people are brought to desire their own oppression: they will then, according to the passage of the preface to the *Theologico-Political Treatise* just cited, 'fight as bravely for slavery as for safety'.

These two facets – desire for change and yearning for stability – form what has been called 'Spinoza's paradoxical conservatism' (Zourabichvili 2002). The paradox consists in the fact that Spinoza actually rejects both sides, arguing, on the one hand, that revolutions necessarily fail and, on the other, attacking frontally the 'theologico-political block' of oppression – and in particular the one of the monarchical state – stating that 'the true end of a republic is liberty' (TTP 20). In the *Theologico-Political Treatise*, this end is to be aimed at through a transformation of imaginary beliefs. In other words, the imaginary is not rejected (which would be an imaginary endeavour in itself anyway) but transformed. Shall we conclude that in the end, this transformation of the imaginary equals its being overcome? As it has become clear, this is not the case, since reason and imagination are not opposed to each other but form two poles within the same continuum. Moreover, these two poles cannot be fully understood on the individual level alone but need to take into account the collective – and thus in the last instance political – dimension.

What is an individual in the first place? Against virtually all philosophical common sense, Spinoza actually conceptualises the individual not as a fixed entity but as a process within a 'web of reference'. The individual is indeed not a given and stable first matter of politics, but individuation is conceived of as a process which is coextensive with politics. The third part of the *Ethics* has highlighted the affective mechanisms of association and transfer (E3 P14–16), mimesis and imitation (E3 P21–34). Affects are associated to one another as well as to diverse sets of objects and they are transferred from one object to another. Moreover, individuals are subject to fluxes of affects among them. There is thus a web of affective references of which the individual human being is but a part. It is not exaggerated to state that the 'actual essence' of the individual is nothing other than the specific place and the specific configuration within this web of imaginary and affective relations (Gatens and Lloyd 1999: 13). Individuality is inherently trans-individuality. A relation of communication between affects, in other words, defines both individuality and the 'multitude', both being strictly the same process, called *affectuum imitatio* (E3 P27 sc), and both relying on communication of affects and communication of individuals through their affects. In this sense, communicative affectivity can be identified as the very essence of the multitude (Balibar 1997: 90). Both the individual and the 'multitude' are nothing but a specific configuration of affectivity.

Understood as a result of the 'confiscation' of the *potentiae*, political power is defined by Spinoza as *multitudinis potentiae*, the power of the multitude (TP 2, 17). And *potentia* is indeed *the* core concept of Spinoza's ethics: virtue being identified with *potentia* (E4 D4), the ethical transformation as such actually consists in nothing other than in the augmentation of *potentia*. However, as pointed out earlier, imagination plays a central role in this process: according to E5 P20, it is through the (imaginative) association with other humans that we can best enhance our imaginative *potentia*. In this sense, it is perhaps not an exaggeration to state that the imaginative power of the multitude is the very essence of politics (see Bove 1996: 237). Politics, in other words, consists in collective agency, which is necessarily supported by imagination. 'Politics at its best' is the most active, i.e., the most reasonable form of collective imagination.

References

Althusser, L. 1976, 'Ideologie et appareils idéologiques d'État', in *Positions*, Paris, Éditions sociales.

Balibar, E. 1997, 'Spinoza, l'anti-Orwell – La crainte des masses', in *La crainte des masses: Philosophie et politique avant et après Marx*, Paris, Galilé, pp. 57–99.

Bove, L. 1996, *La stratégie du conatus: Affirmation et résistance chez Spinoza*, Paris, Vrin.

Foucault, M. 1975, *Surveiller et punir: naissance de la prison*, Paris, Gallimard.

—— 1976, *Histoire de la sexualité I: la volonté de savoir*, Paris, Gallimard.

Frohschammer, J. 1879, *Ueber die Bedeutung der Einbildungskraft in der Philosophie Kant's und Spinoza's*, Munich, Ackerman.

Gatens, M. and Lloyd, G. 1999, *Collective Imaginings: Spinoza, Past and Present*, London, Routledge.

Habermas, J. 1987, *The Philosophical Discourse of Modernity: Twelve Lectures* (trans. F. Lawrence), Cambridge, Polity Press.

Hippler, T. 2000, 'Spinoza on historical myths', in *Myth and Memory in the Construction of Community. Historical Patterns in Europe and Beyond*, Strath, B. (ed.) Brussels, Presses Interuniversitaires Européennes, pp. 95–112.

Horkheimer, M. 1982, *Critical Theory*, New York, Seabury Press.

Horkheimer, M. and Adorno, T.W. 1972, *Dialectic of Enlightenment*, New York, Seabury.

Israel, J. 2001, *Radical Enlightenment: Philosophy and the Making of Modernity*, Oxford, Oxford University Press.

Jaquet, C. 1997, *Sub specie aeternitatis: études des concepts de temps, durée et éternité chez Spinoza*, Paris, Kimé.

Kant, I. 1968, *Kritik der reinen Vernunft (= Werkausgabe III)*, ed. Weischedel, W., Frankfurt, Suhrkamp.

Laux, H. 1993, *Imagination et religion chez Spinoza: la* potentia *dans l'histoire*, Paris, Vrin.

Macherey, P. 1994, *Introduction à l'éthique de Spinoza. La cinquème partie: les voies de la libération*, Paris, PUF.

—— 1995, *Introduction à l'éthique de Spinoza. La troisième partie: la vie affective*, Paris, PUF.

—— 1997, *Introduction à l'éthique de Spinoza. La seconde partie: la réalité mentale*, Paris, PUF.

Matheron, A. 1968, *Individu et communauté chez Spinoza*, Paris, Minuit.

—— 1986, 'Spinoza et le pouvoir', in *Anthropologie et politique au XVIIe siècle (Études sur Spinoza)*, Paris, Vrin, pp. 103–122.

Montag W. 1995, '"The soul is the prison of the body": Althusser and Foucault, 1970–1975', *Yale French Studies*, 88: 53–77.

Moreau, P.-F. 1994, *Spinoza: L'expérience et l'éternité*, Paris, PUF.

Negri, A. 1991, *The Savage Anomaly: The Power of Spinoza's Metaphysics and Politics* (trans. M. Hardt), Minneapolis, MN, and Oxford: University of Minnesota Press.

Norris, C. 1991, *Spinoza and the Origins of Modern Critical Theory*, Oxford, Basil Blackwell.

Zourabichvili, F. 2002, *Le conservatisme paradoxal de Spinoza: enfance et royauté*, Paris, PUF.

Chapter 4

From soul to mind

Psychology and political imagination

Adriano Bugliani
(Translated by Rachel Barritt)

What are the sources of the politics of imagination? This chapter discusses the extent to which politics is a struggle for people's imagination by arguing that such a struggle occurs in the first place *within* human beings before doing so *among* them. While Lentin and Bazzicalupo in this volume look at the way in which social, political and economic structures shape the politics of imagination, I will examine the same relationship from the opposite point of view. By this, I do not mean to sustain that the social dimension does not play an important role, but simply that there is an individual factor that cannot be reduced only to the social.

In particular, by focusing on the relationship between psychology and political imagination, the chapter shows that recent psychology operated a reduction of the complexity of the human soul that is functional to modern politics. The soul, by which we mean here the human spirit in its widest meaning, is the source of images (section 1). As Adorno pointed out, the soul is 'politically incorrect', because it is boundless, inscrutable and cannot therefore be predicted and controlled. Hence the passage from 'soul' to 'mind', which is the superficial, simplest and therefore most controllable portion of the spirit (section 2).

Since the soul, with its ever changing stream and continual production of images is highly irrational, unforeseeable, unstable and inexhaustible, politics needs to repress the soul, because politics needs stability, statistics, trends. Psychoanalysis, by way of contrast, is the rediscovery of the soul in its archaic meaning and reality. Psychoanalysis is image freeing, it increases the soul's vitality – and therefore potentially contributes to render it politically dangerous. What if everyone simply followed her stream of images? What if the power of images themselves were set free (section 3)?

Even before politics starts, human beings are frightened by images and imagination. Power is an answer to the terror human beings feel when faced with the abyss of their soul. Power is everywhere because it is a force human beings exert against themselves in the first place, as individuals and as a group. Before I exercise power over others, I exercise it over *myself*. And I exercise power over others *because* I first exercise it over myself and cannot therefore tolerate in them the freedom that I do not allow myself. This is the reason why power in general and political power in particular, are largely unconscious (section 4).

1. Soul and images

The soul is an unknown and the bulk of my discourse will in the end succeed only in portraying it from a general perspective, ambiguous and undefined. However, I believe there exists a common awareness of the soul (not, that is, a form of knowledge), and here I take this as a basic premise. An entire tradition has referred to the soul without pretending to exhaust its essence and without claiming it could ever do so. Heraclitus states that the soul (*psyche*) is inscrutable (DK 22 B 45). Hegel does not offer a self-contained definition of spirit (*Geist*). Rather, the *Phenomenology of mind* is in effect the extension itself of a meaning that coincides with its own infinite modes, even to the point of becoming dispersed and lost within it (Hegel 2003). The monad is the set of contingencies, the pond teeming with forms of life that descend into the infinitesimal (Leibniz 2005: section LXVII). In Husserl, the succession of prefigurements prevents the fixing of consciousness and its relation with the non-self (Husserl 1980) just like in Fichte (1982). These are all cases where the essence coincides with the accidents and form with content: form and accidents extending boundlessly and uncontrollably, thus constituting a hard to define evanescent entity. The soul shrinks back, becoming extrinsic in the extension, in the gradual expansion of determinations, or hides in the depths, '*psyche* buried in the body' as hinted by Orpheus (Colli 1995: 390) or, closer to us, by Jung and by Freud as well.[45]

Soul, psyche, spirit, subject, self, consciousness, mind, by transposition even 'head' and 'brain' compose a kinship that struggles in vain to gather itself around a centre. What connects it among differences and contrasts is the interiority of the human being, which can be neither seen nor touched. No one is ignorant of the soul, but the soul is assigned different meanings; many do not even believe that it exists, while yet knowing what they deny. As in the case of love (some believe this does not exist) the variety of meanings does not impede the construction of a discourse, and also of dissent. The soul is an extreme example of Peirce's conviction that meaning is the overall set of uses, which confirms Heraclitus on the absence of boundaries of the psyche. Even if one admits that the uses may find a way of coexisting, here more than elsewhere there is no stabilization of a converging meaning.

Despite the polysemy it can be agreed that the soul is the source of images, it is their locus or at the very least their elective intermediary. Thus Kant dwelt on the notion of imagination, productive and reproductive, as the fulcrum of subjectivity (Kant 2003). The idealists glorified a faculty to which Kant

45 Freud did not intend psychoanalysis to define the psyche (see Bettelheim 1982).

himself had attributed a special value. For Fichte, productive imagination was a synonym of self. Naturally, Kant's imagination is a theoretical function, whose creativity is expressed along more delimited paths as compared to the flights of fancy evoked by the Romantics and by the common acceptance of the term. Kant's images are expressed in patterns, frames or structures of experiences. Never are they multifaceted, emotive, exuberant, restless, incoercible; they are predictable and regular. Yet even for Kant the point is precisely this: imagination is equivalent to creativity. Even though creativity fills us with uneasiness – as betrayed by the fact that it is downgraded to the realm of childhood, the naive, the insane or those with an artistic bent – it is the essence of imagining, which does not reproduce a world but extracts it and sets it before us: in a word, *producere*. Psychology and epistemology have accustomed us to the idea that we shape reality even when we proceed in the firm conviction that we merely restrict ourselves to reproducing it. Besides, we shape reality partly by virtue of evolutionary efficiency, because we would be incapable of surviving in the environment if we failed to simplify or metaphorize it.

Fichte designated the self as *Agilität*, pure activity. *Agilität* is a version of Kantian autonomy devoid of the rigid imposition that is characteristic of the law; the self is simply unchained from any antecedence. This spontaneity then condenses into an entire world, objectivizing itself, as Hegel would later say. But at the origin, and in the ever-present core, it knows no limit. In the lecture hall, Fichte roused his audience by reminding them that the liveliness of the self is not an abstruse philosophical notion, far removed from everyday existence, but the interior spark of the person. Consciences must rediscover the responsibility of actions, in the broader sense according to which what is fixed and appears independent – things, the non-self – is the result of spontaneity. A person must recognize his or her actions inasmuch as they are constant extroflections of the soul, incandescent rivers that slowly grow cool and only secondarily acts of the will. Just as in Kant, the subject acts first and foremost theoretically, albeit here individually, establishing that world which becomes the frame for choices (actions in the strict and delimited sense). The same holds true for Hegel: at the root that which is objective is subjective. The productivity of the soul can be hidden away but in no way can it be extinguished. Whether persons recognize it or not, the world is the product of their spirit.

The idealists construe the spirit as a structured dynamics, but their taxonomies have something external. 'Reason', 'science', 'logic', are reflected in formal arrangements that scholars have been endeavoring to put in proper order for fully two centuries – losing on the side of intuition what they gain with systematic performances. In actual fact, the writings of Fichte, Hegel and Schelling have neither bottom nor boundaries. They belong to the tradition that expressed the soul, of which they bear the imprint in the unstable and inexhaustible flux. The Heraclitean and Socratic tradition of the mystery of the soul, not the Platonic, Aristotelian and Kantian tradition of the mind.

María Zambrano is of the opinion that philosophers moved away from the soul very early and ever more so (Zambrano 1993a). After all these years of rational exercise, philosophical discourse is not in a good position to speak of the soul. The discourse has been honed on different referents: on things or on the objectual part, even the material part, of reality. Everything that is not thing related, as Adorno would say, throws philosophical resources into disarray (Adorno 1993). Hence the tendency to make the soul into an object, that is to say, a univocal reality. Through the medium of poetry, the Presocratics had at their disposal an expression that was fitting for the soul; furthermore, they had no desire for a universal communication. Anyone who failed to understand was excluded and the intrinsic effectiveness of the discourse was not impaired. But today, philosophical discourse is no longer artistic (neither is it evocative of initiation rites). At most, philosophy and poetry seem to be irreconcilable (Zambrano 1993b).

Elusive and creative, the soul from whence there emerges the flow of images is the submerged world that slopes down towards the depths of the human being.[46] The images belong to the psychic heritage that substantiates the individual and the collectivity, yet what can be seen is that which is consolidated and there is no awareness of the primary effervescence. Images and constellations of images rise from the deep and are fixed in the cultural universes of the human eras, which subsist as if endowed with a life of their own. But in origin the images are a mode of the soul, inasmuch as the soul is spontaneity that spills out into the world and, with its own imprint, it also restores to the world what it has absorbed from the world itself. The soul is radical imagination (Castoriadis 1987).

2. Psychology: soul and mind

Psychology has taken the place of philosophy as a route to knowledge and treatment of the psyche. According to Hadot, philosophical concern for the health of the soul died out with the demise of the ancient world;[47] since then, philosophers have closed their eyes to the overall state of the spirit, its balance, its harmony, restricting themselves to the ethical issue of being cognizant and to exhortations regarding good and bad, taken as synonyms of right and wrong. (A Greek would have failed to grasp the Kantian separation between happiness and morality.) And today philosophy has almost completely withdrawn from psychic knowledge as well. However, psychology has inherited an ambivalent philosophical attitude as far as the psyche is concerned, on the one hand,

46 Plessner argues that the human being is *unergründlich*, unfathomable, bottomless (Plessner 2003).

47 This is by now a classic statement (Hadot 1995). By contrast, Weil thinks that a method in spiritual things and in everything that relates to the well-being of the soul survived up to the first half of the Renaissance – and I would add, not in the purely philsophical sphere (Weil 2002).

continuing in the footsteps of the Heraclitean tradition of experience of the soul, while extending, on the other hand, knowledge of the psyche as *mind*.

By mind I do not mean the purely cognitive aspects, because psychology also deals with emotions, behavior, etc. Rather, study of the mind is distinguished by its manner of addressing psychic reality and what it obtains thereby. Even if it is conceived in complex terms, the mind is 'reason', the illuminated surface of the entirety of psyche. Like in Freud's metaphor, the soul is the ocean, the mind the Zuiderzee wrested from the sea by protracted philosophical and psychological elaboration. But these lands were barely below the level of the water. The mind coincides with the picture of a scientific type of knowledge defined, its being provisional notwithstanding. Yet, by way of contrast, we said it is impossible to analyze the soul, to decompose it into elements, because it cannot be seen, touched and conceived. (But there are other relations: overhearing, glimpsing, scenting, guessing, brushing against, honoring, respecting, welcoming.)

Let us take J.B. Watson and the behavioral manifesto (Watson 1913). Today, behaviorism retains nothing of its initial radicalness, but Watson's point of view is useful on account of its clarity. It represents the most extreme position among those that consider the psyche as mind. Watson is well aware that psychological knowledge has the aim of controlling people: 'Its theoretical goal is the prediction and control of behavior' (Watson 1913: 158). Likening psychology to the natural sciences, he derives an equation between determinate knowledge and the power of determining. In the case of technological action, its effectiveness relies on ambivalence-free knowledge. If I pinpoint a link, possibly even a causal link, I can act on its elements or its phases. I obtain circumscribed effects – or at least I can convince myself that this is what happens – because I discern components and relations: selective genetic modifications of corn and soybean produce benefits without notable disadvantages, an antibiotic acts on bacteria, not on viruses, surgical instruments are built and operate according to the details of medical science. Vastness and exactitude of knowledge increase the power of intervention. This is the scientific ideal, today as 150 years ago.

But what is determinable? Watson would agree with Heraclitus that the psyche is not. Despite the attempts to regulate introspection, subjective experience that has been lived through is irremediably vague. Naturally, one may opt to limit the field of enquiry to the less complex zones: basic cognitive operations, perceptions, and so forth, where it is possible to localize 'simple elementary constituents' (Watson 1913). But is this a simplicity comparable to that of mathematical, physical, or maybe chemical objects? Furthermore, there is the risk of mistaking the part for the whole, equating the entire psyche with psychophysiological phenomena, with regard to which one or more mathematical laws can be formulated. So why not exclude also the small band of determinable consciousness, obtaining in exchange the entire psychic extrinsication, namely behavior? As far as behavior is concerned, it is possible to embrace and scientifically influence the entire person. Complex though they may be, people are now objects like all other things. I can concentrate on the external surface of the psyche–world interface. The soul is restricted to the mind, the mind becomes a black box, the person a bundle of outputs and inputs. Watson realized that the possibility of controlling the human spirit is proportional to the simplicity of the idea about it which I build up.

If we take mind to signify the psyche which it is possible actually to know, rather than merely intuit, have a hunch about or even be oblivious of (the unconscious), then the overwhelming part of present-day psychology, which interprets itself as science, addresses the mind. In contrast, psychoanalysis and its ramifications are the rediscovery of the archaic psyche, none other than the soul. I fail to see how, by descending into the world of shadows, the nether world, psychoanalysis can call itself science, according to the mathematical-physical model to which psychology conforms or any other model (*Geisteswissenschaft*). Reflection and care for the soul do not exhibit the essential requisites of science.[48] Psychoanalysis is a technique and it is handed down through personal transmission. Freud and Jung had to dig up an entire universe – myth, dream, alchemy – because positivistic culture lacked any bridge into the unconscious; this void was at the very least a therapeutic obstacle, since scientific-technological language is unsuited to unconscious communication and an analyst cannot be missing the 'third ear', which is in effect the most important one (Reik 1983). Thus even though there exist excellent and very clear systematizations of psychoanalysis (Gabbard 2000), they do not represent the science of the treatment of the unconscious, because there is no such science; the relation with the unconscious lies outside any possibility of science. The compendia of psychoanalysis are not written in the language that links analyst and patient. They are tools the analyst is free to use or throw away depending on the therapeutic requirements.

Psychoanalysis has brought back into play an extinct philosophical tradition, if indeed it is to be believed that in the beginning philosophers were not merely theoreticians but also physicians of the soul, although they do not perform this role today (Hadot 1995). Whether we like it or not, this tradition used to have – and in fact still has – an initiatic and esoteric element. One needs only think of oneiric images. Freud was mocked, suspected and attacked throughout his life for having restored dignity to the world of dreams. Even today many psychological theories see no meaning in dreams. And what kind of relation does the man on the street have with dreams? Probably one of disdain or denial. The psychoanalyst, so runs the common assumption, is a shaman of obscure things that do not go beyond the circle of followers. And to some extent this is true. While theories and scientific experiments have a rather general value –

48 Long-term psychoanalytical therapy does not allow assessment of the results, unlike other psychotherapies.

which can thus be shared – psychoanalysis has an incomprehensible side for anyone who has no direct exposure to it. There exist no psychoanalysts who have a merely theoretical grasp of psychoanalysis – but there are many who do not have a great regard for psychoanalytical theories. I think the vast majority of analysts consider the theories as little more than a prop. This could not be otherwise when faced with the disconcerting experience of psychic pathology (if one seeks to engage with it and embark on treatment through a psychological rather than pharmacological approach). There exist no people who are treated by psychoanalysis through the application of a theory. Psychoanalytical practice is not the application of theories. Psychoanalysis is a situation, a relational experience that is lived through, for which there also exists a body of sophisticated, albeit extremely heterogeneous, theoretical tenets. In short, there exists no genuine psychoanalytical theory, but a psychoanalytical tradition.

And what do all the offshoots of this tradition do? They reopen blocked and latent spaces. They expand horizons: one becomes more aware. But above all, the self opens up to the unconscious. This is the basic substance of psychoanalysis. Jung calls it integration. As far as the images are concerned, it implies the freeing up of a potential. Not only do people reappropriate themselves of dreams and perhaps even have a greater number of dreams, but they cease resisting the impulses of the soul, which evokes images from the shadows through the web of a rich and flexible existence. By speaking through dreams, therapy encourages expression of the unconscious, it confronts elements that have been effaced through denial and which inhibit the soul from unfurling its visions. From the very moment when it arouses psychic vitality, psychoanalysis releases the images.

3. The soul is politically incorrect

Adorno's verdict is at least unilateral (Adorno 1974): insofar as psychoanalysis adapts a person to the vital requirements of man's own nature, it renders the person unsuited to external life; and if it nevertheless adapts a person to a profession, family or society, the individual still remains untamed, being restored to others with an energy that contrasts with the depersonalizing collective pressure.[49] Psychoanalysis encourages in the individual the images that struggle to surface from the interior and which very likely do not coincide with either those of other individuals or, above all, with the common image-creating heritage.

What would happen if each person followed the images of the soul or even simply recognized their existence? Visions are revolutionary. The soul

49 'Psychoanalysis is concerned with disadapting the subject, by reawakening in the latter the desire suppressed by denial, which has caused so many troubles: inhibitions, symptoms and anxieties' (Sciacchitano 2003: 206). Cfr. Jung 1953.

ceaselessly produces images and collective imagination is threatened by their innovativeness. The objective spirit is disturbed by the subjective spirit. And since every political regime – including democratic systems – is a consolidated bastion of conservatism that will not relinquish a stable imagination (in fact, more than stable, one would not be far off the mark in calling it inert) the political regime as such is jeopardized by the productivity of the soul.

But the dialectic between order and disorder is first and foremost an individual question. Just as the authentic individual is a danger for a political regime, so the soul is a risk for the self. No one can live in harmony with the irrational and mercurial soul. The health of the person is a dialogue between the various parties, but the soul makes too many intense demands on consciousness. In invoking the concept of integration Jung is suggesting a balance in which the self recognizes the unconscious but is not overwhelmed by it, similar to Freud's compromise among psychic demands. The integrated person lives with the contribution of unconscious energies and contents that are not completely disconnected from one another. An unbridled unconscious would be tantamount to pandemonium, because the soul is the magnificent and the horrendous, the sublime and the most terrible, love and hatred, the set of primordial powers, opposed and in a certain sense infantile, which in the absence of the filter and willpower of the self would overwhelm and crush the person.

It is quite natural for the observant person to harbor a reverential fear of the soul, for although one can draw closer to it, the soul never lets itself be controlled. In particular, the modern culture of disenchantment finds itself totally unprepared to face the lures of the nether regions and the resulting sense of unease easily shades into deadly fear and denial, both on the individual and the collective level. Psychic balance is rare. On all sides our surroundings bear witness to disrupted, coarse and destructive psychicity. Or do we believe we can find a rational justification for the murderous violence of our history, by adducing political, sociological or economic arguments? Rather, the fury of the Erinyes reveals the uncanny dynamics, to use Freud's expression: one's conscience is afraid of that which belongs to it or to which it belongs (the deep) and denies it, engendering a projection of monstrous and unrecognizable forms towards the outside. The tension of the throttled psychic potential spreads throughout all the circumstances of existence: it is the rage springing from a self-inflicted yet intolerable deprivation. The sleepers (Heraclitus) wander among the distorted objectivizations of the soul, perceiving a familiarity that is incomprehensible, yet also repulsive and attractive at one and the same time. The fascination of the lost shadow. The desire and fear of the other half of the self.

The human being fears the soul. The human is terrified of himself, the 'human reality' of which the soul is the essence (Zambrano 1996). Society and the political arena experience in the plural a severance that is already in the single being. Fear refers to the two complementary aspects of psychic energetics, the radical limit of the human condition, the weakness and the creative exuberance that arise as a prodigy from this void (Zambrano 1991, 1993a, 1996). Vulnerability and creativity are the instability of pure energy that the person cannot endure. Freud uses the term civilization to designate the sense of unease that restricts the exuberance of the soul, but he allows the soul to express itself rather than implode or explode. Unfortunately, this coercion oversteps the limit. The soul contracts to the mind. The images fade and fall into pathological oblivion, which is a void of active memory. The images are smothered like the reaction that lies buried beneath the concrete of Chernobyl, a reaction that lingers and remains in a restless, anxious state of forgottenness. A power that is ungovernable, though not hostile and quite plausibly useful and willing to cooperate, is confronted superficially, with summary optimism and becomes transformed into the grim threat of nuclear energy treated without respect, simplified by a deadly ignorance.

Chernobyl, the waste products, global radioactivity show what happens when one makes contact with primordial energies, neglecting the limits of knowledge, with the presumption that knowledge coincides with reality. It is taken for granted that reality offers no resistance to the intellect, whose acquisitions seem to be close to unconditioned possession. But the real exceeds the intellect and psychic reality, both consciousness and the mind. Thus the underestimated and repressed resources of the power of imagination translate into the pettiness of fascist, Nazi and Communist imagination. Their denial does not result in nothingness, but, rather, in the convention of mass imagination. The negation of a reality produces another reality, but a worse one (Zambrano 1996). However, the fascination of simple images, which free the individual from the burden of individuation, also affects democracy, 'totalitarian democracy' (Zambrano 1996: 183). The democratic regime can feed on the propaganda of a petty imagination because even a democratic regime prefers human beings that are as docile as machines and the psyche reduced to the mind is a guarantee against surprises and does not confound the statistics (Marcuse 1964). The imagination of the mind is narrow and naive because the mind is not the faculty of imagining, but instead limits itself to accepting from the mind the few impoverished images it could not do without.

4. Power

An image of the spirit becomes reality and is functional to the collectivity and, in the second place, to politics: the mind that imagines scantily and inadequately. The exacerbation of the dialectics between individual and collectivity is manifested in the contraposition between the mass individual, who does not concede himself the right to imagine autonomously and loses all recollection of the faculty of imagining, versus the few who are authorized to imagine for everyone and who bear the burden of this hypertrophy. Such a state of affairs is typified by the exceedingly unhappy existences of artists (this is a commonplace observation and it is true: one need only think of the film *Pollock* (portrayed by Ed Harris) (Arendt 1998). The anonymity of the objective spirit arises inasmuch as the individual relinquishes any attempt to stimulate common imagination. Imagination becomes petty, oppressive, monstrous, because it is fuelled only by itself and reaches a choking point. The atrophy of the individual produces necrosis of the collectivity.

Oppression begins in the individual, who ceases creating for fear of none other than himself. This is a justified fear, but is does not eliminate pathological repression. Human beings respond to the fear of the soul with *power*. The root of power is sado-masochism towards the vulnerable and fertile soul (Kaplan 1991); it is the need to keep oneself under control, extending from the single individual to the collectivity. Collective power is the delegating of individual autonomy, the objectivization of the act of renouncing, the origin of which is lost to memory and for which it is not possible to bear responsibility. It would be necessary to embark on a journey in order for subjectivity to reappropriate itself of objectivity. But on account of that act of delegating, the subjective spirit is unaware that it is looking at itself in the collective formations where that act of renouncing has been consolidated. Thus it undergoes the apparently extrinsic power of those formations. The individual has exercised power on the soul and has alienated creativity and awareness in the oppression of convention.

In contrast to the opinion put forward by Chomsky, power is rooted down at the bottom (Chomsky 1996).[50] It is the result of the widespread lack of awareness, not of privileged access to truth or other means of dominion. No one is in a position to tell the truth because no one knows what the truth is, not even the intellectuals who, according to Chomsky, ought to be disseminating it. Everyone shares in the privilege of power, for power is a collective rite that sweeps away the disquieting side of mankind. Power is everywhere because it is exercised in the first place by individuals over themselves; it is a question of self against self, not against the other. Collective oppression against single individuals and the oppression that single individuals exercise against one another, without any exception, derive from this original exercise. Before exercising power over others, I exercise it over myself. I exercise it over others *because* I exercise it over myself. How can I tolerate in them the freedom I have denied my own self?

Perhaps there is no remedy to the drama, in the sense that there exists a limit to the understanding of power and thus to the possibility of controlling it. On the one hand, moral principles prevent us from accepting that power admits of no exception: even the evil individual may be confident he does not

50 'Everything is condensed into the assumption that the masses are precluded access to the natural insight of reason. And it is insisted that this is the way things have to be, in order to avert the opposite hypothesis, namely that with full "freedom" the masses might well mount a rejection' (Baudrillard 1979: 111). But Baudrillard sees something positive in this rejection.

exercise it over friends or children, we may suggest. After all, even the tyrant, the criminal, Nazi, terrorist or fanatic has a code, explicit or tacit. But let us go ahead and grant that there may be circumstances in which no morals obstruct power: yet the original exercise still remains unacceptable, because recognition of self-inflicted violence implies the shattering of psychological and cultural premises that are too deeply rooted and are probably indispensable. Even the evil individual may be confident he does not exercise the violence of power against himself. However much he may revel in absolute power, he will be convinced he will never inflict it on himself. Neither will he ever have the faintest idea that he is directing against himself the very apex of that violence. Finally, it's one thing to say, as I am doing, that this is what the situation is. It's quite a different matter to proceed beyond intellectual understanding. I think that profound interpretation is impossible: radical self-inflicted harm is an enigma that no one can look straight in the eye, because no one is capable of descending down into the bottom of the soul. One may peep into the abyss, but anyone who reaches the extremity becomes insane. Such a person sees things that blind you (Oedipus). Power always shows itself under partial aspects, whereas the whole escapes us. We do not accept that it is all pervasive, i.e., truly absolute. Even in the delirium of omnipotence we exclude ourselves, otherwise it would not yield any satisfaction. What would happen if power were to become aware of being the most classic slave of itself (Popitz 1992)?

Power is beyond the reach of consciousness (Hillman 1995) and this renders it insuppressible. It is effective because it lives in no place, at least not the places in which common consciousness sites it. The saying goes: every time a power is overthrown, another rises in its stead; but this happens because power permeates the minimal circumstances of daily existence quite undisturbed. Power is democratic, it belongs to everybody, without distinction. The finger is pointed at the summits, but power draws its energy from below. This is its real life, its triumph. And so the power of repressing imagination does not belong to an élite, but on the contrary it derives jointly from the whole of mankind, from the specificity of every social and political position. Idols and victims together (Nirenstain 1988; Zambrano 1996) sustain a civilization constituted in the excess of repression. There exists no power that controls people's imagination. It is people themselves who set a limit to the faculty of imagining and who detest freedom more than the oppressors (Baudrillard 1979; Fromm 1994). Within each person imagination is waging war against repressive urges. Imagination almost always loses.

Conceiving of power in exclusively political terms is a means of not seeing its ubiquity. If one believes that power concerns only the political arena, or maybe corrupt politics, then one loses the dimension of the phenomenon, precisely the fact of its being beyond measure, measureless, immense. For basically it is reassuring and edifying to think that power is the preservation of (bad) politics. Not that it is wrong to expend time on lengthy disquisitions about the specificity of the political; but the fact is that power is not an exclusively political affair. Quite the opposite: it is so only to a minimal extent. Besides, political analyses actually indicate that the archetype of power, the model of political theories dating back as far as classical antiquity, is the *pater familias* (de Jouvenel 1981). In fact Robert Bly has stated that if aggression is innate, violence is learned and it is learned in the family (Bly 1988). When searching for power we should therefore turn our gaze on the family, before training the spotlight on politics. And first and foremost we should look at the individual before focusing on the family. That is why power is truly universal. And that is why we should not bother ourselves with the details of definitions. Good definitions of power abound (Popitz 1992) and they revolve around the linguistic root itself: capacity, influence, force, threat, efficiency, etc. But the energy expended to grasp the surface of power, such as can be captured in a definition, thus no longer remains available for grasping some of its features which in my view are important. Paradoxically the essence of power is not its nature, but its *situation*, that is, its extension and intensity. It is not difficult to say what power is: rather, what is difficult is to understand where power lies – its place – and how.

All this notwithstanding, our culture excludes the indifference of power. It believes in the asymmetry of oppressing and undergoing: if the culprit is not the tyrant, the oligarchy, the dictator, the boss, then it must be the system, imperialism, capitalism, the rule or the epistemological framework (Butler 2005). An extrinsic negative that must not affect the most pure relations. The ideal rejects power and does not acknowledge that it displays a psychic polarity; the struggle between *Eros* and *Thanatos* is not assumed in the very heart of the subject. However, a utopian (Zambrano) continues to hope that mankind will settle within its own limits; a psychoanalyst believes she can perceive a collective catharsis as in individual therapy, where one draws close to an understanding of psychic ambivalence (Miller 1997). Many other analysts believe that this approximation enables the individual to be not only more aware, but more creative and less destructive; perhaps behind their professional mask they cherish the aspiration that sparks of authenticity will benefit the masses. After all, whoever saves an individual saves mankind (Koran). If an understanding of the limit were to become widespread, democracy could take on the form of the person instead of that of the mass, Zambrano hopes – the imperfect political form suited to that particular imperfection which makes humanity human (Zambrano 1996).

References

Adorno, T.W. 1974, *Minima Moralia: Reflections from Damaged Life*, London, New Left Books.

—— 1993, *Hegel: Three Studies*, Cambridge, MA, MIT Press.

Arendt, H. 1998, *The Human Condition*, Chicago, University of Chicago Press.

Baudrillard, J. 1979, 'L'implosione del senso nei media e l'implosione del sociale nelle masse', *aut aut*, 163: 105–106.

Bettelheim, B. 1982, *Freud and Man's Soul*, New York, Random House.
Bly, R. 1988, *A Little Book on the Human Shadow*, San Francisco, Harper & Row.
Butler, J. 2005, *Giving an Account of Oneself*, New York, Fordham University Press.
Castoriadis, C. 1987, *The Imaginary Institution of Society*, Cambridge, Polity Press.
Chomsky, N. 1996, *Perspectives on Power: Reflections on Human Nature and the Social Order*, New York, Black Rose Books.
Colli, G. 1995, *La sapienza greca*, Milan: Adelphi.
de Jouvenel, B. 1981, *On Power: its Nature and the History of its Growth*, Westport, CN, Greenwood Press.
Fichte, J.G. 1982, *Science of Knowledge*, New York, Cambridge University Press.
Fromm, E. 1994, *Escape from Freedom*, New York, H. Holt.
Gabbard, G.O. 2000, *Psychodynamic Psychiatry in Clinical Practice* (3rd edn), Washington, DC, American Psychiatric Press.
Hadot, P. 1995, *Philosophy as a Way of Life: Spiritual Exercises from Socrates to Foucault*, Malden, MA, Blackwell.
Hegel, G.W.F. 2003, *The Phenomenology of Mind*, Mineola, NY, Dover Publications.
Hillman, J. 1995, *Kinds of Power*, New York, Century Doubleday.
Husserl, E. 1980, *Ideas Pertaining to a Pure Phenomenology and to a Phenomenological Philosophy*, The Hague, Boston, MA, M. Nijhoff.
Jung, C.G. 1953, *The Collected Works*, vol. 17, New York, Pantheon Books.
Kant, I. 2003, *Critique of Pure Reason*, Mineola, NY, Dover Publications.
Kaplan, L.J. 1991, *Female Perversions: The Temptations of Emma Bovary*, New York, Doubleday.
Leibniz, G.W. 2005, *Discourse on Metaphysics, and the Monadology*, Mineola, NY, Dover Publications.
Marcuse, H. 1964, *One-Dimensional Man: Studies in the Ideology of Advanced Industrial Society*, Boston, MA, Beacon Press.
Marocci, G. 2000, *Inventare l'organizzazione*, Rome, Edizioni Psicologia.
Miller, A. 1997, *The Drama of the Gifted Child: the Search for the True Self*, New York, Basic Books.
Nirenstain, A. 1988, 'Quando gli ebrei collaboravano con Hitler', *MicroMega*, 2: 64–76.
Plessner, H. 2003, *Gesammelte Schriften V: Macht und menschliche Natur*, Frankfurt, Suhrkamp.
Popitz, H. 1992, *Phänomene der Macht* (2nd edn), Tübingen, J.C.B. Mohr (Paul Siebeck).
Reik, T. 1983, *Listening with the Third Ear: the Inner Experience of a Psychoanalyst*, New York, Farrar, Straus & Giroux.
Sciacchitano, A. 2003, 'Postfazione', in Zizek, S., *L'isterico sublime: Psicanalisi e filosofia*, Milan, Mimesis, pp. 205–211.
Watson, J.B. 1913, 'Psychology as the behaviorist views it', *Psychological Review*, 20 (2): 158–177.
Weil, S. 2002, *The Need for Roots: Prelude to a Declaration of Duties towards Mankind*, London, New York, Routledge.
Zambrano, M, 1991, *El hombre y lo divino*, Madrid, Siruela.
—— 1993a, *Hacia un saber sobre el alma*, Madrid, Alianza.
—— 1993b, *Filosofia y poesia*, Madrid, F.C.E de España.
—— 1996, *Persona y democrazia: la historia sacrifical*, Madrid, Siruela.

Chapter 5

Imagination, imaginary and the bioeconomic turn of cognitive capitalism

Laura Bazzicalupo

What role does the imagination play in today's economy? The question can be answered on various levels. We are in the midst of the explosion of the *image economy*, from the new economy to the media-led post-capitalism. Image marketing means that even politics is subordinated to the economic code. At first glance it might seem that the problem is the *distortion* that communication and the imaginary undergo when they are controlled by the market. Market domination implies that the spectacular dimension that makes social reality unreal is penetrated by the passive temporality of consumption: the continuous flow of goods, the *enjoyment* that saturates and infantilises. Critical sociology counterpoises economic colonisation to a reality that is itself, however, made into a spectacle. In fact, the two aspects are inseparable and inseparably they are both linked to the political dimension, insofar as politics – as this book claims – manifests itself as a fight for the control of the imagination. In a nutshell, politics is the struggle for people's imagination because it depends on the social imagination, which is the primary location for consensus and/or choices regarding consumption.

We are faced with a structural junction. This is proved by the interweaving of the cultural predomination of the image, the economic-mercantile logic which manages the image and its effectiveness in terms of political consensus. Althusser would have defined it as ideological (1994), because the cultural/ideological dimension does not merely hide (as false conscience) an underlying structural truth (capitalism), but instead gives it its *form*, that is the imaginative condition of commodities.

To use Foucault's expression, we can talk about a productive device of truth/power. The powerful innovation of the Foucaultian perspective, compared to the (albeit brilliant) Marxist critique of the capitalist economy as the matrix of social relations, lies in its abandoning the economicist priority and fully taking on the complex knot of truth/power in which the discursive/imaginative component is structured: subjectifications are moulded by the device, which produces their desires, powers, expressive forms, as well as friction and resistance (Foucault 1988). This perspective has been picked up in various different ways both by cultural studies as well as by the post-Marxism of Badiou, Laclau and Žižek. It is a perspective that allows us to discuss the relationship between imagination and politics, imagination and economics, in a way that is not mechanically overdetermined. The rejection of structuralist economics highlights the role of the imagination and of the collective imagination in all social relations. For a long time this role was considered secondary, an epiphenomenon, the result of manipulable projections and alienations, subordinate to the *truth* of sociopolitical roles in industry. But the function of the imaginary, like that which is phantasmal or symbolic, does not coincide at all with the dichotomy of structure/superstructure and even less so with that between dominant/dominated. As Gramsci pointed out, traditional roles are interwoven and mixed up and the playing cards are scattered: the subordinate classes claim the imaginary and the models of the dominant group as their own (Gramsci 1975: 1584).

Yet, this does not mean that the economy is becoming a secondary field. Far from it. It is precisely the logic, the language and the images of the economy which provide the imaginary where the forms of subjectification are created and where that which is possible to think and desire is defined, culturally but with tangible effects. This leads to that strange but powerful *unquestionability* of capitalism itself, its naturalisation: the framework is perceived as unavoidable, beyond criticism – the universal actually fulfilled, as Žižek and Badiou (Žižek 2005: 241) put it – which has bent all alternative political ideas to its needs. Starting with the observation that an alternative to capitalism is considered unthinkable, we must acknowledge that its image – the imaginary it bears, the powerful game of truth that it represents, the veritative power it exerts – formulates the boundaries of what is thinkable and expressible. It is within these boundaries that we must work to deduce the margins of movements, of transformation and of implosion.

However, the pervasiveness and naturalisation of this collective self-representation implies an obscene repercussion which is unthought of and unuttered: a ghostly flipside upon which we should reflect. So paradoxically, an interest in the imaginary, as opposed to economicist reductionism and its pseudo-materialistic determinisms, leads us precisely to a critical, deconstructive consideration of the material-symbolic machine of the market, which gains credit as the predominant image of society; the self-representation of the economic bond that keeps it united at the global level. This bond is inescapable, very rarely challenged and even sanctioned by those who are excluded and crudely tossed to the margins of society by the very same self-representation.

This brief introduction was necessary because when we discuss the link between economics and political imagination, there is a risk of believing either in the independence of the two fields (politics as separate from the sphere of economics) or in the traditional Marxist objective centrality of economics itself (economics gives shape to politics and the imagination is simply false consciousness). However, the crucial point is the centrality – in the form of naturalisation – of the economic imaginary, which acts as almost transcendental or universal to individual and political subjectifications. In a way, this is a feature of economic relations that the classics of political economy, from Smith to Marx himself, had understood perfectly, while instead contemporary monetarist economic science tends ideologically (and this time the term is appropriate) to suppress.[51] Within this feature the primary object of *economic discourse* is the social relations, while its project is coexistence, communal life, order (Bazzicalupo 2006). Otherwise said, the economic discourse is directly a *political discourse*.

The word 'discourse' is used not in a casual or generic sense: it refers to that significant practice structured around rhetoric, tropes, images and metaphors that organise and legitimate regularities, codes of conduct, institutions and roles that are of importance and have *effects* of power: making them devices, in Foucauldian terms (Foucault 1975: 212, 1977). 'Discourse' is therefore a term that allows us to better understand the complex relationship between structure and superstructure; between forms of imagination, rationality and procedures of domination. The liberal economic discourse of the market portrays a social imagination that provokes behaviours, identifications and subjectifications that exceed the meaning which economic science gives to the market. This surplus of meaning has a political character and rests precisely on the imaginary, metaphorical nature of relations between producers, consumers (today muddled together with the figure of the *prosumer*), patterns of behaviour, hopes and life plans that are based on this imaginary.

Recognising this collective imaginary aspect of the market, which is perceived as natural and therefore performative, leads us to use psychoanalytical, and particularly Lacanian terminology – something which is increasingly common in post-Marxist criticism. And it leads us to the differences that emerge between the *imaginary*, experienced as reality; the *symbolic*, with its subjectifying interpellations; and the *real*, in the Lacanian sense of the word, i.e., that which in symbolisation is foreclosed, untold, and remains unutterable within the image agreed upon by common meaning. For the naturalised market this foreclosure, this spectral reality (to which we will return) is just as much the exclusion of those who are unable to access the market as it is the distribution of the power

51 Monetarism is the set of views associated with modern quantity theory: the primacy of the money supply over investment and government spending in determining consumption and output. Milton Friedman, his most important supporter, rejected the use of fiscal policy as a tool of demand management, and he held that the government's role in the guidance of the economy should be restricted. Friedman's essay 'The methodology of positive economics' (published originally in 1953, reproduced in Friedman 2008) provided the epistemological pattern for the Chicago School of Economics (see also Hammond and Hammond 2006). For Ben Bernanke, current chairman of the Federal Reserve, Friedman and Schwartz identified policy mistakes made by the Federal Reserve. During the financial crisis of 2007–2009, several Keynesian economists such as James Galbraith and Joseph Stiglitz blamed the free market philosophy of Friedman and the Chicago School for the economic turmoil (Lippert 2008).

relationships in the fight between dominants and subordinates, north and south of the world – the effects of violence and of material deprivation which it produces and through which it reproduces.

This spectre or ghost not described by the image of the market should be further discussed (cf. infra). The use of psychoanalytical language in itself causes bewilderment, because it seems to remove the objective, structural, *material* (in Marxian terms) field of economics from the solid, equally structural political struggle and transfer it to ephemeral culturalism or even to the psychoanalyst's couch in order to solve problems that cause suffering in millions. It is clear that it is not a case of bypassing an interest in this potentially antagonistic, conflictual dimension – on the contrary (Laclau and Mouffe 1985). Instead, the complication – Deleuze would say the problematisation (Deleuze and Guattari 1994) of economics, which underlines the imaginary, symbolic or spectral aspects in the quasi-transcendental discourse of the market – is a crucial step for returning it to its contingency, denied by naturalisation and for measuring the trajectories of power which cross through it and change it.[52]

The contingency that is a feature of capitalism is not avoidable, given that we are the discourse which structures us, and therefore we are that contingency: with its imaginary, as well as its subjectifications, its ghost, the return of the spectres, their non-univocal ambiguousness. Only the complex constellation of the imagination allows room for ambivalences in that contingent yet powerful determination which is the current truth of the market, not because the imagination, in the romantic sense, is a place of freedom and anti-systematic creativity, but because it is a place of decentralised, barred subjectification that does not fully coincide with economic determination. It is thus certainly possible that in these complex processes the imaginary neoliberal

52 *Lebensformen* of post-Fordist capitalism would seem to require a standard internal to existing global society and to overcome its local asymmetries: not only preserving capitalism from critique, but sustaining the invisible and unequal world dislocation of class differences. Today's cognitive form of production suspends the question about asymmetries of capitalist power and their global dislocation. The attention at fictional or cognitive economy – virtual, displaced and multiculturalist by definition – promotes a kind of *overcoming* of different, classist and southern world-depending, positions in the economic process and excludes from the field of visibility the actual production process (vegetables and fruit harvested and packed by immigrant workers, tension between global and local political ecologies, inequities underlying belief structures of cognitive capital, genetic trials dislocated in Asian people). For instance, cf. Rajan 2006. This analysis in a multi-sited ethnography of genomic research and drug development marketplaces in the USA and India shows that biotechnologies such as genomics can only be understood in relation to the unequal economic markets, comparing the global flow of ideas, information, capital and people connected to biotech initiatives in the countries of the north or south, east or west parts of the world. The global view of a triumphal fictional, medial capital, which does not know colonial differences, involves a theoretical retreat from the problem of domination within capitalism and a silent suspension of analysis of division of world and of people who support the weight of all suffering.

freedom of an autonomous, ordering self coincides with the direct, immediate (psychotic) incarnation in the symbolic order. Total coincidence is possible, with paranoid, delirious outcomes, but in my opinion it is unnecessary.

Lastly, if economic discourse is a discourse on the sociopolitical relationships organised through logic, language and the images of economics, we cannot deny the affective, libidinal dimension of the social bond (Freud 1921/1955) in general, and specifically of that bond that has been translated into the economic code, a code that manipulates desires, envy, fear, identity, passions, as well as competitive images of the self with varying degrees of power. Affectivity, emotions, passions of identity and competitiveness are now more crucial than ever. They take on imaginary forms which cannot be translated into a lexis, presumed to be rational by economic science whereas in fact it is already full of metaphors, analogies and metonyms. Neither can they be codified into an exhaustive set of symbols. Therefore, the density of the imagination must be fully preserved, as must its surplus of meaning.

Having spelt out in what perspective I want to consider the issue of the role of imagination in today's economy, I will proceed in four steps. I will first explore the role that imagination plays in commodities fetishism, starting with Marx's path-breaking analysis but also going beyond it (section 1). This is necessary because, as I will argue subsequently, cognitive capitalism entails novelty that Marx could not have taken into account (section 2). After exploring such novelties, I will return to the issue of the role that imagination plays in politics through a biopolitical analysis of the dominating image of the *homo oeconomicus* as human capital, as entrepreneur of himself (section 3) to conclude with an analysis of the possibilities to find a moment of friction or resistance within the dominant social imaginary.

1. The surplus of meaning of commodities: stories of fetishes and ghosts

I have mentioned the ability of political economics (and of its critics including Marx) to use the concept of value and valuation to outline a hierarchical network of objective-intersubjective social relations that mutually condition each other by means of cooperation, of the division of labour, of antagonistic and interdependent classes, in short, the market. Marx's perspective cuts through the material consistency of commodities and sees what is no longer visible in the commodity, in the manipulated, transformed object: the hard work, the effort, the life that is alienated in those objects and reified. In capitalism, the humanity of the man–animal is traced back to the reproduction of his means of subsistence: without idealisations, without sublimations, life is embodied in the phantasmagorical immanence of commodities.

Derrida (1994), picking up on Marx's theory of the fetishism of commodities rejected as humanist and Hegelian by orthodox Marxism, points out that Marx was obsessed by the phantasmal, spectral nature of the world of commodities.

As a consequence, while he does not have a theory of the symbolic or a psychoanalytical theory, he throws open the imaginative/imaginary hidden bottom layer of capitalist economics. 'The fetishism of commodities and the secret thereof', the title of section 4, in Chapter 1 of *Capital* (Marx 1999), evokes the imaginary, phantasmal dimension as the main feature (neither an addition nor an overtone) of the relations between people – relations that manifest themselves in the relations between objects which are visible, apparent and concrete while being ghosts and spectres of the relationship of subordination and exploitation resulting from the process of valuation.

The theory of commodity fetishism, thanks partly to Marx's sardonic use of the word *secret*, evokes a magical power, a spiritual force passed down to us from the primitives.[53] 'Fetish' refers to the object invested with a symbolic meaning, the image of something else; its artificial, effective, constructed, *factitious*[54] nature indicates that it supports a semantic shift which transforms the meaning and common value of the thing (its *use*, in Marxian terms) in order to give it a significance that is both individual and collective. An object which satisfies a desire becomes the bearer of value, the material embodiment of social relations.

But from a psychoanalytical point of view it is inevitably interpreted also as the object that *takes the place* of the object of love. Similarly inevitable is the evocation of the sense of uneasiness and powerlessness when faced with uncontrollable events, which is implied in the concept of fetishism. Marx talks about the 'metaphysical subtleties and theological niceties' circulating in capitalist society where, as in archaic societies, objects are not considered for what they are (use value), but for what they are worth, in other words, for their ability to be exchanged for money which, like the primitives' *mana*, is diffused over objects masking their intrinsic nature, their body: a commodity, then, is 'no longer a table, a house, yarn' (1867/1999: section 3). They become something else: the expression and image of their economic value. Fetishism does not make objects sacred; rather, it neutralises their concrete nature, to let loose the spectre or ghost of their exchange value. The more the system grows, the stronger the fascination of fetishism becomes, due to the impossibility of

53 Marx uses unusual words: 'A commodity appears, at first sight, a very trivial thing, and easily understood. Its analysis shows that it is, in reality, a very queer thing, abounding in metaphysical subtleties and theological niceties'; 'mystical character of commodities'; 'the enigmatical character of the product of labour'; 'a mysterious thing'; 'There it is a definite social relation between men, that assumes, in their eyes, the fantastic form of a relation between things. In order, therefore, to find an analogy, we must have recourse to the mist-enveloped regions of the religious world. In that world the productions of the human brain appear as independent beings endowed with life, and entering into relation both with one another and the human race' (1999: Part I, Chapter 1, section 4).

54 The Latin word corresponding to *fetish* is *facticius* (from *facere*, to make) as made, constructed; Marx: 'This I call the Fetishism which attaches itself to the products of labour, so soon as they are produced as commodities, and which is therefore inseparable from the production of commodities' (1999).

grasping the object without passing through the artifice, the fetish: what is talking is not the objects themselves, but the code which expresses them all, because it is expressed in all of them.

The role of the imagination in economics cannot disregard the chapter on human alienation and reification in the fetish of the commodity, which is displayed, sold, valued, while 'the human world is devalued'. Marx was also the first to evoke in the phantasmagoria of commodities the spectre, the foreclosed of that which is real, namely effort, labour, the living person. Behind commodity fetishism there is the real and Marx indicates the deconcretisation process which envelops things themselves: their incessant loss of meaning, of concreteness, to become a pure sign or image of economic value.

When they enter the magical circuit of valuation, things and living bodies that are apparently highly appreciated (but appreciate means to put a price on) lose themselves (assuming they have a history, memory, meaning and *use* for pleasure, for communication). They empty themselves in a process of virtualisation, sucked in by the only power that determines value: money, the exchange relation. The bewitching power of commodities increases. This is not due to the obsession of desire, which actually weakens despite the relentless stimuli, but due to the fact that it is impossible to grasp the concrete object without clasping only its factitious, fictitious value as a fetish, a simulacrum. The simulacrum of an inconsistent relationship with the other. Furthermore, on the market, money is the non-material key, the image of the system in which commodities circulate. The virtual nature of money, which is now more obvious than ever in its digital version, is proof of the replaceability and interchangeability of all things and for Benjamin this declares its devaluation (2009).

A humanistic reading of fetishism presupposes the possibility or the utopia of a transparent social relationship. In capitalism, 'relations between people' are imagined as free/voluntary and equal and the domination relationship is shifted (and ghosted) onto the relation between objects: the revolution will bring emancipation and transparency. But relationships between people are never transparent. Leaving Marx to one side, the shift is structural, cardinal, in that 'there is no immediate, self-present living subjectivity to whom the belief embodied in things can be attributed, and who is then dispossessed of it' (Žižek 1997: 154). 'Our access to this "reality" is always-already "mediated" by the symbolic process', suggests Žižek, in Lacan's wake (1997: 143).

This is a key question because, as we will see when it comes to the productive role of the imagination in post-Fordist capitalism, the mediation of the symbolic order in which we are immersed, i.e. the market, does not produce total symbolisation. The fetishistic reification is never complete, as proved by an imagination that, while it does depend on the collective, is disordering: the subject is precisely this failure of the symbolic in the imagination.

What interests us here is that the fetishism of goods reveals the symbolic efficacy of the economic sphere itself: 'The commodity form affirms the image of the social character of men's labor . . . There it is a definite social relation between men, that assumes, in their eyes, the fantastic form of a relation between things' (Marx 1999: Part I, Chapter 1, section 4). Benjamin picks up on this metaphor of the phantasmagoria of commodities in his visionary Parisian *Passages*, in which the concreteness of objects shines out of their spectral, phantasmal nature. Benjamin vigorously points to their oneiric density. The phantasmagoria of commodities is a sequence of illusory images, a dance of ghosts who stir and involve the imagination of the observer, of the *flâneur*, of the crowd (Benjamin 2006: 14–19, 108–109). The Marxian fetish becomes more and more an allegory and a pretence; that is, an empirical, nominalistic sign containing nothing, which can be replaced with anything else and is totally disconnected from material need, from concrete necessity, because it is the dematerialised image of interchangeability.

Benjamin sees in this the fantasy of a collective subconscious between dreaming and waking, which creates images that elude the grasp of semiotics. The world of commodities is the new, which is always the same. With Benjamin we are closer to today, but still in a Fordist world of things offered up for consumption: he is not interested in the ideological meaning but in the surface, in the visible image. The shift he stamped on the theory of fetishism grasps the transformation into a simulacrum, an allegorical literalness which affects the image (Benjamin 1996: vol. 3, section 5). For Benjamin, a materialist physiognomy, which deciphers the inside from the outside, arises from *this bodily object*. '*Value*, as the natural burning-glass of semblance in history, outshines meaning. Its lustre is more difficult to dispel. It is, moreover, the very newest' (2006: 138; emphasis mine). The fetish character of the commodity is allegorical. 'Marx describes the causal relation between economics and civilisation. What matters here is the expressive relation' (2006: 13). The 'burning glass' of the process of valuation destroys the object, delivering it to allegory, which empties the meaning of things into interchangeability and whose constant object is death, like the true spectral inhabitant of those *passages* (Benjamin 2006: 137–138).

Guy Debord also sensed the perverse fascination of representation and the current developments of immaterial reality, founded on the commodity-spectacular dogmatism which allows just one ideology. Debord projects a new transparency onto the Marxian spectres which inhabit the commodity form. After Benjamin and Lukács, Debord is among the few who put the fetishist essence back at the centre of capitalism, as the matrix of the alienation/reification of social relations. The spectacle of the commodity spreads totally and *necessarily*: 'The spectacle is capital accumulated to the point that it becomes images' (2004: 7, section 34). A contemplative, passive dimension, typical of the spectacular, is incorporated into the frenetic, cold, calculating work of production. Thus the old figure of fetishism collides with the future, now current one of capitalism. Debord burst onto the scene, ahead of his time, ahead of mass production, which at that point was still Taylorist, with his description of the world of absolute appearance. This consists in the information technology world of telecommunications, populated by chains of numerical systems, of simulacra, of virtual electronic ectoplasm, avatars, digital essences, cybernauts. The capital in his view appears as a pure phantasmagoria, a measureless accumulation not of commodities but of spectacles, of images to be watched and interacted with, complying with their logic. Simulacra claim no truth; instead they claim the commonplace, the disjointing and atomisation of every meaning.

This new world is also obsessed by phantasms and Marx is still useful, because as Derrida says, 'he continues to address the question of life, the spirit, the spectral, *la vie–la mort*, beyond the opposition of life and death' (1994: 40). Such is the phantasm 'between life and death', the non-dead, the spectre that nests in the un-realised world. 'The spectacle is a concrete inversion of life, an autonomous movement of the non-living' (Debord 2004: 1, section 2). Derrida develops the theme of the spectre by adapting it to media capitalism, in *Echographies of Television* (Derrida and Stiegler 2002). The visual object appears to be colonised by allegorical signs, by numerical entities, by the linguistic-communicative network that envelops it, which creates its charm and affective seduction. All cognitive and affective images define relationships of power. 'Political-economic hegemony and intellectual or discursive domination passes, as never before to this degree or in these ways, through the power of technology and the media . . . It is a power, a differentiated set of powers, which cannot be analyzed and potentially fought – support here, attack there – without taking into account so many spectral effects of the new capacity for apparition (in the ghostly sense) of the simulacrum and of the synthetic or prophetic image of the virtual event, of cyberspace and of the control of apparitions or speculations which are today disclosing unprecedented powers' (Derrida and Stiegler 2002: 113).

But can one possess or grasp a spectre? Are we not grasped and possessed by it? In actual fact, one cannot cancel the ghost to see reality: the fetish cannot be passed through. The spectre is appearance, which removes the being from view; it is the incorporeal in the body, the suprasensible in the sensible; or the weight of subordination behind the virtuality of creation. As soon as there is production for a market, there is fetishism, idealisation, automation, dematerialisation, spectral incorporation. In the shift towards the de-realised totality of the current market it is not possible to return to the authentic presence, to real, living time as opposed to that of the simulacrum. The techno-world allows the fetish to spread and saturate all that is real. For Derrida, we should leave things be. Let the imaginary be. The identity of structure and superstructure – belonging to the allegory, to its nominalism and its immanence – indicates the total incorporation of figures into economic–social processes.

Furthermore, with the society of the integrated spectacle, as Debord so cleverly predicted, the very sign itself is threatened, along with its representative capacity. Baudrillard, paradoxical and visionary, announces 'it is precisely when the sign and the real are no longer exchangeable that reality, now left alone and meaningless, veers off exponentially and proliferates infinitely' (2005: 9). Provocatively, turning upside down the common assumption whereby reality succumbs to the hegemony of the sign, of images, of the simulacrum, Baudrillard demonstrates that what has been lost is the sign, to the benefit of absolute reality, of the hyper-real. The dissolution of the transcendence of the sign, overturned by vertiginous deregulation, drags all 'the universe of meaning and communication, which is subjected to the same deregulation that affects the markets' (2005: 9–10).

Signs, images, allegories cease to have a differential function. 'No more gaze, no more stage, no more imaginary, no more illusion even, no more exteriority, no more spectacle: the operational fetish has absorbed all exteriority, all interiority . . . the realization of utopia' (2005: 11). In other words, it is a psychotic universe. The only judgment remaining is that of the absolutely interchangeable valuation of the market. Total immersion in the flow of images is the price of this infinite availability of infinite combinations. In a psychotic, factual, ready-made universe, all the culture of metaphor risks being sucked into an objective dimension made of images, but without the 'fuzziness of gesture', without the tremor, 'the imprecision which attests that tremor of the world'. Images become impoverished, 'the simulacrum does not mask the truth, it masks the fact that there is no truth at all' (2005: 25–29). The contingency of the product replicates itself infinitely, a simulacrum without an original. As they say in *The Matrix* – chosen not coincidentally by Žižek as the hyperbole of the anxiety caused by radical virtual and technological transformations and by the emancipation from the body: 'Welcome to the desert of the Real.'[55]

2. An immaterial matrix: the novelty of post-Fordist cognitive capitalism

This new media reality is exploding like the field of a vast economic investment, inexhaustible and inconsumable in a way that material production could never be. But does it really annul the invasiveness of the body, i.e. of affectivity, emotiveness, imagination, the intellect and therefore language? Does this psychotic virtual hyper-reality not still need language or the image, albeit replicated infinitely? Does it not need the icon and the simulacrum, however literal they may be? Are these still or no longer the *use value* of language, of communication, of social relations? In Žižek's ironic commentary, *The Matrix* is the symbolic matrix, the Lacanian Big Other, the *discourse* that structures us, from which we are constituently alienated; that which, like the Frankfurt School, he calls the 'social substance', meaning capitalism in its latest new

55 Žižek 2002: 241.

economy, digital, immaterial version (2002: 244). We are inside it. Through the system of subjectifications, of the production of desires and of virtual life forms of the bioeconomy, we are inside the network of extreme transformation of the symbolic. We must ask ourselves whether being inside it makes it possible to establish a distance, to be opposed to it. Whether the subjective work, the live work – which produces value through creativity, emotions and imagination – creates some kind of friction, a non-concurrence with the paranoid universe. We must ask ourselves whether the absorption into the symbolic/imaginary order to which we belong is total or if that productive imagination put to work, which as such subjectifies us, has margins of non-colonisation. What is social substance if not the collective, shared imaginary (since we act as instruments for the reproduction of what Žižek calls the *jouissance* of the Big Other), which we participate in like halved, decentralised subjects?

Once again, fetishism and the ghostliness of the stage come to the rescue. The spectre also resides in virtual production, in the imagined and imaginary spectacle, in the life experience which dominates him who has lived and produced it: the ghost which the collective imaginary overshadows and yet returns to, the obscene fact of the expropriation of the living being, of its creativity.

Thus the imaginary plus the phantasm seems to be the real that will enable the distance, the non-concurrence. But let us proceed in order. The linguistic shift of post-Fordist capitalism consists of a series of processes to reconvert the production system that radicalises (and partly overturns) the schema of alienation underlying the fetishism of commodities. We have discussed the commodity simulacrum. Communication and information flows become a constituent part of the innovation production process. This means the 'overlapping of production and communication, instrumental action and communicative action' (Marazzi 1999: 17). Not only does logical-formal language (symbols, signs, abstract codes) *produce organisation*, but communicative action also brings into play a sensorial, intuitive and, above all, imaginative ability to manage symbolic acts.

The linguistic nature of social relations and of aesthetic production extends to the relational and cognitive economy of post-Fordism, which takes it on structurally, transforming the productive paradigm: what is produced are not things, but signs, imagines, symbols loaded with emotion and suggestion. As a consequence, images prevail over words themselves, to meet the growing demand for a relational nature, for social meanings that once again the economy offers to satisfy. Social meanings that the economy in turn produces, first of all by producing consumers–producers, *prosumers*, for whom the consumption of a service or a commodity replaces the experience itself. The shift in cognitive capitalism coincides with the extraordinary development of a tertiary industry or the service economy; the latter is much less technological but has in common with the former the centrality of the social and relational dimension of the immaterial economy. Services do not produce things but performances, relations, *praxis* not *poiesis*: and the difficulty of measuring them makes valuation difficult in the exchange of capital for labour.

Marazzi discusses the 'return of the social in the understanding of economic phenomena' (1999: 40). In my view, social relations are, always, the meaning of economics: the theory of commodity fetishism bears witness to that. Economics means that these communications, this information, and indeed these bonds, these dependencies, these services have a (perhaps not exhaustive) profile of means, of commodities; they are relational situations that are expressed in the code of the market. In it, they are translated and betrayed, saturated, perverted. However, just as the life of the person producing the services continues to move ghostlike within these immaterial performances, in the same way the person using them fulfils a scrap of his relational needs in the unnatural yet live form of a service that is paid for.

Thus the service commodifies the life of the worker, his availability, his intuitive and affective capacity, his flexibility and psychological penetration into the desires and anxieties of the user and the customer. The last, in turn, acquires care and sociality in the form of commodities. Similarly, in cognitive capitalism the worker is called on to use all his fantasy and creativity to manipulate symbols, to create images that are capable of arousing interests, passions, dependency, dreams and satisfactions, whether dreamlike or imaginary; in doing so, he must actively relate with the psychic world of the consumer (a practice increasingly similar to Arendtian action).[56] In the service economy, just as in cognitive, immaterial capitalism, that which is economic is of a relational nature, is by definition communication.

In synthesis, the imagination is now required to *work* inside the economic process: so not just the imaginary of the phantasmagoria of commodities, and not just the spectral sensitive-insensitive semblance of object commodities, through which the phantasm of alienated work passes. Here, the imagination is called on to offset, making them economically accessible (for services and information, performances and promptness come at a price), the vast emptiness of spontaneous social relations, which come undone and disappear in the 'fact of the market'. It compensates for the emptying of the system of symbols which were once thick with meaning, with cultural recognition: relationships must be established from scratch, created especially to fill the 'lack' of individuals; a lack which has worsened with the dissolution of family, country, belonging, in the de-territorialising flow of capitalism (Deleuze and Guattari 1987: 453–456).

56 Arendt 1998. The tripartite division between the human activities of labour (repetitive, never ending, necessary to sustain life), work (Greek, Aristotelian: *poiesis*, with a beginning and end and that leaves enduring artefacts) and action (Greek, Aristotelian: *praxis* that takes place in the public realm, through which the agent is disclosed) are confused in post-Fordist capitalism. Cognitive production has characters of praxis: frail, public, unpredictable and consumers are active users of creative means of communication.

But *substitute* images and emotions can only be simulacra: they replicate and repeat indefinitely only the form – as Benjamin had already understood – without the symbolic density of 'territorial' realities. They float on themselves, offering the resemblance, the standardised repetition typical of the simulacrum, of what used to be the major, substantial densities of everyday life: friends, family, love, filial affection, the protection of the group. Everything is reproduced, we find it all offered in the market of the imagination, but all of it in a perverse form that is expressly modelled to fit the demand of the presumed consumer: so with that slight exasperation, that stereotype, which betrays the *papier mâché* quality of pure simulacrum, which an image has when it is repeated infinitely in order to strategically satisfy the customer.

Or not? Or perhaps when the gesture of welcome, the image of hospitality, is given with a smile or the right words for the face of the new guest of a hotel, there is something alive and true in that gesture; a surplus of spontaneous friendship that frees it from being totally commodified and servile? Or does imagining an advertisement script or a sketch to sell beer mean going beyond, producing a deviation from the alienation of one's own fantasy, one's own memories as a young man going to the bar with his friends? Does it also mean freeing one's own subjectivity, expressing it and giving it a form that goes beyond the commercial exchange? Thus evoking, if nothing else, grief for that relational nature which is sought after by the person buying beer: that group friendship shaped by economics as it sells, and sells off cheap desire and its momentary satisfaction?

The post-Fordist shift brings *live work* into play, meaning life as work, with no separation between work time, mechanical wage earning and free time in terms of life, feelings and self-fulfilment. It brings subjectifications into play. By and large (although here distinctions and exceptions should be made) work becomes alive, inseparable from the producer, different for each person who carries it out because it involves their specific life, in the entirety of their subjectivity and their psychic and cultural dimension. In other words, it includes the whole of that person's memory, emotions, fears and dreams.

This involvement, however, bears witness to the belonging and dependency of each individual, as a producer and/or consumer, on the collective imaginary. Some have called it the 'general intellect' to suggest that the idea is a patrimony in which everybody participates.[57] The general intellect seems to refer to the

57 'General intellect' (perhaps a kind of *volonté générale* of Rousseau or of *nous poietikos* of Aristotelian *De anima*) is an expression of Marx, in the famous 'Fragment of machines' from *The Grundrisse* (1997: 690–712) 'The developments of fixed capital indicates to what degree general social knowledge has become a direct force of production and to what degree hence the conditions of the process of social life itself have come under the control of the *general intellect* and been transformed in accordance with it' (1997: 706; emphasis mine). Here, Marx bears evidence of prominence of knowledge on physical work, and proposes a new hypothesis of emancipation through common intellectual knowledge. Hardt and Negri

indivisibility of the heritage of images, intellectual and mental knowledge, symbolic forms emerging from the bottom up, new figurative aspirations, visual and visionary trends that cognitive entrepreneurship metabolises and transforms into marketable images. In fact, it is the social body, through a series of interactions, knowledges, paradigms and communications, that is the guardian of this knowledge; it, therefore, could operate the productive machine to the benefit of all, for all. This common language which is currently dominant in communication is a repository of resources; while it is inexhaustible and not easily appropriated, it does not possess, as Marx hoped, an emancipative force in itself (1997: 704). In its ambivalence it is strongly creative; it establishes analogies, assonances; it conveys codes of conduct, beliefs that are more or less loyal to the *discourse*; but it is also available to be subjectified by the market through commoditisation mechanisms.

Lastly, let me mention another aspect of the new capitalism that is relevant to the theme in question: the role played by belief, expectation and imagination in financial activities, which represent an increasingly crucial dimension of the economic system. All stock exchange transactions, in particular their new generations such as derivatives or hedge funds, are based on the psychological imagination.[58] They rely on representation, not of the actual value of what is sold and even less so on the objective and material solidity of the products. What is exchanged are the reactive expectations of those participating in the transactions, because the latter are based on how stock exchange traders imagine the world. Yet, this is an imaginary scenario with very concrete effects, as we have seen in the recent financial crisis.

3. The dilemmas of human capital and its limitless imagination

Does the collective imaginary of the market represent *us*, an image among images, a sign among signs? The latest, most persuasive version of *homo oeconomicus* represents itself as a subject who is the entrepreneur of himself, of his own life, as human capital. To fully understand the meaning of this image, let us refer to the positive/productive nature of biopolitical power, with the literal meaning of something that can 'posit' and 'produce'. The biopolitical nature of this power points to the ambivalence of the subjectification processes which it builds: it is a 'power of incitement, of reinforcement, of control, of

(1994), Virno (2004) and other neo-Marxists have emphasised the ambivalence of the new way of production and the revolutionary input of sharing of ideas, knowledge, relations. Similar to the *doxa* of Bourdieu or to popular wisdom, the use of the expression 'general intellect' is closer to economic production and has the role of extended and anonymous human capital, in Marxist areas.

58 About hedge funds, see ECB 2006; *derivative* is a financial instrument that is *derived* from some other asset, index, event, value or condition (known as the underlying asset).

increase of force' (Foucault 1976: 183). Biopolitics means that the economic power that organises our lives spreads its productivity through truth games – since the definitions of human nature and the living are games of truth – directed towards the effects of power.

Power is a tool for production, not just in the now less important sense of the production of things, but in the more radical sense of producing subjectivities by encouraging attitudes that are functional for the system and therefore are themselves productive. Power produces an anthropological icon that supports and confirms the social substance, the collective imaginary with its imperative to produce and enjoy by consuming endlessly, thanks to the limitless immateriality of production itself. The crux, then, is in the subject, in the representation of an active, productive subject who is able to take risks, who can be more responsible for her/himself than ever as he has direct access to the main production tool of the economy: intelligence, imagination, psyche.

Thus the lynchpin is the imagination; as an inventive, productive faculty, it is the feature which sticks out from the otherwise given, static, symbolic order, the feature that makes that order dynamic – as is required by the rule of infinite increase that distinguishes capital and biopolitics. The subject that is adapted to our great Other has his desires and plans moulded by the consumerist imaginary of commodities; but due to the new *live* character of the commodities themselves, he is able to draw innovations from this pool of common images, he can disarrange the schemas, combine the fragments. In other words, he *has imagination*, he creates emotions and images, he is an innovator and is able to enjoy applying his talent as well as its results. *Vae victis!* Damn the weak spirited! And just as Kant and Hegel had already intuited, as Heidegger and Sartre knew, as Lacan stated and Žižek now repeats, the imagination is what is at stake. With immaterial capitalism, the imagination is put to *service* as an infinite, always renewable resource; a resource that is human and very personal, but also social, linguistic and relational; it *serves* in the process of valuation and is subordinated to the economic code.

The image of human capital guides the social imagination ambivalently: within the empire of signs and images, but potentially against it too. On the one hand, it confirms the subjection to the economic–symbolic cultural device, which has control over all of human life; on the other, this subjugation – based precisely on the imagination, the mental faculty which constitutes the subject but denies it full control – could be reversed, with unpredictable forms of resistance.

The imagination is the place of identification. It is where the individual rubs against the whole and, paradoxically, it is the capital which determines the subject's value while at the same time subordinating it entirely to the exchange relation: its subjective essence is in fact strategic. The imagination, then: we do not re-propose the romantic creative imagination. Instead, going beyond the roles defined by symbolic interpellation, what we call subject is precisely that energy of the imagination (largely negative and dissolutive) which indefinitely takes apart and recomposes the order. The subject is the impossibility of total subsumption into the logic of capital. It manifests itself in a *fold* – such is the imagination – which resists; it may reiterate the simulacrum to infinity and thus empty it of meaning, or perhaps it opens up a passage, a new causal series. Hence the extreme mockery, but also the paradoxical truth of the theory of human capital.

The subject is defined by means of and as a movement – even just a movement of deviation, evasion, folding. The imagination is never the faithful reproduction of reality. It is the dissolutive or creative deviation (the simulacrum does not have an original, does not have a truth) compared to the replica: said deviation, which is man himself compared to the order that forms him, is included in the exchange, but is not exhausted in said exchange. Incidentally, I would like to point out that the first image of *homo oeconomicus* – thought up by the forefathers of political economy precisely in relation to the social function of economic relations – defined him as being lacking, imperfect, in need of the unsociable relationship with others in which to mirror his own desires, his own lacking and his own identity, also defined him as a power, *dynamis*, of believing and inventing.[59] Interaction and social dependency did not cancel out the contingent beginning, the event and the difference which is not metaphysical but purely empirical, emergent, 'spontaneous', germinative. It is this that makes a subject a subject and not a clone: perhaps a subject that works to invent clones, giving shape to anxiety about risk by which he is seized.

Otherwise stated, what makes the subject is believing and inventing, therefore being inside the fact while at the same time protruding from it: dismantling, denying it, going beyond it. It is true that all economic theories (*homo oeconomicus* and his logic) are aimed at controlling and governing that original image. But the suggestion of this idea of subjectivity, which even now exerts its libertarian, contingent fascination, lies in the combination of germinative power and social contextualisation, with no synthesis whatsoever. Invention and belief are facts of the imagination – i.e. the places of the subjectivity that emerge from fact. In the form of creativity, trust and credit they can also be the key to the implacability of live work today, faced with the processes of subsumption and assimilation of the market itself. This surplus, this non-objectifiability, is constantly sought after and grasped at by the economic mechanism of capitalism, and is 'put to use'.

Economics is the social substance or the collective imaginary which gives shape to these subjects who are immersed in a consumption/enjoyment that folds in on itself, producing ever newer images and initiatives. They are 'realist' subjects, detached from debts and from solidarity, capable of enterprise and personal risk; the weight of their fragilities cannot be seen. The image of *homo*

59 See Hirschman 1977; Horne 1981; Mandeville 2001; Smith 2000: Part I, Section II, Chapter V.

oeconomicus runs across all sectors of society. He is his own entrepreneur, even when he consumes, even when he acts as a criminal and when he sells, or rather invests, his own creativity.

This image could not have emerged if the very same capitalist process of valuation had not extended so far as to include intelligent machines and that intelligent, flexible, creative and surprising machine which is man. It would not have been possible if *valuation* had not been, with biopolitical capitalism, a legitimation that obscures the dynamic of alienation and heteronomy which the word 'labour' brought with its etymology.[60] Valuation and therefore self-valuation, the spontaneous, voluntary translation of one's self, of one's own baggage of images, memories, hopes, ideas, experiences lived and used (use value), into an exchange value.

Thus, economic strategy becomes the logic behind political, social and family life: a libidinal economics that is both individual and social. A framework that perfectly integrates the post-modern narcissism that is bound together with the imaginary, which never becomes adult as it is kept at the stage of a substitute satisfaction, of the *jouissance* of the Other; but which also contradicts it, because it radically denies the subject any dependency, *defaillance*, inequality: and as we know, negation generates phantasms. This kind of narcissistic subjectivity lacks structuring prohibitions and takes ownership of the imaginary ideal: like the infamous hackers, paid to spend time on their hobbies in front of the computer; those who are contractually obligated to be what they are, to follow their own tastes and inclinations; those who fulfil the utopia of overcoming the opposition between the alienation of working for money and doing hobbies in their free time.

But taking on such an ideal exposes them to their own superegoic pressure, focused on their personal creativity and difference. This is much more oppressive than the old moral pressure to do one's duty. They are exposed to psychotic outcomes of infinite self-ordering. This paradoxical pattern of dis-alienation also overshadows the tension between creative impulses and the society that appreciates them, gives them a price and wants to normalise them. In this imaginary of '*no workers, but all capitalists*', there is no hint of spectres and foreclosures: indeed, commoditisation is totally accepted as a voluntary investment in oneself and there is no effort, work and alienation to be phantasmatically concealed, because the image, the dream produced carries with it the subject at work and identifies with the subject. But the phantasm will never die altogether, in total immanence, without transcendence. They tell us that this is the desert of reality: welcome, you cannot and you must not do anything except adapt, without the Marxian *dream of a thing* and without spectral nightmares. Everybody is alone with his gift, with his talents and with the need to put them to interest by enjoying them.

60 The etymology of 'labour' comes from Latin *labor*, that is fatigue, effort, pain, sorrow, throes or labour pains.

Young creative types offer inventions and images taken from their social life, hoping to draw financial gain from them, but they also consume images, experiences and enjoyment while they produce, mixing production time and satisfaction time, alienated experiences and their own experiences. Mothers invest their time in their children's success: the better the quality of that time, the more likely the success of an educational *enterprise*; old people invest energy in physical exercises and diets in order to *obtain* a long, pleasant, easy life. These are images that replicate stereotypes so widespread and unchallenged that, without realising, we approve the logic behind them. The subject considered as an enterprise – individual, collective, cooperative – that handles its life according to a plan of investments, risks, expected earnings, innovations, speculation as though it were a business plan. The subject can do this because, in fact, the capital lies in its total availability: this is its life, its imagination, its emotions.

And yet something is excluded from the hyperrealism of these lives, something remains spectral and obscene: for example pain, melancholy, the unpredictability of desire, the destructive drive, the residual freedom of the imagination that lies within the stereotype but causes a little friction, bends in another direction, is distracted by other images that mess up the *economic* project to invest in one's own live capital. This spectre makes possible a traversal of the fantasy.

4. Traversing the fantasy

Total acceptance of the new imaginary is necessary. This does not mean accepting the radical depoliticisation of the economy, in other words accepting the state of things as natural and objective. In order to repoliticise the economy, that which is foreclosed in the collective imaginary needs to be left to circulate, in whatever form the spectre is able to take on according to context, favouring either the socio-symbolic life forms of the system (gender, cultural, ethnic, religious or environmental conflicts) or the form of economic struggle which tends towards a universalistic concentration of pluralities.

What is fundamental is that, either way, it should be possible to make out the spectre of the colonisation of the market logic; this, among other effects, causes the imaginary sensation of being autonomous spheres, not implicated in the economy, capable of free choice. The social relations of subordination, the material basis and the selective action of the bioeconomic governmentality over those lives that do not have the ability to access the market or which are made precarious and marginalised within it, become the phantasm of that which is obscured by the social and individual imagination. Going through the social phantasy means not averting one's eyes and being able to see freedom, powers and subjectifications in the imaginaries – the repressed content of dominion, of subordination, of suffering (Žižek 1989: 69).[61] Acknowledging the reflexive commoditisation of our vital spheres threatens the standard of the free, autonomous subject; it forces us to process the obscene need for subjugation and dependency in the post-Oedipal society, populated by psychotic narcissists, without being dazzled by their self-celebration.

Cutting with a deviation through the imagination and imaginary in which we are immersed; touching the spectre with our hands; listening to the real voices of those involved, warm with affectivity and anxiety – all this means giving weight to existence, guaranteeing a minimum of corporeal reality in a universe of simulacra. If the term 'labour' has practically fallen into disuse due to this *communicative action* and we talk of professionalism, of enterprise, of risk yet autonomous initiative, then the phantasm is the wages, dependency, heteronomy: the obscene of the entrepreneurial scene, which has finally cancelled out antagonism and subordination. The obscene is the dissymmetry of powers, subordination and – an outdated image – the fight between unequal forces that was once called the class struggle.

Class itself is a spectre, an evanescent invisible, compared to the much more emphasised images of differences of gender, race or culture: it is outdated and embarrassing to talk about it, as indeed happens with obscenities. However, this too is proof of the strength with which this imaginary mainstream has penetrated even the socialist vision of the world of work, proof of its incredible capacity for popular involvement, for projecting itself into the model of the successful entrepreneur as an identifying force. This penetration erodes a tradition of social expectations that are oriented towards the state, to the heteronymous government, but also towards social justice, to solidarity.

The result is that the traditional discourse on subordinate classes has been disjointed, specifically within the imaginary. 'The circle of dominant ideas *does* accumulate the symbolic power to map or classify the world for others; its classifications do acquire not only the constraining power of dominance over other modes of thought but also the initial authority of habit and instinct. It becomes the horizon of the taken-for-granted: what the world is and how it works, for all practical purposes. Ruling ideas may dominate other conceptions of the social world by setting the limit on what will appear as rational, reasonable, credible, indeed sayable or thinkable' (Hall 1988: 44). Television dramas, the extolling of popular icons of success – these obviously pass through the image much more than through reasoning, in which it would be problematic to explicitly empty acquired rights, long-settled benefits.

61 In order to avoid a clash of fantasies we have to learn to 'traverse the fantasy' (what Lacan terms 'traversing the *fantôme*'). It means that we have to acknowledge that fantasy functions merely to screen the abyss or inconsistency in the Big Other. In 'traversing' or 'going through' the fantasy 'all we have to do is experience how there is nothing "behind" it, and how fantasy masks precisely this "nothing"' (Žižek 1989: 47–48).

And so? This is the bioeconomic collective imaginary and the effect it has on lives. Once again we are faced with the question of the contras, of the tension regarding the imaginary training which orders lives: not outside the matrix, but inside it. Not outside of the imagination put to work, but inside the imagination itself. This is the key question of *bios*: biovalue, creative work, alive, entrepreneurial, autonomous work understood as a surplus of biopolitical subjugation; it is an element of power, if power is change; it is a human element, if it is creativity, the surplus of the living human being beyond the repetitive routine of the biological and the servile/operational. Is it perhaps the surplus of the *bios*, of the imagination itself that rescues it – as some euphorically hope (Negri 2008) – from subjugation? Through which fields of concrete possibility does it come about? In other words, which conditions render it a power of transformation? Is it freedom? Is there space for freedom in that power that has a direct hold over bios, which guides it and governs it? Or is the innovative action of the imagination free and contingent, but at the same time structurally subjected to the control of the entry code to the market? And is subsumption into systemic alienation total and necessary?

These questions are crucial from a bioeconomic point of view, for the following reason. Neo-Marxian theories insist on the total commoditisation of *bios*, the total loss of the self in cognitive capitalism and in the concurrence of life and working life. These theories correspond to the interpretations of the biopolitical paradigm in terms of the vital, affirmative power of the masses.[62] Both paths preclude the genealogical work that disjoints the mesh of powers, logics and languages within the seemingly monolithic imaginary.

In actual fact, the factors determining the processes of subjectification are powerful, but not cohesive or all consuming. A recursive, proliferative logic is in force, rather than a deterministic causality. The network economy deals in commodities that are largely social and are not easily appropriable: their characteristic is that they are cumulative and iterative and their value depends on their distribution. They cost next to nothing to reproduce and are disseminated with a net form that is commonly found neither in the market nor in political state institutions. This network brings to mind a rhizomatous process: its model is not mechanical, but biological, emergency based, in a dialectic relation with the social and human environment, which is neither neutral nor inert. Exchange, which is the social meaning of commercial relations, and which determines the positions of subordination and domination, is no longer linear: this is not to say that it no longer exists, but that the imagination produces forms, ideas and stimuli which tend to multiply and which can be appropriated – in form but not in substance – by the employer.

62 See the Deleuzian and neo-Spinozist group of the review 'Multitudes' and Hardt and Negri 2000.

The cession of rights does not lead to true alienation and separation between the producer and product. The processes of expropriation become more complex and control is exerted laboriously through the sometimes unsuccessful standardisation of stereotype imaginaries.

Neo-Marxist determinism perceives the automatic capture of the areas *of use* of resources and of the 'free' spaces of communication, creativity, technology, knowledge and social relations. However, immaterial work cannot be easily reduced to measures, to valuations and to checks; it implies that this special life commodity has the capacity to produce, on consumption, a higher amount of value than that which was put into it. Images live on and are multiplied in the consumption which they generate, making themselves productive in turn. Subjective, living work makes up the source of all value: therefore it overturns (or can overturn) its relationship with objectified work, in other words with capital itself, as it considers capital part of itself. However, resistance cannot limit itself to remaining within the imaginary. It must interpret its own inventive and imaginative strength so as to recognise and work through the relations of domination that have been repressed.

There was a time, around the 1990s, when it was thought that new technologies could hold a great capacity for emancipation: both in the fervour surrounding the potential of the internet to escape the control of political and economic power and, conversely, in the race towards purely speculative wealth accumulation, which is wholly tied in with the productivity of the imaginary. This illusion has now been scaled down somewhat: the transformations, which all take place within the imaginary, disregard its efficacy on people's lives in terms of subordination and subjected subjectification. They repeat the same repression that generates the phantasm of materiality, of inequalities, of the hardness of relations that are increasingly precarious and flexible in the sphere of creative work, the service industry and the manufacturing industry. The imaginary restricts vision, and literally excludes those who are unable to gain access to the economic scene; those who do not speak that language, or cannot manage to translate their lives into it. The imaginary literally excludes those who lose out; but also, by extolling entrepreneurship, courage and challenge, it does not see, it eclipses the shadows of those who do not manage to take up the challenge, or who lose the competition – shadows, spectres, neither alive nor dead: zombies of the economic imaginary. If the capitalist economic imaginary has become the naturalised game of truth, perhaps all that is left is to de-naturalise it, summon the phantasms, invite them onto the stage and listen to their voices.

References

Althusser, L. 1994, 'Ideology and ideological state apparatuses', in Žižek, S. (ed.) *Mapping Ideology*, London, Verso, pp. 100–140.

Arendt, H. 1998, *Human Condition*, Chicago, Chicago University Press.

Baudrillard, J. 2005, *Violenza del virtuale e realtà integrale*, Florence, Le Monnier.
Bazzicalupo, L. 2006, *Il governo delle vite. Biopolitica ed economia*, Rome-Bari, Laterza.
Benjamin, W. 1928/2009, *Origin of German Tragic Drama* (trans. J. Osborne), London, Verso.
—— 1996, *Walter Benjamin. Selected Writings vol. 3 (1935–1938)*, Cambridge, MA, London, Belknap Press.
—— 2006, *The Writer of Modern Age. Essays on Charles Baudelaire*, Cambridge, MA, London, Belknap Press.
Debord, G. 2004, *The Society of Spectacle*, London, Rebel Press.
Deleuze, G. and Guattari, F. 1987, *A Thousand Plateaus: Capitalism and Schizophrenia*, Minneapolis, Minnesota University Press.
—— 1994, *What is Philosophy?*, New York, Columbia University Press.
Derrida, J. 1994, *Specters of Marx, The State of the Debt, the Work of Mourning, and the New International*, New York, Routledge.
Derrida, J. and Stiegler, B. 2002, *Echographies of Television: Filmed Interviews with Bernard Stiegler*, Cambridge, Polity Press.
ECB (European Central Bank). 2006. 'Hedge funds', *Financial Stability Review*, June: 133–142.
Foucault, M. 1975, *Surveiller et punir*, Paris, Gallimard.
—— 1976, *La volonté de savoir*, Paris, Gallimard.
—— 1977, 'Le jeu de M. Foucault', *Ornicar*, 10: 62–93.
—— 1988, 'Truth, power, self: an interview with Michel Foucault', in Martin, L.H., Gutman, H. and Hutton, P.H. (eds) *Technologies of the Self*, London, Tavistock: pp. 9–15.
Freud, S. 1921/1955, *Group Psychology and the Analysis of the Ego*, London, Hogarth Press.
Friedman, M. 2008, *Milton Friedman on Economics: Selected Papers*, Chicago, University of Chicago Press.
Gramsci, A. 1975, *Quaderni dal carcere*, vol. 4, Turin, Einaudi.
Grossberg, L. (eds) *Marxism and the Interpretation of Culture*, Champaign, University of Illinois Press, pp. 35–37.
Hall, S. 1988, 'The toad in the garden: Thatcherism among Theorists', in Nelson, C. and Grossberg, L. (eds) *Marxism and the interpretation of Culture*, University of Illinois Press, pp. 35–74.
Hammond, J.D. and Hammond, C.H. (eds) 2006, *Making Chicago Price Theory: Friedman-Stigler Correspondence, 1945–1957*, London, Routledge.
Hardt, M. and Negri, A. (1994) *Labor of Dionysus: A Critique of the State-Form*, Minneapolis, Minnesota University Press.
—— 2000, *Empire*, Harvard, Harvard University Press.
Hirschman, A.O. 1977, *The Passions and the Interests*, Princeton, NJ, Princeton University Press.
Horne, T.A. 1981, 'Envy and commercial society: Mandeville and Smith on "Private vices, public benefits"', *Political Theory*, IX: 4.
Laclau, E. and Mouffe, C. 1985, *Hegemony and Socialist Strategy*, London, Verso.
Lippert, J. 2008, 'Friedman Would Be Roiled as Chicago Disciples Rue Repudiation', *Bloomberg News*, December 23, 2008, http://www.bloomberg.com/ apps/news?pid =newsarchive&sid=a3GVhIHGyWRM.
Mandeville, B. 2001, *The Fable of the Bees: or, Private Vices, Publick Benefits*, Oxford, Oxford University Press.

Marazzi, C. 1999, *Il posto dei calzini. La svolta linguistica dell'economia e i suoi effetti sulla politica*, Turin, Bollati Boringhieri.
Marx, K. 1997, *Grundrisse der Kritik der Politischen Ökonomie*, London, Penguin (1993 in Marx/Engels Internet Archive (marxists.org)).
—— 1999, *Das Kapital. Kritik der politischen Oekonomie. Band 1: Der Produktionsprocess des Kapitals*, Hamburg, Marx/Engels Internet Archive (marxists.org).
Negri, A. 2008, *The Porcelain Workshop: For a New Grammar of Politics*, New York, Semiotext(e).
Rajan, K.S. 2006, *Biocapital: the Constitution of Postgenomic Life*, Durham, NC, Duke University Press.
Smith, A. 2000, *The Theory of Moral Sentiments*, New York, Prometheus Books.
Virno, P. 2004, *A Grammar of the Multitude: For an Analysis of Contemporary Forms of Life*, New York, Semiotext(e).
Žižek, S. 1989, *The Sublime Object of Ideology*, London, New York, Verso.
—— 1997, *The Plague of Fantasies*, London, Verso.
—— 2002, 'The matrix: or the two sides of perversion', in Irwin, W. (ed.) *The Matrix and Philosophy*, Chicago, Open Court, pp. 240 –266.
—— 2005, 'Concesso non dato', in Boucher, G., Glynos, J. and Sharpe, M. (eds) *Traversing the Fantasy: Critical Responses to Slavoj Žižek*, Aldershot, Ashgate, pp. 219–255.

Chapter 6

Imagining the west, perceiving race

Social sciences and political imagination

Alana Lentin

Abstract

Despite the taboo surrounding race in Europe, racism continues to define its sociality. The postwar drive to expunge race has not overcome the effects of race thinking which structure conceptions of Europeanness and non-Europeanness. The inability to see race allows European states to declare themselves non-racist, or even anti-racist, while continuing to imply an inherent European superiority which determines both international relationships and those seen as 'in but not of Europe' within its domestic spheres. I conclude by asking what the repercussions of this envisioning of a Europe always less homogeneous in reality than it is commonly imagined to be.

> Race disappears into the seams of sociality, invisibly holding the social fabric together even as it tears apart.
>
> David Theo Goldberg (2006: 339)

Introduction: tolerating diversity

Western, postcolonial societies are imbricated in an imagined idea of themselves – of their constitutive nature – as non-racist or, indeed, as anti-racist. However, this general consensus on racism as an evil that has no place in today's democracies is belied by the facts: racism, while undoubtedly changing and constantly taking on new forms, as Stuart Hall (1997) reminds us, is far from being a memory from the dark past. As made clear in the Introduction to this volume, if anything, since 9/11 and the launch of the United States' 'war on terror', racism – as active policy – is on the rise. The prevalence of the 'clash of civilisations' discourse has given racism new legitimacy (Bottici and Challand 2010). A renewed Orientalism manifesting itself in bellicose foreign policy and domestic Islamophobia also enables a revised history of European colonialism (cf. Ferguson 2003). While before, what Barnor Hesse (2007) calls the 'European colonial relation' was treated as a blind spot of history, in both France and Britain, for example, a growing number of historians and policymakers have promoted a cleansed history of colonial rule, presenting a sanitised view of imperial domination as largely beneficial to 'natives' and 'metropolitans' alike.[63] Daily racism continues, too, the brunt of the impact borne by the asylum seekers and migrants who face detention, deportation, exploitation, poverty and destitution.

This chapter founds itself on the proposition that the collective political imagination of the west today is based on a *projected image* (to which I shall return) of itself as both inherently non-racist and as unique and, by implication, superior. These two suppositions are interlinked. The image of the state in western Europe as non-racist is built on the presumption that it is because of its uniqueness in terms of civilisational, and hence political, progress that it is also superior to other polities in the non-western world. The uniqueness of the west is purported to be found in its democratic traditions and it is this that is said to be at the heart of its commitment to tolerance, equality and anti-racism. This has two implications. First, other societies that have not developed these traditions of democracy are the true fomenters of prejudice and intercultural hatred. Second, the west has the right, and indeed the duty, to lead by example, a belief that is demonstrated not only by the wars on terror in Iraq and Afghanistan, but also by the viewing of the west's relationship to the non-economically dominant majority world through the lens of humanitarianism (cf. Douzinas 2005).

The idea that Europe/the west commands an unruly mass of generalised 'others' is not new. It underpins what Hesse (2007) calls 'racialized modernity', expressed through the administrative structures of colonial rule, the racialisation of domestic class structures (Balibar 1991) and the territorial demarcations that geographically divide European insiders from outsiders. It is when this relationship of inherent inequality is seen to persist in creating and recreating such divisions in contemporary western societies that it creates a rupture. The call for assimilation (or today, integration) that has accompanied each moment of crisis that immigration is said to bring is experienced as profoundly paradoxical by those it targets. Integration is not perceived as neutral by 'immigrants' and 'minorities' because it is unilateral, always signifying an inward process, rather than an outward one that is transformative of society as a whole. Integration implies a national script that is known by the insiders and only knowable by those outside (or those who are trying to enter) under precise, often shifting, conditions. It supposes a priori knowledge of a way of doing things which, because it is intimately associated to notions of heredity, is naturalised, therefore probably making it an ultimately impossible

63 In February 2005 French parliament voted in favour of a law on the teaching of the history of colonialism that recognises the positive role played by French men and women. It states that 'school curricula recognize particularly the positive role played by the French presence, notably in North Africa, and accord the history and the sacrifices of soldiers of the French army from these territories the place of eminence that is owed to them' (*Loi française* no. 2005–158).

goal. Integration is hence always only a promise. This paradox lurks within and disrupts the collective political imagination. It is as though the pixels in an image of national unity and cohesion were to become scattered and dislodged kaleidoscope like, coming together again in different ways on different screens (see also Buck-Morss in this volume for a discussion of images and political imagination). What results is a totally different image of society that depends on what screen is being looked at or, more precisely, what lens one views society through. The lens is inevitably shaped by the lived experience of inclusion or exclusion from the national project that for many is still defined by perceptions of race and class, ethnicity and religion.

My purpose in this chapter, therefore, is to look at why the image of 'unity in diversity'[64] has become so central in western political discourse and why its attached condition for success – integration – is failing to create the socially cohesive societies projected by western leaders. I will do this by arguing that unity is unachievable under the present conditions because the west has done nothing to transform the bases on which we conceive of the nature of inclusion and exclusion. Despite the official banishment of race from the political lexicon, the classificatory power of race continues to hold us in its grip. Race, so easy to laugh off and overwrite, yet so perfectly open to malleable interpretation, remains the signifier par excellence out of which the west is imagined, always in relation to its racialised opposite. What follows is divided into three sections. The first considers the link between race and the modern political imagination and explains the significance of a race-critical approach to understanding the persistent salience of racialisation to Europe (section 1). The second examines the shifting of race from the centre of politics and discourse to their unacceptable margins. Lastly, I show how race, nonetheless, continues to determine the way society is conceptualised and imagined. The modern social and political imaginary is ordered by, yet discursively conceals, a system of classification that is racially underscored (section 3). In doing so, I show that the politics of imagination is the result not (only) of a psychological struggle that takes place within individual human beings, as Bugliani argues in this volume, but also of social structures that shape the way in which we imagine them.

1. Racialising imagination

Why frame a discussion on what could be termed 'the problem of difference' or of living together in culturally diverse societies around race and racism? My answer, echoing David Goldberg (2006), is because 'race refuses to remain silent' despite, as we shall see in what follows, the effort made to expunge it. Goldberg (ibid.: 337) goes on to say that race is still with us because:

64 The phrase 'unity in diversity' is borrowed from UNESCO and is referred to in particular by Claude Lévi-Strauss in his 1983 essay 'Race and culture'.

> [I]t isn't just a word. It is a set of conditions, shifting over time. Never just one thing, it is a way (or really ways) of thinking, a way(s) of living, a disposition.

In other words, it is, as Stuart Hall (1997) argues powerfully, a floating signifier. Race is a very useful concept, constantly adapting and readapting itself, chameleon-like to the changing political and social landscape. It is for this reason that race is central to political imagination in a constitutive sense: it plays a formative role in constructing images of societies that are easily transmittable. It is a shorthand for ordering and making sense of the problem caused by the observation of difference that has not diminished despite official denunciation.

This is not to say, however, that race is either inherent or perennial. On the contrary, the race concept is borne of the possibilities opened up by Enlightenment methodologies; most importantly, the capacity to order and classify, to rationalise everything from immaterial objects to plants, animals and human beings themselves (Hannaford 1996). As Balibar (1994) argues, race is the necessary counterweight that helps demarcate the boundaries of what constitutes 'man'. Racism and universalism, argues Balibar, each 'has the other inside itself' (ibid.: 198) because establishing the contours of a generalised humanity after Enlightenment is dependent on the parallel definition of non-man. Race develops into a fully evolved system for the hierarchical ranking of humanity, from superior white to inferior black, over a long period of 200 years. This process, which leads finally to the 'Golden Age of Racism' of the late 19th century, is an emphatically political one. Despite the roots of race in science and the continued significance it has in the realms of genetic determinism (Gannett 2001), race must be seen as a cultural and political product of its place and time; namely European modernity.

The modernity of race, and therefore its comparative recentness and its contextually dependent evolution, is paramount to an analysis of race that is the central focus of 'race critical theory'. Theorists such as Eric Voegelin, Hannah Arendt, Etienne Balibar, Michel Foucault, David Theo Goldberg, Paul Gilroy, Howard Winant, Ivan Hannaford and Barnor Hesse, among others and in different ways, have been committed to establishing the centrality of race to modernity. Their work cannot be read without equal attention being paid to the historians and theorists of colonialism and the lived experience of racism, such as Frantz Fanon and W.E.B. Du Bois. A race critical perspective seeks not to unquestioningly dismiss race as a redundant, because scientifically unviable, concept. Rather, race is seen as a central ordering principle of modern western societies because of its consequence: the belief in racially demarcated hierarchies that produces racial discrimination. Race is significant, not in itself, but because of its inability to exist solely conceptually and in the absence of racism.

A critical perspective on race and racism is central to my general concern with drawing attention to their conceptual utility for politics. Both Eric

Voegelin (1933, 1940) and Michel Foucault (1997), two theorists who are not remarkable for their particular concern with the specificities of racism in conditions of colonialism or slavery for example, have nonetheless placed race centrally in their analyses of the state and governmentality. It is probably impossible to link these two authors theoretically in any other way, yet both Voegelin and Foucault agree that race, though uninteresting in itself in their opinion, is the prime lens through which the construction of the nation-state in modernity – as a regime for exclusion as much as inclusion – may be viewed.

In particular, Voegelin's scheme of 'body ideas' – 'any symbol which integrates a group into a substantial whole through the assertion that its members are of common origin' (Voegelin 1940: 286) at the core of his theory of state – gives prominence to the political idea of race. Race is so significant because the state takes action, according to Voegelin, on the basis of a vision of the type of people belonging to its political community and an assumption about the type of collective moral experiences they have had. At the time of Voegelin's writing *Rasse und Staat* in 1933, the belief that racial categorisation was the sole means of making sense of human difference and the consequent organisation of society had reached its peak. The amalgam of science and politics used to bring the 'race idea' to full fruition meant that it was particularly prone to the type of myth making that perpetuated its appeal.

Read alongside other theorisations of the importance of race in the ideological formation of nationalism and the nation-state (cf. Balibar 1991), Voegelin's emphasis on the centrality of race insists on its political significance. While certainly not reducible to one another, racism and nationalism, as Balibar (1991) has argued, entered into a relationship of 'reciprocal determination' over the course of the 19th century. The power of race was in its applicability as an immediately recognisable reason – buoyed up by the weight of scientific 'proof' – for the need for separately constituted and increasingly hermetic nations. The significance of the relationship between racism and nationalism, particularly for the constitution of what today appears to be the indispensability of borders, passports and the other institutionalised demarcations of national inclusion, has been discussed at length elsewhere (Lentin 2004, 2005). My purpose here in reminding that race is not neutral and not dissociable from either nation building or imperialism is to place emphasis on its political role. The embarrassment caused by race, following its official refutation after the Second World War, has led to its being stripped both of its *politics* and of its *modernity*. Race, and consequentially racism, have been assigned to the realm of the pre-modern and the primordial. Commonsense sees race in all ages of history and as a characteristic of all human beings. Banished from modernity, it has therefore become a disposition, an attitude, a pathology. Banished from reason, it has become unmodern, a hangover to be found only in those who have not, due to lack of education and maturity, been able to see the error of their ways.

The post-war pathologisation of racism and the marginalisation and infantilisation of those who continue to hold such 'attitudes' is, of course, painfully ironic. It is the irony of race that what emerged from and was made conceptually possible by the dawning of the Age of Reason was later to be discursively rejected on the grounds of unreason. However, it is this too which is at the heart of the conceptual and imaginative power of race. Because of what Hesse (2007) refers to as race's 'undecideability', it holds within it the possibility of remaining present while the conditions and discourses to which it adapts itself are transformed. Hesse argues that whereas 'race critical theory' insists on the centrality of the politics of race to modernity and emphasises the salience of racism while rejecting the biological significance of race, it nevertheless continues to define race in terms of signifiers such as skin colour. In other words, race continues to be exclusively about the Other. For Hesse, race is much more definitive of Europeanness and non-Europeanness, which constitute themselves in the relationships in and with the conditions of 'coloniality'. Race is made to mean through the interaction of the oppositional, yet mutually dependent, relationship between Europeanness and non-Europeanness:

> On this account the biologisation of the colonially constituted 'European'/ 'non-European' distinction and its territorialization onto diverse human bodies is but one historical symptom and political formation of race through modernity.
>
> (Hesse 2007: 6)

I read Hesse's proposition as saying that viewing race as primarily corporeal may in fact be a *distraction* from its true purpose as a means to define Europeanness and modernity in relation to their opposite – non-Europeanness and primitiveness. Understanding this, I think, is central to understanding the persistent allure of race. Race is still relevant because of its undecideability or the fact that there is a continuous search for the *essence* of identity and difference in the context of the modern European relationship to its constituted Other(s). Hesse argues that, in this search, it is whiteness that is more important than blackness. What constitutes the other as black (or as corporeally oppositional) is the European Enlightenment obsession with the aesthetics of its own whiteness. As such, the sign of blackness is assigned to the geographical, historical, climatic, etc., differences that divide between Europe and non-Europe. It is symbolic of what is *not* European, and therefore constitutive of what Europe *is*.

Falling short of being arbitrary, race as physiognomy is a shorthand that encapsulates all those differences that set Europe apart and above, and consequentially, legitimate its hegemony.[65] Most importantly, because race in

65 Space prevents my engaging in a fuller discussion of Hesse's ideas. However, on this point, he usefully introduces the concept of 'governmental racialization' (2007: 19) to describe

the 18th and 19th centuries is defined scientifically and anthropologically as determinant of genetics and culture, there is little questioning of its political origins or its purpose, either in relation to the constitution of nation-states in Europe or in the institutionalisation of racialised hegemony in the colonies. This continues to affect our thinking on race in two ways. First, because of the persistent primacy of science as a legitimatory discourse, race as science can be separated from race as politics, as if no connection ever existed. Second, because of its dissociation from any act of self-definition it has easily been retold as an aberration from the natural course of modernity's trajectory, from Enlightenment to democracy. In the next section, I shall look at how race officially undergoes this process of expulsion from both science and politics.

2. Banishing race

In his 2007 essay, Hesse deals mainly with Habermas's reading of Hegel on modernity.[66] He does this in order to establish the point that race is absent from the canonical analysis of the constitution of European modernity, despite the fact that the histories of colonialism, slavery, the Holocaust and postcolonial immigration all point to the entanglement of those staples of modernity – rationality, liberalism, capitalism etc. – with race. Race and racism are not seen as subjects for mainstream social theoretical discussion. Unlike a Voegelin or a Foucault, contemporary social theorists seem to view the discussion of race as a special interest subject, their belief aided perhaps by the establishment of disciplinary areas in the vein of 'racial and ethnic studies'. Most social theories of the state and modernity fail therefore to treat race as central to their concerns. As a consequence, race in the sense that Hesse and other race-critical authors talk about it, namely as constitutive of European modernity, is simply left out. It is this absence of race from the realms of social and political theory that has made it possible both to banish it from the political lexicon and, crucially, to allow it to continue to intervene in the world of the natural sciences, most commonly biology and genetics.

I wish to focus on the expunging of race from European public political discourse in order to reveal how it continues to work unfettered in the ways

the way in which 'although both the native Americans and Africans lie outside of its [world history's] remit of evolutionary rationality, they are required to succumb to its regulatory force'. Governmental racialisation works through the institutionalisation in administrative practice of laws and disciplinary measures exercised by white Europeans over non-white, non-Europeans. I would add that the transposition of colonial arrangements into post-colonial immigration regimes in Europe (Kundnani 2001) and the relative impossibility to transform existing political systems in Europe to include non-Europeans in their governance leads to a perpetuation of this governmental racialisation in the contemporary European context. A clear contemporary example of this is the prevalence of racial profiling in 'anti-terrorist' policing.

66 In the *Philosophical Discourse of Modernity* (Habermas 1989).

that Hesse and Hall, among others, describe, namely as concerned with much more than mere physiognomic difference. This should help us understand how it continues to shape contemporary formulations of diversity and integration in postcolonial Europe. The basis of my argument has been developed at length elsewhere (Lentin 2004), but I shall rehearse it briefly here because it remains central to my analysis of the relationship that Europe has to race, as something that happens somewhere else.

The idea that race is external to Europe is of course blown apart by the event of the Nazi *Shoah* and the lead-up to it. While, at the end of the 19th century, race had certainly become a guiding principle, a means of classifying humanity, it was rarely associated directly with barbarism.[67] 'Race was all', as Disraeli famously stated: racial hierarchy was a *fact* that legitimated the excesses of colonial rule (which mainly happened out of sight of European eyes) and the keeping of the proletariat in 'their place' (Macmaster 2001). It explained the growing need for national frontiers and for the social divisions that prevented much cultural intermixing. Moreover, in western Europe, the prevalence of the idea of race coexisted, paradoxically perhaps, with a growing democratisation of the polity and the concomitant inclusion in society of formerly pariah groups, in particular the now emancipated Jews.

As Goldberg (2006) notes, the *Shoah* is definitive of race in Europe, with good reason. However, the persistent questioning of how it was possible for such a genocide to occur on European soil (raised again, albeit to a lesser degree, during the Balkan wars of the 1990s) led to a concomitant erasure of Europe's colonial legacy: 'Colonialism, on this view, has had little or no effect in the making of Europe itself, or of European nation-states' (ibid.: 336). The Holocaust was Europe's tragedy, colonialism someone else's. What therefore had to happen in its aftermath was for race to be publicly negated in order for Europe to be cleansed and to allow it to get back on the trajectory set out for it by the Enlightenment project. Building on the example of the UNESCO 'Statement against race and racial prejudice', this work of reform both tackled the problem of race and proposed a solution to it (Lentin 2004, 2005).

The spirit of the UNESCO Statement, first drawn up in 1950, continues to dominate the approach to racism of most western governments. UNESCO's approach is based on two central premises. First, it was proposed that racism had to be tackled on its own grounds. The panel of UNESCO experts believed that racism was a pseudo-science rather than a political idea. Therefore, to defeat racism, it was sufficient to disprove the theory of race from a scientific point of view. Second, once this was achieved, it was believed racism would no longer hold water. Race, therefore, was not seen as a political idea at its origins.

67 Exceptional voices could be heard such as those in the inter-war period of the anthropologist Frantz Boas and his students and the African-American scholar and activist W.E.B. Du Bois, who used racial science against itself to unprove the theory of white supremacy.

For the social scientists gathered by UNESCO to write the Statement, race had to be disproved on scientific grounds, and this task was, for them, easily achievable. There was no scientific value in the concept of race. Rather:

> The division of the human species into 'races' is partly conventional and partly arbitrary and does not imply any hierarchy whatsoever. Many anthropologists stress the importance of human variation, but believe that 'racial' divisions have limited scientific interest and may even carry the risk of inviting abusive generalization.
>
> (UNESCO 1968: 270)

Directly after the publication of the Statement, it was followed by an alternative Statement written mainly by geneticists also involved in the UNESCO project. Scientists such as Theodosius Dobzhansky (Gannett 2001) argued that race continued to be of scientific usefulness for describing 'groups of mankind possessing well-developed and primarily heritable physical differences from other groups' (Comas 1961: 304) and should not be confused with politics. However, the political climate of the day was unfavourable to this point of view. The official response to race was to shut the door on its period in history.

Race, as Eléni Varikas (1998) has pointed out, was literally banished from publicly acceptable discourse, particularly in continental western Europe. For Goldberg (2006: 336), after the *Shoah*, 'race is to have no social place, no explicit markings. It is to be excised from any characterising of human conditions, relations, formations.' This does not mean, however, that it ceases to be implicit. Just as anthropologists and geneticists agreed to disagree, leaving the latter free to develop theories of racially underpinned intelligence and proneness to disease, race was not uttered but could not be unthought.

This is evident in the solution proposed by the UNESCO project which, though denying the scientific validity of race, nonetheless recognised the importance of being able to explain human difference. Particularly in light of the rise in inbound European immigration after the Second World War, the first-hand experience of non-Europeanness, already afforded by the presence of black servicemen during the war in many European countries (Levy 2004), became extremely significant. Race had come home, but it could not be known as such. Anthropologists, most famously Claude Lévi-Strauss in his *Race and History* (1975), argued for terms such as ethnicity and culture to replace that of race and for ethnocentrism to be used in the place of racism. It was recognised that the horrors of the *Shoah*, steeped in the taint of race, were not dissociable from the difference made evident by the appearance of non-whites in the European midst. Yet it was by association with the *Shoah* that the products of colonial rule (the postcolonial immigrants) were to become 'ethnic minorities' and 'cultural groups', rather than races.

The evident outcome of the simple replacement of race with 'culture', 'ethnicity' or, even more euphemistically, 'origins' or 'identity' is the consequent banishing of *racism*. Race should not indeed be reinstated to its pre-war status (although the activity of racial scientists today hardly masks the double standards at work). Yet, as Goldberg and others argue forcefully, race is given meaning by the persistence of *racism*. The continued practices of institutionalised injustice founded on a ready-made hierarchical schema that divides between Europeans and others demonstrates that officially negating race does little to remove its consequences. In Goldberg's terms, Auschwitz has left us unable to speak about race. It has therefore been '[b]uried. But buried alive' (Goldberg 2006: 338). Race still lives in our minds. As a result, the millions of non-Europeans, often the descendants of those emerging from the 'racialized governmentalities' of the colonies into the post-racial metropole, have no words to express their negation. If race were a bad word, it was, at the very least, historically explanatory.

3. Integrating into a race-free world

The west, increasingly defined by its multiculturality, is mired in the problems arising from the hushing up of race. It is at the heart of the mismatch of discourse and practice that, I contend, denies the possibility of collectively imagining an inclusive Europe. Having expunged race, Europe, like the USA after Jim Crow, has been declared post-racial. Yet, more than the United States that, after all it is argued, was built on/with slavery,[68] Europe has returned to its original status as *non*-racial, a status displaced only by the short and regrettable years of Nazi domination. Because of the absence of race from the official writing of the history of European modernity and its relegation to the realms of science in which it has a confined legitimacy, race acquires the status of aberration. Like a weed that inexplicably grows in an otherwise lush garden, race came to disturb the peace of European democracy, civilisation and universal values. But, as soon as it came, so it went. Europe is reinstated, old stories neatly archived.

After having closed the door on this 'regrettable' period of history, Europe immediately began on its quest for explaining and assimilating the difference that nonetheless assaults the senses. This is a quest that is ongoing. Furthermore, by constantly searching for new ways to make sense of the differences between human beings and the problems they give rise to, yet shutting the door on race as past history, it may well be an eternal one. Race, it is worth repeating, stands here for the crimes that it is responsible for, rather than any invocation of differences in human biology: the indelible experiences that mark and shape whole groups of people, often for generations. It is imprisonment and enslavement, forced labour and lynching. Death. But

68 This Europe–USA distinction, of course, ignores the significance of slavery for the domestic European economy.

it is also assimilation through education and cooptation – the historicist racism (Goldberg 2002) that proffers progress as an always promised, but never quite achieved, prize.

Unable/unwilling to speak about the effects of race, Europe, through the vehicle of its institutions, has transformed race into 'identity'. In other words, race is no longer something that is imposed on subjugated others. By anaesthetising race and labelling it 'ethnicity' or 'culture', it becomes something that is possessed, rather than something that is unwillingly acquired. In Hesse's (2007: 16) terms, '"race" was understood proprietarily as a form of *possessive communitarianism*, rather than relationally as a European articulation of colonial differentiation'. Race, now dissociated from its crimes, becomes a mere descriptor among others that, because of the discomfort it evokes for Europeans, has been replaced with other, less threatening, terms. This translation process denies what Fanon (1967) describes as the lived-experience of race: the process of dehumanisation and infantilisation that is fundamental to racialisation. By taking race away from the racialised, the 'badge' of race is also denied them (du Bois 1940). Du Bois's badge of race refers not to biology, but to the 'physical bond' that the 'common history' of those who 'have suffered a long disaster and have one long memory' are compelled to carry with them (du Bois 1940, cited in Appiah 1985: 33).

It is against this backdrop, of the unspoken yet ever present spectre of race, that Europe struggles to imagine its sociality. Successive decades have given rise to assimilation, multiculturalism and now diversity as policy directives for coping with the consequences of the heterogeneous cultural, religious and national makeup of most contemporary European societies.[69] Each model spawned a variety of reactions that led to crisis being invoked at every turn. In the late 1960s, the British Conservative MP, Enoch Powell, imagined the country flowing in 'rivers of blood' as the attempt to assimilate immigrants would lead to the eradication of Britain and Britishness. Today, the multiculturalist proposals made by French President Nicolas Sarkozy are painted as damaging the values of the secular *république*. What unites these policies and the reactions to them is the need for *coping* with difference, for doing damage control, that results from the realisation that Europe is no longer (as though it ever were) culturally homogeneous.

In other words, it is difference per se that is problematised by the various debates and policies that frame what is no longer known as race in Europe. The spectre of race lingers in the sense of discomfort that impels us to find solutions to the 'living together' (Touraine 2000) of culturally (racially) different and, it is implied, incompatible groups. Moreover, this is portrayed by the liberal establishment as something that is called for and expected by monolithically

69 It is worth noting, although not central to my argument, that there are significant differences between models of 'integration' proposed in various European countries.

named 'minority' groups. The framing of the grievances of the racialised as identity politics, as I have argued (Lentin 2004, 2005), means that what have mainly been unsuccessful policies are put down to the recognition claims (Taylor 1994) of these marginalised 'minorities'. The call of the racialised to stand against racism is translated into a call to recognise (my) identity. Yet, this entirely overlooks why identity or race as a du Boisian badge takes on the importance it does in the first place. Du Bois' explanation of what drew him to Africa, where he lived out the final years of his life in Ghana, demonstrates that 'the physical bond is *least* and the badge of colour relatively *unimportant* save as a badge; the *real essence* of kinship is its social heritage of slavery – the discrimination and insult' (du Bois 1940, cited in Appiah 1985: 33; emphasis mine).

Whereas it could be argued that the multiculturalist model, by allowing at least for cultural self-governance, went some way to recognising the autonomy of non-white groups, the current backlash against it can be described only as regression. While I have warned against the facile nostalgia for the good old days of multiculturalism following its rejection in Britain in 2004 by several public figures (Lentin 2005), the current focus on diversity and social cohesion marks the wholesale rejection of the significance of du Bois' badge of race. Although translating race into culture and hoping that racism would disappear did little to dull the 'discrimination and insult', there was an, albeit misguided, hope that it could be better coped with through culture, a hope that has been shared, for example, by the proponents of negritude.[70] In the post-9/11 world, it is precisely the freedom granted to those who are *in* but not *of* Europe (Hall 2002) to practice their 'culture' that is perceived to be at the root of the global clash of civilisations as it plays itself out in the metros of London or Madrid.

Today, the professed need for integration and social cohesion has superseded the 'leave them to it' attitude of multiculturalism. However, while anti-terrorist policing and the racial profiling multiculturalism relies on has certainly increased the pressure on non-whites, particularly the brown skinned, it is not this aspect that represents a radical break with multiculturalism. Whatever policy has been publicly endorsed, black people have always suffered criminalisation whether or not their 'culture' was being celebrated for its 'vibrancy' at the same time. What the insistence on social cohesion and integration and the concomitant espousal of national values through the establishment of citizenship tests for new immigrants, for example, have done is to shift responsibility for societal success onto its outsiders. The avowed Britishness of the 7/7 bombers notwithstanding, the message is integrate into 'our way of life' or be cast out.

70 Let me add, however, that those who invoked Black Power in the USA, the UK and the former colonies most notably did not do so without, at the same time, taking a stance against the racism of the state. Cultural authenticity was never a solution to racism (cf. Fanon 1967).

4. Conclusion

It is at this point of course that we must remind ourselves of the ambivalence of race within the western political imaginary. The implication of integration is that outsiders, condemned to be so regardless of citizenship, must integrate into and be integrated by Europe in order for its societies to become socially cohesive. There is no need for Europe to integrate into its outsiders. This is unnecessary because Europe stands for universal values such as democracy, human rights and the rule of law. Under this trinity, there is no room for race. Indeed, race, as we have been told, came to blight Europe for a brief period but was banished as quickly as it settled. Europe (and by extension the west) is therefore the standard against which all else can be judged. It is perhaps unnecessary to recall that this very assumption is racist in itself because, mirroring whiteness, it holds Europeanness up as the norm and condemns all else to its moral hegemony (Goldberg 2002). What is less evident perhaps is that requiring all to integrate into a Europe that denies its raciality – past and present – is an impossibility. It is impossible because it is incoherent and this incoherency is at the root of the problem of commonly imagining a unified future. Imagination breaks down at the point when the image presented of Europe so obviously belies that which is experienced as true. Simply by refusing to see race, by covering it over with alternative signifiers and therefore, most crucially, blinding itself to its consequences, Europe sends a message: race is not our problem, it is not ours. It is yours.

By giving race back to its bearers – the racialised, the wearers of the badge of race – the west is demanding for it to be taken away. In other words, integration implies not only the assimilation of western ways of doing things and the acceptance of its 'values'. This in itself *is* possible and would even be desirable. It would be desirable if race was not in fact so deeply embedded in what Europe is to make it impossible to extricate Europeanness from its opposite – non-Europeanness – from the constant reminder of the crimes committed in the name of 'European universals' (Hesse 1999). For those still thought of as non-Europeans, integration means denying the significance of the experience of race. Yet its constant reminders come back to haunt us: the detention centres and deportation flights, racist policing and profiling, the orange jumpsuits and demonised imams.

How then can political imagination be thought of as anything but a struggle? If the aim is to unify and find commonalties, a shared vision of future sociality must be found. The pixilation must reconstruct itself just so in everyone's mind's eye. Yet this struggle is one between the powerful and the powerless, between those with the capacity to racialise and those who must bear (eternally?) that infernal badge of race. It is between a vision of society's tolerance and a reality of profound deception. Race structures our imaginative capacity while hiding itself from view. The bodyguards at race's door are indefatigable.

References

Appiah, A. 1985, 'The uncompleted argument: du Bois and the illusion of race', *Critical Inquiry*, 12 (1): 21–37.

Balibar, E. 1991, 'Racism and nationalism', in Balibar, E. and Wallerstein, I. *Race, Nation, Class: Ambiguous Identities*, London, Verso, pp. 37–67.

—— 1994, *Masses, Classes, Ideas: Studies on Politics and Philosophy before and after Marx*, New York, Routledge.

Bottici, C. and Challand, B. 2010, *The Myth of the Clash of Civilizations*, London, Routledge.

Comas, J. 1961, '"Scientific" racism again?', *Current Anthropology*, 2 (4): 3010–3340.

du Bois, W.E.B. 1903, *The Souls of Black Folk*, Chicago, A.C. McClurg & Co.

—— 1940, *Dusk of Dawn: An Essay toward an Autobiography of a Race Concept*, New York, Oxford University Press.

Fanon, F. 1967, *Black Skins, White Masks*, London, Pluto Press.

Ferguson, N. 2003, *Empire: The Rise and Fall of the British World Order and the Lessons for Global Power*, New York, Basic Books.

Foucault, M. 1997, *Il faut défendre la société: cours au Collège de France, 1976*, Paris, Gallimard Seuil.

Gannett, L. 2001, 'Racism and human genome diversity research: the ethical limits of "population thinking"', *Philosophy of Science*, 68 (3), Supplement: Proceedings of the 2000 Biennial Meeting of the Philosophy of Science Association. Part I: Contributed Papers: S479–S492.

Gilroy, P. 1987, *'There ain't No Black in the Union Jack': The Cultural Politics of Race and Nation*, London, Unwin Hyman.

Goldberg, D.T. 2002. *The Racial State*, Malden, MA, Oxford, Blackwell.

—— 2006, 'Racial Europeanization', *Ethnic and Racial Studies*, 29 (2): 331–364.

Habermas, J. 1989, *The philosophical discourse of modernity: twelve lectures*, Cambridge, MA, MIT Press.

Hall, S. 1997, *Race, the Floating Signifier*, Media Education Foundation Film.

—— 2002, '"In but not of Europe": scattered speculations about "the myths of Europe"'. Paper given at the conference Figures d'Europe – Figure d'Europa, Images and Myths of Europe, jointly organised by the EUI, HEC Department and the City of Florence, 11–13 April 2002, European University Institute, Florence.

Hannaford, I. 1996, *Race: The History of an Idea in the West*, Baltimore, MD, Johns Hopkins University Press.

Hesse, B. 1999, '"It's your world": Discrepant multiculturalisms', in Cohen, P. (ed.) *New Ethnicities, Old Racisms*, London, Zed Books.

—— 2007, 'Racialized modernity: an analytics of white mythologies', *Ethnic and Racial Studies*, 30 (4): 643–663.

Kundnani, A. 2001, 'From Oldham to Bradford: the violence of the violated', *Institute of Race Relations*, http://www.irr.org.uk/2001/october/ak000003.html.

Lentin, A. 2004, *Racism and Anti-Racism in Europe*, London, Pluto Press.

—— 2005, 'Replacing "race", historicizing "culture" in multiculturalism', *Patterns of Prejudice*, 39 (4): 379–396.

Lévi-Strauss, C. 1975, 'Race and history', in *Race, Science and Society*, New York, Whiteside & Morrow for UNESCO.

—— 1983, 'Race et culture', in *Le Regard Eloigné*, Paris, PLON.

Levy, A. 2004, *Small Island*, London, Headline.
MacMaster, N. 2001, *Racism in Europe 1870–2000*, Basingstoke, Palgrave.
Taylor, C. 1994, *Multiculturalism*, Princeton, NJ, Princeton University Press.
Touraine, A. 2000, *Can we Live Together? Equality and Difference*, Cambridge, Polity Press.
UNESCO. 1968, 'UNESCO statement on race and racial prejudice', *Current Anthropology*, 9 (4): 270–272.
Varikas, E. 1998, 'Sentiment national, genre et ethnicité', *TUMULTES*, 11: 87–97.
Voegelin, E. 1933/2000, *Race and State*, Baton Rouge, LA, London, Louisiana State University Press.
—— 1940, 'The growth of the race idea', *Review of Politics*, July: 283–317.

Chapter 7

Politics and the Messianic imagination

Armando Salvatore

To what extent is religion a relevant dimension of politics understood as a struggle for people's imagination? This chapter addresses the question by focusing on an often neglected yet crucial aspect of religion: the Messianic imagination. In order to understand the mechanism through which this kind of imagination came to operate in modernity, the chapter reconstructs its genealogy. The so-called Axial Age (ca. 800–200 BCE), whose importance is now popularized by the best-selling author on comparative religion Karen Armstrong (2006), is interpreted as the "pivotal" age of human history that started around the middle of the first millennium BCE and in which, according to Karl Jaspers who first employed the term (1953 [1949]), a momentous revolution in thinking took place simultaneously across Eurasia. Particularly in its western part, the revolution laid the bases of the political theology that generates Messianic imagination.

This chapter discusses the type of political theology grounded on the idea that the subject (the *ego*) gets entangled in a new realm of transcendence via the institution of a strong nexus between the transcendent *Alter*, a divinity with the character of omnipotence but also mercifulness, and the concrete *alter* faced by *ego* in the experience of the world. It is in the context of the deep transformations of the Axial Age in the western part of Eurasia (characterized as much by biblical prophecy as by Greek philosophy and religion) that the Messiah was first imagined by late prophets as a way to bridge the gap between *alter* and *Alter* (section 1). The Messianic imagination fully erupts at the sunset of the Axial Age and reaches a first climax with the as yet enigmatic figure of Jesus of Nazareth and especially with his ingenious interpreter Paul of Tarsus, but has had an enduring historical impact well into modern political phenomena.

It is not by chance then that an author like Jacob Taubes, who lived in the troubled years of the aftermath of Nazism and the Holocaust, provided the most acute reflections on this topic: simultaneously wired into the Pauline doctrine and into contemporary political theologies. As Taubes argues, Messianism both helps out the constitution of the modern agent of political order, i.e., the state, as the administrator of the profane realm of immanence before the procrastinated second coming of the Christ or even as the agent that "holds down" evil (according to its so-called "katechontic" function, from the Greek *katechon*, the one who holds down or restrains) and its subversive challenger, the movement of the anti-state. At the same time, Jacob argues, the phenomenon also aggregates and provides some coherence to the neo-Messianic frustrations of diasporic Judaism, after that it became the object of persecution and genocide in the context of modern European state building (sections 2 and 3).

After introducing the concept of connective justice, the "Axial triad" that configures the *ego–alter–Alter* relationship by projecting an obligation to care for *alter* onto the *ego* and the authority to sanction such a care onto the transcendent *Alter* (sections 2 and 3), the chapter shows that in the alternative between the authoritarian political theology of Carl Schmitt and its subversive reading by Walter Benjamin, Taubes privileges the latter because in his view Benjamin's concept of the Messiah prefigures an almost post-modern completion—or exhaustion—of the power of the Axial triad (and not its plain transgression). The final "price of messianism" decried by Taubes is the potential of violence incorporated both in the katechontic nature of the powerful European state and in its replica via Zionism. Yet Taubes also unveils a different price, which might be paid more eagerly by modern individuals. This price comes close to the "end of history" of global society and its ultimate nihilism described by Benjamin's *Theologico-Political Fragment*. Such a scenario exalts the sovereignty of the self and the "liquidity" of the political imagination. It nourishes human happiness in the immanent order of the world based on the consciousness that Messiah is not coming, but is absorbed in the process of erosion and "liquidation" of the order of the world (section 5).

1. Ego–alter–Alter/Theos

Modern global society is heir to a fundamental rupture in human history, through which the human grasp of symbols of godly majesty and divine intervention on both nature and human society is replaced by a reflexive rationalization of their meaning. It is not necessary to venture here in discussing when and in which parts of the globe this rupture is to be located, whether it is a monopoly of the west, or not. What counts is that the transformation has been either celebrated—as, e.g., in the approach to Axial civilizations (Wittrock 2005)—as, a swift transition from *mythos* to *logos*, or decried as the progressive liquidation of human community and its incorporation into the iron cage of the power-saturated, anonymous relations of global modernity (Gauchet 1997 [1985]: 43–46). The reflexive rationalization of the relation of God to the human world is in both views considered a necessary premise to making the sources of order of human society immanent to it—a step that will be fully accomplished with the modern breakthrough.

We need here a definition of political theology articulated on two levels. The first level consists in the political effects of a certain representation of divine presence or intervention in the world. A theology including a representation of such a power is supposed to support specific political effects: a certain form of government, and the patterns of its legitimization. The second level needs a longer elaboration, since it concerns the often neglected, necessary nexus between transcendence and immanence, without which that reflexive elaboration on divine transcendence would not be possible. This level embraces the way through which transcendence becomes immediately present to the subject, to *ego*, by instituting a privileged axis between the transcendent *Alter*, the divinity, and the concrete *alter* faced by *ego* in the world.

In a situation that precedes such a reflexive turn the concrete and most threatening type of *alter* is represented by a nomadic, semi-savage "stranger." The change here is effected by a rupture of the ritual compactness of archaic religion and by the consequent differentiation of models of community based on ritual and representation from those where the *Theos* was present in immediate, not metaphorical terms: ritually invoked, not reflectively evoked. This process opened up a new type of reflexive transcendence integral to a new politics of differentiation within society (Eisenstadt 1982; Gauchet 1997 [1985]: 47–66). While in macro-societal terms the main differentiation led to the building of a separate apparatus of domination in the form of highly stable and entrenched state-like entities governed by rulers with a particular close connection, or affinity, to the divine realm (as in ancient Egypt and Mesopotamia), at a micro-societal level the differentiation was as simple as a micro-politics of imagining other, now not just "given" by his/her strangeness but demanding to be—theologically—redefined, in terms of the duties incumbent on the self toward him/her.

The *ego–alter* opening tension is thus both the empirical ground and the reflexive terrain for testing the new tension between mundane and transcendent orders. The world is no longer a reflection of cosmic order; rather, the cosmic tension as the source for order is simultaneously mundane and opens up the mundane–transcendent divide. The engine of the mechanism lies in the operation through which the terrestrial *alter* is projected onto the *Alter/Theos*, endowed with attributes of sovereign majesty. Against all conventional distinctions between monotheism and polytheism, Jan Assmann has spoken of a cosmotheistic type of imagination (Assmann 2005). From there on, order, including what we, by privileging the Greek component of the Axial Age, call "politics," can only be stabilized by evoking *Theos*.

This crucial dimension of a "political theology" involving the basic micro-societal bond then shows how such a type of theology cannot be reduced to a mere ideological blueprint providing legitimacy to the ruler and to his power apparatus. The articulation of this level of political theology also elucidates the link between the level of construction of the social bond and the political order proper. The key phenomenon here is the production of a surplus of meaning and an excess of normativity through the projection of *ego*'s tension towards *alter* into their double connection to *Alter/Theos*. This normative excess—an excess which is, in many ways, the condition itself of possibility of normative force—is both internal and external to how the norm that regulates the Axial triad is shaped and supported. The excess is reflected in how the norm is conceived as emanating from divinity itself, whose power exceeds by far all that is human.

We should bear in mind that in the so-called Axial breakthrough, which superseded the cosmologies of the ancient empires and, in many ways, defied them directly (in particular through the "Mosaic distinction," the Hebrew paradigm of Exodus from Pharaoh's tyranny: see Assmann 2005), meaning and normativity are, so to speak, extra-systemic, or at least produced at the system's borders. They cannot be contained any more within a ritual reconstruction of *cosmos*, but are produced by marginal social forces (like the tribes of Israel that had settled in Egypt) through a movement of exit from the system, the paradigm of Exodus. Ritual is not eliminated, but instead of reflecting *cosmos* and reproducing order becomes a source of increasing instability, since it is linked to a reflexive imagination of *Theos*, who, narratively endowed with "anthropomorphic" characters, is rather interfacing with the human world of signification by both representing and veiling a more impersonal reality of ultimate Being, which the late Voegelin effectively called the "It-reality" (in turn narratively dependent from an It-story, condensed in myth and scripture: Voegelin 1987). God's utterances of wrath and, more rarely, mercy, are conveyed and elaborated on through the voice of the prophets and those who recorded and transmitted them. This type of prophetic imagination, which precedes the Messianic imagination, takes the upper hand in the (never accomplished) attempts to stabilize the norm.

Let me here caution on the use of "norm," originating in *nomos* (and, for the later development of the argument in this chapter, on the concept of "antinomianism," a movement of thought and practice that challenges and subverts the norm in order to fulfill it). The model of this kind of transformation is here mainly the biblical unfolding of Israel out of Egypt. Therefore, it is not primarily a Greco-Roman *nomos* that is at stake, which is still the main reference of Schmitt's *Nomos of the Earth* (2003 [1950]) and of its canonical interpreters, but the Axial triad as framed by biblical prophecy. Yet it is true that the implications of the high degree of instability of the Axial norm once inscribed within the triangle *ego–alter–Alter* will be also elaborated on, in the history of the west, through Greco-Roman categories, so justifying the term antinomian for all movements aiming at subverting the norm in order to fulfill it, including those that are not directly heir to biblical prophecy.

Eric Voegelin's parallel analysis of Hebrew prophecy and Greek philosophy is helpful here in that it lays the focus on what is shared by both streams within a longer and more suffered trajectory of transformation that finally affects the "west" as a whole, including—or especially—its modern political developments. The biblical narrative and the role of the prophets retain a certain primacy in this approach (Voegelin 1956). In this sense, transcendence means, across the Hebrew–Hellenic divide, reflective participation in the experience of human becoming, whose kernel is located in the previously mentioned triad of *ego–alter–Alter* (Salvatore 2007: 33–67).

The crux of Voegelin's argument consists in disclosing a chain of subsequent, momentous shifts in the prophetic discourse that targets the socio-political order. At a crucial stage of prophecy where it laid the seeds of the Messianic imagination, according to Voegelin, the progression of the prophetic warnings assumed a "metastatic" character. Metastasis here consists in the fact that the waves of instructing–exhortative, prophetic discourse happened to depend on a densely creative, exponential reassembling of symbols of mundane and transcendent order and divine majesty that could no longer be contained within the norm of the axial triad, as enshrined in the Ten Commandments, and more in general in the Torah. The exit from the Axial triad implied for Voegelin a kind of recourse to "magic," via a metastatic proliferation of the symbols previously contained within the Axial triad. His main example is Isaiah, who "can indulge in the magic phantasy [sic] of forcing the End of the It-story on the end of a war with Assyria by a royal act of faith that will transfigure the pragmatic conditions of warfare into the final victory of the It-reality" (Voegelin 1987: 33). Taking into account the metastatic branching of the Axial process, this imaginative syndrome reveals its potential of subversion that unsettles the conventional interpretation of the Axial revolution as a quite linear development of the self's reflexivity and a neat differentiation of functions and rules. The Axial momentum appears here rather as a cut into the self and his/her relation to transcendent order, a trauma with momentous and enduring collateral effects: particularly at the level of how imagination triggers off expectations of radical transformation. The metastatic character of the prophetic discourse that opens up the chasm between mundane and transcendent orders lies in the experience that can no longer be contained in the vocabulary of the Ten Commandments oriented to the Axial triad. Foreign occupation and exile mark new traumas for the Hebrew people. Salvation is transposed to the end of time. A Messiah, a "just, suffering servant," starts to be imagined by the late prophets in order to bridge the widening gap of transcendence, to be a living bridge between the mundane and the transcendent order. Messianism is a mature stage of the prophetic metastasis described by Voegelin and a symptom of the intrinsic, now perhaps irreversible instability of axial transcendence and of the normative frameworks derived from it. A static norm can no longer contain the dramas of history, so the fulfillment of the norm can no longer be confined to deeds that execute the normative injunctions.

2. From Messiah to the antinomian imagination

The author who has most incisively discussed the long-term political implications of the process of Messianic imagination as the outcome of this metastatic movement is Jacob Taubes. A synthetic presentation of his life and career is here in order, because his contribution is tensely inscribed in the periods of political upheaval he lived in, at different stages of his life. He was born in Vienna in 1923. Due to Nazi persecution, his family emigrated to Switzerland and his father became the Chief Rabbi of Zurich. Jacob Taubes graduated as a rabbi at the yeshiva of Lausanne in 1943. His PhD thesis *Occidental Eschatology* represents the only monographic study of his career. Politically, he was critical of the Zionist project and its justification as the sole post-Holocaust solution to the issue of survival of the European Jewry. He moved for a while between the USA, where he worked with Leo Strauss, and Jerusalem, where he entertained close contacts to Gershom Scholem. By the early 1960s he was back to Europe. He received a call to a professorship at the Free University, Berlin, where in 1966 he inaugurated the Institute of Hermeneutics, which became a major intellectual centre of the 1968 student movement. In the last phase of his life, Taubes edited three books as the result of a series of conferences organized by a working group on *Theory of Religion and Political Theology*. His life and career climaxed in a seminar held in Heidelberg in January 1987 on Paul's Letter to the Romans, on the basis of whose transcripts a book was published after his death, which is probably to date the best-known publication authored by him. On several occasions, including in his Heidelberg seminar, he stressed that his relation to Carl Schmitt and his political theology is central to his own elaboration on the Messianic problem.

It is Taubes himself who reveals to us a key episode that occurred to him when he was a Research Fellow in Jerusalem in 1949, right after the proclamation of the state of Israel and the armistice with its Arab neighbors, one that is of great help to frame and understand the main *problematique* of his oeuvre and life. Hebrew University's campus, on Mount Scopus, was situated across the armistice line, an enclave in the hands of the new state; while the library was still on the hill, the courses and academic life took place downtown. The young Taubes had to give a seminar on "law." So he felt that he needed Carl Schmitt's *Verfassungslehre*. Yet in no way could he get it from the library quickly enough for using it in the seminar: in the quite complicated procedure to get a book down from Mount Scopus, three months was the average time needed. He filled in the loan form, but with no hope to get the book on time. Yet after just three weeks he got a call from the library: the book was there. He wondered how, and they told him that the book had come all the way from the Ministry of Justice, which had received it on loan from the library with utmost urgency—and now it had made good use of it, Taubes was allowed to take it. Apparently the minister had wanted the book in order to solve some difficult problems in the production of a draft for the constitution of the new state of Israel (which, incidentally, was never issued) (Taubes 1987: 18–19).

It cannot be too surprising that in spite of his left-oriented stance Taubes had an intense exchange with Carl Schmitt, in particular during the last part of their lives. The political theology of Carl Schmitt, well known for seeing in the "state of exception" the essence of the modern state formation and its claims to sovereignty, is, in Taubes' interpretation, a genuine theology of the *post Christum*. The *post Christum* demarcates the state of politics within the late medieval *respublica christiana* of Latin (western) Christianity, and its most original modern successor, the "state." Accordingly, the European state is the administrator of the profane realm of immanence before the procrastinated second coming of the Christ. This state is powerful, but intrinsically static. It is a "state," the state of waiting for the second coming. Its mandate is to govern profane time before the millennium. It is the force *qui tenet* or *katechon*, "holding down" evil and preventing the coming of the Antichrist that necessarily precedes Christ's second coming. The "katechontic" state so prevents, as long as humanly possible, the millennium. Yet the realm of the humanly possible *is* the profane realm, the secular domain. Secular formations in Europe *are* nested in the regime of the *post Christum*.

According to this interpretation, the katechontic function of the modern state, while opening up the door to the realm of the secular, contributed to keep alive the medieval idea of a *respublica christiana* and the renewal of Roman law. Yet it also justified the formation of the autonomous, centripetal forces of national states. It is noteworthy that the *nomos* of the emerging states is new, and therefore not a simple reformulation of Mosaic Law. Here comes to sight the previously mentioned hiatus between the *nomos* of the norm, articulated in terms of the Greek notion of politics, and the Hebrew concept of the Law, enshrined in the Mosaic and Deuteronomic legacy. The *nomos* inherited by Europe is a new law ultimately legitimized by the antinomian opening of Paul who deactivated Mosaic Law from within, through proclaiming Christ's coming a specific type of Messianic accomplishment of the law. It is not post- Christian in the sense of secularly overcoming Christianity or the *respublica christiana*, but as a full, though original accomplishment of the Pauline regime of the *post Christum*. Messiah represents here an anti-Law potential, the source of radiation of antinomian impulses, yet this process did not necessarily lead to upheaval and subversion but could be employed for a process of law reconstruction finalized to the restoration and stability of the socio-political order.

Taubes saw a symmetry between Carl Schmitt's and Walter Benjamin's programs of political theology as two opposing yet coherent developments of the Pauline regime of the *post Christum*. Taubes is very eager in reporting the deep admiration (along with a profession of indebtedness) nurtured by Benjamin towards Schmitt, as expressed in a letter of 1930: not by chance one expunged from the edited correspondence of Benjamin by Theodor Adorno and Gershom Scholem published in 1966 (Taubes 1987: 27). Taubes tenaciously followed this track since after the 1960s, at the cost of widening the gulf separating him from leading scholars of the caliber of Adorno and Scholem. But what is mostly remarkable is that his interpretive hypothesis was corroborated by the correspondence and finally by a meeting he had with the late Carl Schmitt between 1977 and 1980 (Stimilli 2004: 7–8). We cannot consider the importance of this development apart from the historical–political context of those troubled years, which saw dramatic developments both in Europe (the post-1968) and in the Middle East (the wars of 1967 and 1973, the Iranian revolution of 1978–1979 and the concomitant Camp David peace agreements).

Walter Benjamin's early *Theologico-Political Fragment* (Benjamin 1978: 312–313) is key to understand the connection between the two, opposing yet symmetrical political theologies of the former pro-Nazi theoretician and of the ingenious precursor of critical theory. Over the years Taubes deepened his conviction that Benjamin remained faithful to the vision of this fragment till his late *Theses on the Concept of History* (Benjamin 2000: 71–80). It is a vision of corrosive, liquid modernity of profane time activated by the Messiah, unsettling the static and repressive character of the state. Taubes believes that when Benjamin mentioned the Messiah at the beginning of the fragment ("Only the Messiah himself consummates all history, in the sense that he alone redeems, completes, creates its relation to the Messianic") he meant it quite literally and precisely as Paul did (Taubes 2003 [1993]: 97–100). This interpretation is at the origin of Taubes' view of Benjamin as a successor to Paul, or, even more strongly, to Paul's radical follower Marcion and his gnosticism (a further complication of Messianism making an even more intense use of imaginative constructions of divinity and self originally rooted in the simple Axial triad). Benjamin's perspective, however, includes a crucial difference to Schmitt, marked by his overt opposition to the katechontic *nomos*, which Schmitt had theorized by invoking the authority of Paul himself. In other words, the only possible opposition to the Schmittian *katechon* as the force that holds down the coming of the Antichrist and that founds the political theology of the modern state and of its state of exception is to evoke the Messiah as ineluctably present and as consuming all history. No reason to hold down the Antichrist, if Messiah is already there. History cannot go faster than the fear and hopes generated by the ongoing expectations of Messiah's coming: so, no need for a second coming, for the corresponding waiting, and for the type of authority justified by the waiting.

3. Connective justice

We can interpret Taubes' reasoning on the issue of Messianism and of the end of history as reflecting a new politics of imagining and constituting Other. This imagination grounds the crucial nexus *alter–Alter*, or immanence–transcendence, and the extent to which the irruption of Messiah onto the scene of human history either eases or complicates human relations to Other—depending on the approach to Messiah, on how it is imagined. As a result, the price to be paid for Messianism might turn out to be cheap or dear. Another scholar who has been closely linked to Taubes, and figures among the editors of Taubes' political theology of Paul (Taubes 2003 [1993]), is Jan Assmann. In order to provide an adequate background to the issue of the Messianic imagination it is useful to introduce Assmann's notion of "connective justice" as a point of departure defining a certain kind of politics, a quite un-Greek one—yet one with a certain resilience, cutting through several conventional epochs, the pre-Axial, the Axial, the medieval, the modern, and the post-modern. Connective justice is the potentially universal social force—though locally defined in specific cultural terms in various contexts—imposing on *ego* an obligation to care for *alter* and projecting the authority for sanctioning such care (and the failure to do so) onto a transcendent *Alter* (Assmann 2000: 199–204). Thus conceived "connective justice" defines an important type of micropolitics constituting the social bond, both preceding and surviving Messiah, both preceding and surviving the *katechon*.

Jan Assmann also engages directly with Carl Schmitt's political theology of the modern state, and even with the notion itself of political theology and the *nomos*. An Egyptologist by training, Assmann devoted a particular attention to the political theology identified with the genesis of the Mosaic opposition to the Pharaoh's state in ancient Egypt. This process marked the beginning of the "Mosaic distinction," as the condition for all future, sceptical approach of both Judaism and Islam (since the Mosaic narration has a prominent place in the Qur'an) to the pretensions of the state to be the ultimate warrant of social cohesion and of larger notions of mundane order. The Mosaic distinction is based on the idea that solidarity is a pattern of social relationships sharply distinguished from those organically provided by a structured division of labour covered by the sacredness of key symbols of the collective and by the institutional forms of their cohesion (the accomplished state and its historical antecedents). Solidarity has instead to rely on the connective justice guaranteed by the triad *ego–alter–Alter*.

The key to this type of solidarity did not consist in subverting the state but rather in constructing a higher, transcendent instance of guarantee of the social bond. Through the mediation of a common fellowship in God, *ego* and *alter* are called to be fair to each other and thus build the cell of a larger socio-political body without the intermediation of a ruler. The exact limits and the precise shape of this larger body are nonetheless unsupported by clear normative injunctions. Thus law cannot be the law of a state. The problem of the justification of political order remains elusive, or rather suspended. There is here no vertical political theology and no notion of an inherent, immanent *nomos*: we have here even its pre-emptive rejection. From now on the way is open to a different concept of order, whereby the accomplishment of order is projected into an indefinite future. This is the mechanism that triggers out, via the failure of successive prophetic warnings to care for the *ego–alter* bond which unleash the previously mentioned symbolic metastasis, first a series of waves of apocalyptic thought and finally a full-fledged messianism (including its gnostic spinoffs).

Messianism is, however, only one option among many in order to exit this state of suspension. Connective justice still operates as the carrier of Messianism, transported by notions of transcendence that are only problematically present in—though not completely extraneous to—Greek notions of politics and of the organisation of the social bond. In Judaism and Islam, whose orthodoxies have either functionally stabilized Messianism or put it at the margin of the orthodox sphere, the fundament of solidarity remains anchored in the triad *ego–alter–Alter/Theos*. Doing good to the other is not only a test for God's judgement, but is the only practically effective way to relate to God. Outside of a largely surpassed, archaic, cultic framework, the endeavour of connecting to the absolute *Alter* is only afforded through connecting to the concrete *alter* found in everyday interactions. This tension and openness of the daily intercourse between *ego* and *alter* absorbs—as it were—the subversive potential of a Messianic exit from human society and historical time. In other words, the endurance of the Axial triad within Judaism and Islam reposes on Exodus, but not on a Messianic exit of the kind just described.

Yet Jan Assmann reminds us that the injunction to see God in the weakest other—and so to fear divine justice, God's wrath, as the sanctioning of the violation of the *berith*, the biblical deal or "covenant" between *ego* and *Alter*—was instituted in ancient Egypt before the Mosaic distinction came to maturation. This was evident in the Egyptian obligations of solidarity with orphans and widows, which later became a key religious obligation both within Judaism and Islam: God provides for those who are not provided for, but this can only occur through the solidarity-oriented behaviour of the pious and faithful. Post-Exodus, prophetic discourse brought this injunction to a high level of conscious elaboration, yet this heightened reflexivity on the simultaneous complexity and necessity of a solidarity-oriented social bond led some prophetic voices to despair about the possibility of connective justice on earth. The progressive affirmation of a model of connective justice does not prevent the daily realization of its structural failure: human society is unjust, rulers are sinners, the forces of evil conspire against justice—prophesy gives way to apocalyptic visions. A further step to apocalypse, and a possible, though not necessary complement to Messianism, is the gnostic vision, for which *Alter* is the creator of this unjust world, no longer transcendent but to be transcended. The solution for *ego* lies then in plugging into the secret realms of the self. This step amounts to transforming the *ego–alter–Alter* triad into an *ego–ego–Ego*/as/*Alter* triad. The new, supreme *Alter/Theos* is no longer the creator of the world but the repository of the superior dimension of human existence, its spirit or *pneuma*. The cataracts to the Messianic imagination are opened at the moment when the social bond and the Law that commands its care (reflected in the second part of the Ten Commandments) appear to be ineffective, caught in a senseless repetition that evades the "spirit" of the Law.

The Jewish philosopher and sociologist Martin Buber has proposed that connectivity means relational openness, even dialogue. There is no Messianic solution to the human limitations to connective justice to be accomplished via a Christ who symbolically pre-condenses the meaning and the outcome of connectivity, by taking on himself all human suffering. In this sense, apocalypse and Messianism risk to dissipate the ethical prophecy that elaborated on connective justice (Buber 1992). Taubes partly agreed and partly disagreed with Buber's ensuing idea of a "Messianism of continuity" of Judaism as opposed to Christian and post-Christian Messianism and its metastatic developments—and price. Such developments unfolded through the history of the European state as of the *post Christum* and paved the way to the apocalypse of the two world wars and the Holocaust. While Taubes acknowledged the peculiar European appropriation of Paul through the katechontic *post Christum*, he considered Buber's dichotomization between two opposing forms of Messianism (one as a breakdown of biblical prophecy, the other as its completion) too much of a token of sterile anti-Christian polemics.

Against this view, and in line with the earlier analysis of Eric Voegelin, Taubes saw a metastatic logic at work within biblical prophecy itself. Voegelin had stressed that the metastatic character of the prophetic discourse lies in the prophets' efforts to stubbornly push forward the boundary between the mundane order and the transcendent order, up to a breaking point: the critical threshold when Hebrew prophecy, although still rooted in the vocabulary of the Ten Commandments, was no longer concerned with the restoration of the Covenant with Yahweh. A notion of "salvation" emerges in the process and crystallizes through the power of prophetic imaginative discourse (Voegelin 1956: 428–513). According to Taubes the development of prophecy that led to apocalypticism, Pauline Messianism, and gnosticism was not a deviation from the path. Paul remained located half way between the vision of a Messiah that cannot come back, and the gnostic implications of this Messianic postponement, which were only drawn by Marcion through his view of the Christ as the herald of a hidden God. Taubes considered Benjamin a true heir to the deepest implications of Paul's Messianism, almost a modern Marcionite. This is due, first, to Benjamin's neat separation, in the *Theologico-Political Fragment*, between the realm of human happiness (the profane realm) and the drama that stages the coming of Messiah (that is inevitably theological), and second—quite paradoxically—due to Benjamin's attempt to mend the radical separation, an attempt that constructs the inevitability for the human realm and even for nature itself to cry for Messiah.

I will try to draw the implications of this radical political theology (irrespective of the question whether Taubes' appropriation of Benjamin is acceptable or not), yet not before going back to its antagonistic, yet mirroring conception, the Schmittian vision, whereby the radical separation between this world and the thereafter is exactly what justifies the state of necessity—and then of exception—that determines the regime of the *post Christum*. As we know from Agamben, who relies on the critical thought of Adorno and Horkheimer, the Holocaust can be interpreted as the latest outcome of the development of the state as a techno-rational machine, or, in Hobbes' words, *machina machinarum* (Agamben 1998 [1995]). In an essay of 1983 published in the first volume of his three-volume edited series on *Theory of Religion and Political Theology*, Taubes, a major inspirer of Agamben, goes beyond Schmitt in interpreting Hobbes's Leviathan as a direct metamorphosis of the Christ into a mortal God or supreme super-person. This is also evident from the frontispiece of the original edition of Hobbes's Leviathan, where this is represented not as a biblical monster, but as a *magnus homo* holding the pastoral on his left and the sword on his right: exactly the opposite of the medieval representation of a *respublica christiana* as a unified body whose head is the Christ (Taubes 1983, 1987: 41–42, reproducing a letter of Jacob Taubes to Carl Schmitt, September 18, 1979). The modern state is just an inversion of the hierarchy of powers of the Church, spiritual and temporal. The state's mandate is katechontic and it cannot be otherwise, due to its origin. Clearly, the emerging of an autonomous and sovereign *saeculum* did not expunge the spiritual realm: it just appropriated to itself the power to define the borders of the religious sphere (Stimilli 2004: 139–152).

For Schmitt, the katechontic nature of the modern state was a response to the crisis of contingency in the *saeculum*, which justifies the state of exception as intrinsic to the norm or *nomos*. In this sense, theology is absorbed into a political mechanism and even into a juridical procedure. *Theologia* becomes *ancilla politicae* if it wasn't always—and from its inception—such. Taubes is more Schmittian than Schmitt, in that he reverses the relationship between theology and politics when he stresses that the core of Hobbes's political theology is a christology of the Leviathan. He derives from this acknowledgement the conviction that in spite of the theory of the state as a *machina machinarum*, the operation of reducing the state and legitimate modern politics to a static rationalistic tautology is a blunt misunderstanding of the European post-Christian state, since this modern secular state reposes on an inversion of the Christian myth, facilitated by the Pauline opening to the *post Christum*. The theological imagination cannot be expunged from the making of the modern secular state since it is essential to the *nomos*, simultaneously internal and external to it. It is one with the state of exception, and cannot be reduced to its *ex post* justification. The secular–katechontic *nomos* of the *post Christum* is in the final analysis legitimized by the Christ, in spite of the profane incorporation and the immanent state *of the* state.

Neither is this development a purely modern phenomenon facilitated by the sheer power of the modern state machinery. Partly in conjunction with, partly in opposition to the long genesis of the Leviathan out of the medieval *respublica christiana* as the body of the katechontic Christ, several religiously oppositional and radical movements, especially in the late middle ages and early modernity, imagined the profane realm as God's Kingdom, almost a paradise on earth. Most radically, Joachim a Flores, for Taubes (as much as for Voegelin) the ancestor of the modern European radical intellectual, imagined the temporal realm, the new era, as the full accomplishment of the spirit. As in the original Pauline imagination, the spiritual and the temporal realms are sharply separated, yet to be reconnected in new ways that completely unsettle the balance of the Axial triad. For sure, the modes of reconnection are different in the political theology of the state and in the opposition to it. Yet both Schmitt as the theoretician of the state and Benjamin as the herald of the movement of a liquid, corrosive modernity have a common Pauline root—and late-medieval ancestors who inaugurated a neo-gnostic era.

According to the gnostic myth, the radically transcendent God is a kind of Super-*Alter*, which cannot be accessed through a laborious work of connective justice like in the triadic model, but only by reaching down deeply into the arcane of the self. The modern self's absolute sovereignty is the product of an ever more liquid type of modernity that unfolds as a reflection of Super-*Alter*'s disconnectedness from the limitedness of creation. Taubes is no less vehement than Voegelin in showing how this dialectics has become a normalizing theology, although he also stresses that the gnostic momentum, unlike its Hegelian normalization into a dialectics of reconciliation, perpetuates the gulf between the *ego* and creation or nature (Stimilli 2004: 54–61). He prefers to see the root of this movement in Paul's posing as a second Moses, renewing Exodus as an exit both from creation and from biblical religion, both caged in the triadic nexus *ego–alter–Alter* (Taubes 2003 [1993]). Taubes also stressed the extent to which Freud himself, while rereading Moses, reiterated a Pauline motive by inaugurating a normalizing psychoanalysis that targeted the primordial human guilt for the killing of God-Father, the creator, and the substitution of the Father by the Son, through the sacrifice of the Son (ibid.: 122–131). In the Pauline reading this is the momentum that reinstitutes the social bond no longer as an *ego–alter–Alter/God-Father* triad but as a new community of *egos* longing for the kingdom of the Son and therefore trapped in a dialectical dispositive governed by the impossible removal of primordial guilt; this community is the Christian (or, better, Pauline) *ecclesia*. Its legitimate successor—via the intermediation of the late medieval *respublica christiana*—is the society that finds its principle of organization in the modern state.

4. Completion, not transgression

Taubes cannot stop at this diagnosis of the long-term impetus of Pauline Messianism. Its next station is a hypersensitive, yet ambivalent reading of Benjamin's *Theologico-Political Fragment* which shows the price to be paid for the ultimate replay of the Pauline motive, the acute Messianism of radical secular politics heralded by Benjamin. This politics prefigures not the end of the world, but the end of classically intended politics and the dawn of a new era of nihilistic "world politics," which is today called globalization. If the luringly "secular" state of grace promised by Leviathan can only rationalize violence, a radical rejection of violence can be equated to the institution of an alternative state of grace, which prefigures a new opening but also new dangers—since the opening can widen into a cataract from which an ever more incontrollable violence can spring. This danger recalls the "political religions" (a Voegelinian term) of the 20th century, which build the immediate backdrop to Benjamin's quandary. Benjamin provides a plastic representation of this last station of political theology: it is his image, in the *Theses on the Philosophy of History* (an image recently reread by Slavoj Žižek in a twisted neo-Christian perspective: Žižek 2003) of the puppet of historical materialism representing the allegedly autonomous force of history, which is nonetheless secretly piloted by the dwarf of political theology.

In Taubes' interpretation of Benjamin's image, the order of the profane or secular realm, as the harbinger of the quest of a free humanity for happiness, assists, precisely by virtue of the deceiving lightness of its being profane and non-committed, the coming of the Messianic Kingdom, which is now clearly intended as the end of politics. A sobered out connective justice of free-floating *egos*, close to Agamben's "coming community" where redemption is "the irreparable loss of the lost, the definitive profanity of the profane" (Agamben 1993 [1990]), ushers into a sort of neo-limbo. This hyper-profane realm is kept together by a soft antinomianism that does not subvert the norm but dwells in its ongoing process of becoming superfluous. This scheme inoculates the inhabitants of this truly secular "coming community" against an exposure to the fading normativity of the state-bound, katechontic *nomos*. Their Messiah is so immanent to the world to converge on the line of profane time and on a peculiar search for happiness. This consists in an old–new type of connectiveness that redeems the fundamental *ego* centeredness of the modern Benjaminian subject: "Law is not the first and last term, since even between man and man there are situations that transcend law—love, forgiving" (Taubes 1987: 35, letter to Armin Mohler, February 14, 1952). Benjamin's Messiah so becomes in Taubes' eyes a completion of Axial Law with its triadic structure, not its transgression. Relying on both, the cryptic and suggestive "coming community" of Agamben acquires more plausibility.

It is also worth noticing that at times Taubes seems to suggest that Spinoza, who was also quite sensible to the long-term reach of Paul's teaching as a metamorphosis of Mosaic Law, was moving in a similar direction (Taubes 2003 [1993]: 106–110), while de-Messianising, in a quite "Islamic" way (since for Voegelin Spinoza's secular ethics possesses a key Islamic trait: his *acquiescientia* meaning only and simply *islam*, i.e. surrender: Voegelin 1999: 129), the Pauline figure of the Christ, who so becomes a "lay," honorary Messiah (quite like in the Qur'an). This should not be too surprising, if we situate the work of the Sephardi Spinoza in a line of continuity with the Bible criticism of the Andalusi philosopher Ibn Hazm. We should not forget that Spinoza was also a countercharacter to his contemporary, the most famous and successful Messiah after Jesus, Sabbatai Zvi.

This extraordinary character of the mid-17th century, a Jewish Messiah who later converted to Islam, and to whom Scholem dedicated an important part of his work (Scholem 1973), incited waves of Messianic fever that even penetrated the sober and prosperous bourgeois world of Spinoza's upcoming modern Europe. As observed by Taubes, Dutch *marranos* like Uriel da Costa, a key inspirer of Spinoza, and Spinoza himself, came close to theorize the dogmatic indifference between Judaism, Christianity and Islam, if seen as based on the minimum common denominator of prophetic imagination, common *pietas*, and a soft political theology of human power sharing in a *saeculum* liberated from any "after" and "not yet" (cf. Taubes 2006: 119, in a letter of Taubes to Scholem of March 16, 1977). The diametrically opposed trajectory of their contemporary Sabbatai Zvi, who, on the injunction of the Ottoman sultan, accepted conversion to Islam, could be also recruited in support of the idea of a secular convergence, erasing the excess of sense of the Messianic imagination by zeroing into a world without waiting—except for the Spinozian lapse between potency and act as intrinsic to human action and its power.

Zvi's antinomian climax was marked by an exit from a Law and the entry into another (indeed functionally equivalent) Law: from *halacha* to *shari'a*: perhaps a hint to their indifference, provided a kernel of triadic nexus is preserved. Against the quite obvious, far from esoteric meaning of the outcome of the career of the second most famous Messiah, Taubes criticized Scholem's idea that the most significant legacy to Zvi's message was the radically antinomian, Sabbatean movement of Jacob Frank, an antecedent to the French Revolution. This inheritance would then be too easily interpreted as the folding of Messianic illumination into political Enlightenment, carried on as a trajectory of exit from Jewish tradition and symbolism, almost an "alternative modernity" *ante litteram*. Culminating in the French Revolution (during which the Frankist Junius Frey found his death on the scaffold along with Danton), this radical antinomianism erases the differences between *ego* and *alter* and can only justify the violent suppression of the other, the refusal of diversity, the impossibility of a convergence absorbing Messiah's presence into the living social bond, without waiting or transgression.

Yet Taubes' critique of Scholem went much further and found expression in the former's vehement opposition to the latter's cultural Zionism along with its ultimate indulgence towards the theological–politically motivated political identity of the state of Israel, "the 'ghost' of Calvinist Geneva, of Cromwell's and Mikon's England" (Taubes 2006: 60; Stimilli 2006: 137–142). Visiting Israel again towards the end of his life, after revisionist Zionists had taken over power from old Labor pioneers and a sustained policy of settlements in the occupied territories was underway, Taubes apparently saw in neo-Israel the best accomplishment of the Schmittian idea of sovereignty incarnate in the state of exception, which Benjamin had fairly and astutely countered with his acute Messianism "from below." In 1949 the Minister of Justice had found a good reading in Schmitt's book on constitutional doctrine. It is perhaps not surprising that a constitution was never issued for the new state of Israel. No state boundaries were drawn. They still haven't been.

The resilience of connective justice on the ground and the adequacy of calling for its protection and promotion through dialogue was the continual object of attention of Martin Buber. Taubes elaborated on this approach and so played Buber against Scholem, yet by avoiding falling back into a dialogic rhetoric that absorbs the Messianic tension into the social bond without residues, a rhetoric invoking a "Messianism of continuity" or "concrete Messianism" based on a permanent dialogue between *ego*, *alter*, and *Alter*. Taubes does incorporate this tension, thanks to his interpretation of Benjamin, into the double *ego–alter* and the *alter–Alter* tension, but without belittling the ongoing, unsettling and antinomian potential of Messianism as just a problem of Christianity and the west (Taubes 2003 [1993]: 53–64).

5. Conclusion: the price of Messianism and the liquidation of politics

The incidents of 1949 (the appearance of Schmitt's political theology in Israel's aborted constitutional process) and 1966 (the occultation of Schmitt's political theology from the corpus of Benjamin's writings) prompted Taubes to discuss what he called the "price of Messianism" for modern politics, which he saw—albeit operating in symmetrical opposite fashions—in both Schmitt's *katechon* and in Benjamin's "acute messianism." For the west, there was no way to avoid paying such a price. It was just a matter of paying it the way of Schmitt, in a reactionary and potentially fascist fashion, or the way of Benjamin, via a radically revolutionary approach that can finally be folded into the liquid modernity of nihilistic world politics. It was not completely clear to Taubes if paying this price still allows for some sort of politics or prepares its ends—from right to left.

Taubes' combined interpretation of Benjamin's and Schmitt's symmetrically opposing political theologies suggests that a twist in Messianism's logic justifies the concentration of power in the secular realm of immanence preceding (and delaying) the second coming of the Christ. Yet the process also coagulated the neo-Messianic frustrations of diasporic Judaism, whose own "katechontic" regime was the stateless rule of rabbinic doctrine and practice, and that due to this statelessness easily became the object of persecution and genocide in the context of modern European state building—an intolerable situation that finally opened the way to the radical political Messianism of Zionism.

The "world politics" evoked in Benjamin's fragment reframes Messianism within a life form, yet one dense with political significance, therefore ambivalently ingrained into the biopolitics of global modernity. Jacob Taubes kept a keen sense for the level of reality where the lifeworld-based micropolitics feeds into world politics and constitutes a type of political subjectivity that is the legacy of what he called the trajectory of "Occidental eschatology," the title of his first (and only) book (Taubes 1947). Here the price of Messianism comes close to the theorized "end of history" of global society and its ultimate nihilism, well epitomized in Benjamin's *Theologico-Political Fragment*. This hyper-modernity exalts the sovereignty of the self and allows for the antinomian imagination to liquidate the legal dimension of the social bond, the Law. It nourishes human happiness in the immanent order of the world, based on the consciousness that Messiah is not coming for the simple reason that *it* is absorbed in the process of erosion and "liquidation" of the order of the world. Yet the doubt remains that the Axial triad and its Law of connective justice continue to lure behind any such vision of a "coming community." Taubes' interpretation of Benjamin's political theology attempts to close (or perhaps square) the circle by relocating the apocalyptic politics of the 20th century into its Axial rails.

References

Agamben, G. 1993 [1990], *The Coming Community* (trans. M. Hard), Minneapolis, University of Minnesota Press.

—— 1998 [1995], *Homo Sacer: Sovereign Power and Bare Life* (trans. D. Heller-Roazen), Stanford, CA, Stanford University Press.

Armstrong, K. 2006, *The Great Transformation: The Beginning of Our Religious Traditions*, New York, Knopf.

Assmann, J. 2002 [2000], *Herrschaft und Heil. Politische Theologie in Altägypten, Israel und Europa*, Munich, Carl Hanser.

—— 2005, "Axial 'breakthroughs' and semantic 'relocations': ancient Egypt and Israel," in Arnason, J. P., Eisenstadt, S.N. and Wittrock, B. (eds) *Axial Civilizations and World History*, Leiden, Boston, Brill, pp. 133–156.

Benjamin, W. 1978, "Theologico-political fragment," In *Reflections: Essays, Aphorisms, Autobiographical Writings* (E. Jephcott, ed. P. Demetz), New York, Schocken Books.

—— 2000, "Theses on the philosophy of history," in Schirmacher, W. (ed.) *German 20th-century Philosophy: The Frankfurt School*, New York, Continuum.

Buber, M. 1992, *On Intersubjectivity and Cultural Creativity* (ed. and intro. Eisenstadt, S.N.) Chicago, University of Chicago Press.

Eisenstadt, S.N. 1982, "The Axial Age: the emergence of transcendental visions and the rise of clerics," *European Journal of Sociology*, 23 (2): 294–314.

Gauchet, M. 1997 [1985], *The Disenchantment of the World. A Political History of Religion* (trans. O. Burge), Princeton, NJ, Princeton University Press.

Jaspers, K. 1953 [1949], *The Origin and Goal of History*, New Haven, CT, London, Yale University Press.

Salvatore, A. 2007, *The Public Sphere: Liberal Modernity, Catholicism, Islam*, New York, Palgrave Macmillan.

Schmitt, C. 2003 [1950], *The Nomos of the Earth in the International Law of the Jus Publicum Europaeum* (trans. and annotated G.L. Ulmen), New York, Telos.

Scholem, G. 1973, *Sabbatai Sevi: The Mystical Messiah, 1626–1676*, Princeton, NJ, Princeton University Press.

Stimilli, E. 2004, *Jacob Taubes. Sovranità e tempo Messianico*, Brescia, Morcelliana.
—— 2006, "Der Messianismus als politisches Problem," in *Der Preis des Messianismus. Briefe von Jacob Taubes an Gershom Scholem und andere Materialien*, Würzburg, Königshausen & Neumann, pp. 131–179.
Taubes, J. 1947, *Abendländische Eschatologie*, Bern, A. Francke.
—— 1983, "Statt einer Einleitung: Leviathan als sterblicher Gott: zur Aktualität von Thomas Hobbes," in *Religionstheorie und Politische Theologie, vol. I, Der Fürst dieser Welt. Carl Schmitt und die Folgen*, Munich, Wilhelm Fink, pp. 9–15.
—— 1987, *Ad Carl Schmitt. Gegenstrebige Fügung*, Berlin, Merve.
—— 2003 [1993], *Die Politische Theologie des Paulus*, Munich, Wilhelm Fink.
—— 2006, *Der Preis des Messianismus. Briefe von Jacob Taubes an Gershom Scholem und andere Materialien*, Würzburg, Königshausen & Neumann.
Voegelin, E. 1956, *Order and History, vol. 1, Israel and Revelation*, Baton Rouge, LA, Louisiana State University Press.
—— 1987, *Order and History, vol. 5. In Search of Order*, Baton Rouge, LA, London, Louisiana State University Press.
—— 1998, *The History of Political Ideas, vol. IV, Renaissance and Reformation*, in Morse, D.L. and Thompson, W.M. (eds) *The Collected Works of Eric Voegelin*, vol. 22, Columbia, MO, University of Missouri Press.
—— 1999, *The History of Political Ideas, vol. 7, The New Order and Last Orientation*, in Gebhardt, J. and Hollweck, T.A. (eds) *The Collected Works of Eric Voegelin*, vol. 25, Columbia, MO, University of Missouri Press.
Wittrock, B. 2005, "The meaning of the Axial Age," in Arnason, J.P., Eisenstadt, S.N. and Wittrock B. (eds) *Axial Civilizations and World History*, Leiden, Boston, Brill, pp. 53–85.
Žižek, S. 2003, *The Puppet and the Dwarf: The Perverse Core of Christianity*, Cambridge, MA, MIT Press.

Chapter 8

Religion and the struggle for people's imagination

The case of contemporary Islamism

Benoît Challand

Introduction

It is perhaps not by chance that the idea of this book's collection originated from a reflection on the role of religion in the contemporary world. Religion seems to have become one of the privileged sites for the politics of imagination. As a system of beliefs, religion must be able to impose its image of the world to gain support. As an aggregation of followers, it must be able to convey the sense of a united community. As a creed, it often resorts to representing threats in order to survive the challenges of our epoch. In other words, in all these basic functions religion has to rely in one way or another on imagination.

This chapter argues that there has been a transformation of the role of imagination for religion in our contemporary epoch. There is a need for a renewed sociology of religion that comes to terms with the limits of Christian-centric categories of analysis and that acknowledges the different cultural settings and meanings involved with non-western religious forms and manifestations (see Salvatore's contribution in this volume for such an attempt). This cannot be simply done by professing some commonalities (a 'Judeo-Christian tradition', or a common process of cultural translation) or by lamenting fundamental divergences (resistance to democratic secular orders of certain religious traditions), but by taking a wider comparative approach which includes the centrality of imagination (and tensions around it) in our globalised epoch. To do so, we will look at the case of Islam.

Indeed, talking about Islam today is unlike talking about any other religion: Islam has gradually emerged as one of the most significant Others of our epoch and has often served as negative counterpoint to the representations of modernity, democracy and western identity. There is a long tradition of discourses about Islam that depicts it as a homogenous block and associates it with concepts such as 'traditionalism', resistance to 'modernity' or political violence. One only has to think of the classic 18th- and 19th-century representations of the so-called 'oriental despotism' where an attitude towards despotic forms of government was explicitly associated with Islam. In a more recent vein, the propositions of 'neo-Orientalism' (Sadowski 1993) is a readaption of older classical orientalist *topoi* originally based in literature, music and art and so skillfully analysed by Said (1978). Neo-Orientalist themes are a revamp of old themes with more direct political consequences to explain some of the current problems in the Middle East. Such reductive representations of the 'Orient' as negative mirror of the 'Occident', which have for centuries been the object of an ambivalent despise and fascination, have not disappeared from the contemporary global imaginary, where they still exercise their power, although at times in a much more nuanced way. Therefore, when talking about Islam one should indeed be aware that this religion has indeed served, among other differentiation markers such as barbarian, savages, etc., (Hartog 2005; Pagden 2000), as a differentiation factor for modernity, its categories and its self-representation (Bracke and Fadil 2008; Stauth 1993). One runs the risk therefore of simple tautological answers when one questions the compatibility of, say, Islam and a liberal public sphere or Islam and modernity. In other words, a normative judgement on religions with regard to secular orders should involve a critical study of the techniques of self-representations around themes of modernity, liberalism and individualism. Thus, the self-referential tendency of modernity demands scrutiny.[71]

Let us take the issue of the relationship between politics and religion. Be it in the secular thesis, or in the many discussions on the theologico-political nexus (Assmann 2000; Benjamin 1986; De Vries and Sullivan 2006; Gauchet 2005), one basic premise is that religion and politics have been conceived as separated realms in a modern polity. While theories of modernisation remain of analytical importance to understand the disenchantment of the world and processes of social differentiations leading to the gradual erasure of religion from public spheres, it is important to question such an underlying presupposition when working with the issue of religion nowadays. This is even more the case when dealing with Islam.

Critical to such dichotomous views, we will argue that religion and politics still have many points of entwinement (Lefort 1986) and that such points of entwinement are hindering a sound and dispassionate discussion of the interplay between Islam and politics. Because of the eurocentric approach prevailing in the definition of 'modernity', 'democracy', 'liberal state', etc., there is a constitutive bias towards Islam: whereas in the west, religion was perceived as separated from politics (at least until very recently), from politics of the Middle East and in particular from the Arab world has been misleadingly characterised as living examples of the resilience of religion in the political realm. There is therefore a widely relayed opposition between the image of the secular way of doing politics in the west, on the one hand, and the 'Oriental' (Muslim) tendency to mix religion and politics on the other.

71 See incisive remarks on that point by Buck-Morss 2003: Chapters 3 and 5. For critical examples, see Bottici and Challand 2010: 66–75 or Smith 1995.

The problem is that such representation is highly problematic, for two reasons. First, as convincingly argued by, among others, Lefort (1986) and Asad (2003), there has been a permanence of the Christian theological categories and worldviews in western liberal politics. The concept of secularisation risks being more the result of a self-representation than a living reality. Asad insists on considering the secular as 'neither singular in origin nor stable in its historical identity' and underlines how 'secular political practices often stimulate religious ones' (Asad 2003: 26). Thus, religious motives have been transformed in the sacralisation of liberal themes, in the belief that liberalism must redeem the world, but such moral ideas often have a religious basis ('toleration', 'universalism', etc.). Moreover, even admitting that there had actually been in the past a complete process of secularisation of politics, this is no longer the case in many western countries. The trend towards a post-secular society is firmly established in the discursive field (one needs to think about the many recent debates on religion and the public sphere to come to grips with this fact) and there are many signs suggesting an increasing role of religions in the European public sphere.[72]

Second, the opposition between Islam and modernity also hides the fact that not only Muslims living in the west, but also Muslim-majority countries have witnessed a more or less advanced process of secularisation – or that at least they have imagined themselves as living such a process for a long time. Indeed, most of the Middle Eastern states are formally secular regimes, with the few significant exceptions of the Islamic Republic of Iran and Saudi Arabia. And as we will see, even if religion has regained an important role and Islamism has emerged as a powerful political ideology, this is not primarily due to cultural reasons, rather to some straightforward political reasons. Halliday explains very well how the creation of secular states in the late colonial Middle East period was a way to reinforce weak states and to keep religious authorities at bay.[73]

The current predicament of Muslim-majority polities is due not to an essential role of religion in formal politics, but to the emergence of an ideology (Islamism) of opposition using the discourse of Islam against autocratic states. It is indeed crucial to distinguish between them conceptually speaking: Islam (as the millenarian religion) and Islamism (as a recent political ideology aiming at the instauration of an Islamic state) are two different things. The fact that people tend to conflate the two terms – or the three different adjectives 'Muslim', 'Islamic' and 'Islamist' – is a sign of the persistence of Orientalist stereotypes in the contemporary global imaginary and that part of the problem is a struggle for the political imagination.

72 For a recent discussion, see Ungureanu 2008.

73 Secularism, above all, as a policy to reinforce the state, '[o]nce created little intention of surrendering their power' (Halliday 2005: 76).

Islam is therefore not a homogeneous block, either in space or in time. In this chapter, I distinguish between different key moments for the history of religions: first, their foundational moments, second, the modern phase of encounters with secularity and finally the current epoch of a globalised ('post-modern') world. It should now be clear that when I talk of categories such as 'modernity', I am not primarily referring to empirically observable phenomena, but rather to self-representations, ways of representing and imagining self and others. And, as we will see, imagination matters.

Starting from the modern representation of a separation between religion and politics, we will suggest that the emergence of Islamism (the ideology) created the possibility for a sort of externalisation of religion that has negative consequences on the capacity of large social groups to define their autonomous political projects. There are multiple roots for the spilling over of Islam into politics, but in all of them the 'struggle over people's imagination'[74] has been a crucial element. With the rise of Muslim politics, politics ceased to be a simple Leviathan (admitting that it has even been the case) and became a symbol maker (Eickelman and Piscatori 1996: 9).

In order to show this, I discuss the consequences of the emergence of secularism as a systematic way to rule Muslim majority societies in the early 20th century (section 1). I then look at the trajectory of the nascent ideology of Islamism in the context of independent and sovereign states and the role that imagination played in that period of reinvigoration of the various Islamist movements (section 2). Section 3 will introduce the idea of an externalisation of religion and link it to a possible consequence, that of a double heteronomy (section 4), before reaching our final conclusions on the meaning of such a process, not only in the Middle East but also in the west.

1. Islam(s) and secularisation: towards a modern Islamist ideology

Islamic and Islamist rhetoric has become very important for Middle East politics. In order to understand the process through which Islamism has turned into a political ideology becoming thus the site of a struggle for people's imagination one has to address the historical, ideological, sociological and political roots of this success. This also serves from the very outset to stress that the link between Islam and politics is not an automatic one. Islamic rhetoric is not yet Islamist rhetoric: 'Islamic' simply denotes a neutral qualification for who/what has to do with Islam in general, whereas 'Islamist', on the contrary, serves to describe a distinct political project that wants to subdue political order to religious ethics and principles. There are very different cases

74 The phrase 'struggle over people's imagination' stems from Eickelman's and Piscatori's seminal book (1996) unearthing what 'Muslim politics' (not Islamic nor Islamist politics) is about.

and forms of what is branded as Islamism (or 'political Islam').[75] The emergence of Islamism has distinct historical origins as it was only created in the period between the two World Wars (Ayubi 1991) but its emergence, far from being a simple residual of primordialism, is linked with the specific conditions of modernity.[76]

Asad's seminal study on the formations of the secular is a stark reminder of the blind spots of secularism: the latter is a political ideology that never totally rids itself (although it claims to do so) of the religious overtones built in the grammar of modernity (Asad 2003). In his work, Asad shows that secular political practices far from relegating religion into the private sphere often stimulate religious ones, but with a silent and ethnocentric preference for Christianity. For instance, as he shows, the rhetoric of human rights and the propagation of democracy or liberalism as a redeeming mission are based on the recycling of religious moral duties and grammar (Asad 2003: 21–66, in particular, 25f., 127–158).

Secularisation, as both a political project born in and carried out by Europe around the late 19th and early 20th centuries and later by the USA and as a self-representation, has been central for the emergence of Islamism. According to some interpreters colonial interventions have presented a legal challenge undermining 'values indigenous to Islamic societies' (Smith 1995: 29) which then led to the creation of the political ideology named 'Islamism'. Secularisation policies by colonial powers in the Muslim world implied thorough changes in the legal systems, putting *shari'a* aside, therefore giving to religion only 'qualified freedom' (Asad 2003: 205ff.). This generated the imaginary association of secularism and colonial oppression. It is not by chance that the most influential Islamic thinkers such as Mawdudi, Qutb and Qaradawi all wrote in open opposition to what 'secular' meant. The pillars of their intellectual endeavour (some would say ideology) is the forging of new concepts merging religious principles with political ones opposing secularism.[77]

This does not mean that the representations of modernity have always been one sided. There have been other encounters with political modernity in the late 19th century prior to the encounter with secularisation described in these pages. We are thinking of important writers such as Afghani (d. 1897), Abduh (d. 1905) and Rida (d. 1935), the so-called 'modernists' or 'reformists' (Laroui 1987). They called for a merger of rationality, scientific progress and modernity, on one hand, and Islamic authenticity, on the other. In this way,

75 For a discussion of the various forms of Islamisms, see Karam 2004: 4–8.

76 There are origins going back to the late 19th century. Thus we spot the beginning of pan-Islamism in the 1870s. See Esposito 2003.

77 On the various interpretations and connotations of 'secular' in Arabic, see Asad 2003: 206 fn 2, Filali-Ansary 2002: 21, Ghalioun et al. 1993: 78, Masud 2005: 370–375 and Smith 1995: 21.

they contributed to creating a different political imaginary which still survives in a large strata of the population.

Still, the historical, geographical – and I would add imaginary, to follow Olivier Roy (1994: viii) – encounters between Islam and secularism have greatly influenced the ideological content of Muslim contemporary thoughts (Masud 2005: 363–366). Masud distinguishes between four areas of encounter. First, in Turkey secularism was synonymous under Atatürk's modernisation plans with westernisation and has always been defended as a positive feature by Turkish politicians, at least until the rising challenge of Turkish Islamic parties from the 1980s onwards. Second, in the Arab world, secularism was seen for the pan-Arab movement in the beginning of the 20th century as a way to get rid of the Ottoman yoke. It therefore originally had a rather positive appeal for Arab nationalists seduced by the European positivist project of nation building. Things changed with the 1967 defeat by Israel: pan-Arabism was gradually substituted after the Six-Day War by a more pan-Islamic appeal, making of secularism the avowed enemy. Third, in South Asia and in particular for the Muslims of India, the abolition of the Caliphate by Atatürk in 1924 was seen as a western (British) plot to weaken Islam and therefore Muslims' position in a decaying empire. It is not by coincidence that Mawdudi (1903–1979), a founding father of modern Islamic political theory was based in Delhi in the 1930s. His writings, calling for the creation of an Islamic state based on Islamic ideology, stood in violent opposition to secularism.[78] Finally, in South-East Asia, the political economy has requested historically a form of religious tolerance. Here, secularism was easier to accommodate within the local political imaginary because it posed a less direct challenge to fragmented subgroups.

These four geographical areas of encounter are also the description of four *types* of adaptation to or rejection of secularism. Masud interprets these different reactions as a result of political and cultural processes and sees the influence of the power relations between majority and minority. In his view, 'when the minorities [felt] threatened', politically and culturally, 'they protected their religious identity in political terms. Political secularism, thus does not necessarily negate religion, rather it stresses religious freedom as a basic right' (Masud 2005: 367). Islamisation, that is, the attempt to erect a political project based on religion, implied a reaction against the threat of secularism and a call for 'cultural unification and centralization' (ibid.). The ideology calling for Islamisation has its historical roots in the encounters not just with secularism, but also with colonial domination and can be described as a movement in *reaction* to the imposition of a new order by colonial powers.

78 His work became very influential for, among others, Sayid Qutb (d. 1966), the leader of an increasingly radical Muslim Brotherhood in Egypt in the 1950s and 1960s, when his writings were translated into Arabic (Arjomand 2010).

It is only in the latter setting that Islamism will gradually evolve to entail all the components for a definition of ideology, understood as a 'set of ideas by which a social group makes sense of the world', and which 'provide[s] some explanation of how things have come to be as they are, some indication of where they are heading (to provide a guide to action), criteria for distinguishing truth from falsehood and valid arguments from invalid, and some overriding belief [. . .] to which adherents may make a final appeal when challenged' (Jones 2003).

Islamism, as we suggest later, will then adapt to new challenges and become a political ideology having little to do with Islam the faith (Laroui 1987: 83).[79] Its success stemmed from the capacity to strike the popular imagination by 'invok[ing] the symbols of those [normative] codes to reconfigure the boundaries of civil debate and public life' (Eickelman and Piscatori 1996: ix) within independent states. With the rise of Muslim politics, politics ceased to be a simple Leviathan and became a symbol maker (ibid.).

This new radical project was also refusing modernist Muslim attempts (such as those of Afghani, Abduh and others) to reconcile western modernity with a return to a cultural Muslim identity proposed by the reformist (Laroui 1987: 82f.). Still, the success of Islamism is not just a reaction to modernity, but also a product of it. In the first place, it is intrinsically linked to the modern contexts of nation-states. The transformation of the first ideas of authors such as Mawdudi into a full-fledged political programme and the implementation of Islamism will only be possible within the framework of independent nation-states – as opposed to the previous political context characterised by political fragmentation, cross-cutting loyalties and absence of clearcut boundaries. It is the emergence (or imposition) of the form of the modern state as a homogeneous political space that created both the political context and the imaginary resources for the emergence of the Islamist project. Further, to understand the role of Islamism in the contemporary world to which we now turn, one cannot prescind from an analysis of the role played by contemporary media.

2. Islamism within independent states and its imaginary appeal

If the colonial rule over the Middle East gave the initial spark to Islamism, it will be the context of independent secular states and then of the regional conflicts and revolutions that will set aflame the political imagination of Islam and make of Islamism the ideology that is as widespread as we now know it.

The constant in the two phases[80] is that Islamism continues to function as an ideology *in reaction* to political developments. In the first phase, Mawdudi

79 Laroui's full quotation illustrates our point: 'L'Islam dont on parle tant aujourd'hui est un néo-Islam qui est plus une idéologie politico-sociale qu'une théologie ou une pratique sociale.'

80 For a more articulate transformation, see Laroui 1987: 83ff.

wrote against the abolition of the Caliphate and the creation of a secular order in the 1930s and 1940s. In the same opposition vein, the Muslim Brotherhood was founded in 1929 by Hassan al-Banna (d. 1949) in Egypt in 'reaction to the division of Arab countries into spheres of influence for European powers, the abolition of the caliphate in Turkey, and Western influence on Islamic culture' (Esposito 2003). In a second phase, Sayyid Qutb (the follower of al-Banna) wrote 'against ignorant or "pagan" societies, both Western and secular Islamic' in the 1950s and 1960s (ibid.). The Muslim Brotherhood under al-Banna was keen to support the Free Officers' coup in 1952 to overthrow King Farouk (considered a pawn in the hands of the British), but quickly came into opposition to Nasser's regime under Qutb's leadership, paving the way to more radicalised fringes of the Muslim Brotherhood to resort to political violence against their own leadership (the assassination of Sadat in 1981 is a prime example).

This illustrates the shift from the first to the second step: many of the Islamist movements came in the second phase to oppose their own government, while, in the first step, they were together with secular Muslim leaders calling for the end of western colonial power in the Middle East. A quick panorama of the political setting in this second phase demonstrates our point – at least until the 2011 Arab revolts – the main opposition in Egypt is the Islamist one; Islamic opposition grew in opposition to the Shah's rule in Iran until the revolution in 1978/79; the Algerian Islamist party (FIS) presented the strongest challenge to the FLN, the heir of the Algerian revolution, up to the 1991 elections. In all other Middle East countries, the strongest opposition has been from the Islamist milieux (Afghanistan, Morocco, Palestine, Tunisia, Turkey, Yemen, etc.).

So how is it that these Islamist movements/parties became so strong? There are usually two strands of explanation: both of them point to a capacity to strike collective imagination. The first type of explanation is a sociological one; the second is political.

There have been many changes affecting the composition and profile of Middle Eastern society, including the higher urbanisation rate, the spread of literacy and the development of mass media and transportation. 'Rapid urban growth was accompanied by a renewed vitality of religious activity', a phenomenon that access to literacy and higher education reinforced. As Arjomand (2010) argues, mosques and other religious associations provided a sense of community that was lost after the dislocation from the villages. This explains the imaginary appeal of Islamist rhetoric: it provides the very much needed image of a united community. Far from being a simple negative reaction to modernity, the rise of Islamism is also a consequence of it. Indeed, it is in modern times that one needs and moreover can think of oneself as part of an imagined community (Anderson 1983), in this case the Muslim *ummah*.

Furthermore, the imaginary appeal of Islamism cannot be conceived outside the technological revolution which usually goes under the name of 'globalisation'. With new mass media such as internet and satellite TV channels,

Middle Eastern societies have reached a level of 'conscientisation' of their being 'Muslims' that was unknown in the previous epochs. Conscientisation is no longer the unique privilege of *ulama* (clerics) but also part of the mental equipment of 'lay intellectuals, mothers, government leaders and musicians' (Eickelman and Piscatori 1996: xi). Millions of people scattered around the globe perceive of themselves as part of the Muslim *ummah* through the apparatus of images that enter their houses every single day.

The success of Arabic international channels such as Abu Dhabi TV, Al-Jazeera, Al-Arabiyya, etc., is a case in point. This also highlights the extent to which politics has become about the capacity to portray different alternative imaginaries. It is not by coincidence that the recently launched TV channel Al-Jazeera International insists that it provides a different coverage. Not only does it expose the dark side of world politics that no other news channel has done so far (and indeed, it does show the crude reality of politics not only in the Arab worlds, but also in Africa, Latin America and South(-east) Asia), but it also insists very much on the *cultural* image of the Arab/Muslim world. For instance, there are many talk shows and interviews analysing the representation of the Middle East in mainstream western media and presenting alternative points of view of Arab filmmakers and artists. It is as if the purpose of Al-Jazeera International was not about 'Setting the News Agenda' (its motto), but about rectifying the image of the (Arab) Middle East in the west, where it is often depicted in a simplistic if not biased way. What is at stake is not only an imposition of a given social imaginary, but a real struggle for its definition.

To take an even more striking example, the existence of global jihadi groups such as al-Qaeda often entirely depends on such contemporary media (Gerges 2009). Indeed, the only tangible proofs we have of the very existence of al-Qaeda is a series of writings and images that circulate on the web, on TV and via digital support. Gilles Kepel, while analysing the written sources produced by al-Qaeda, highlights how the organisation is based on a piecemeal and at times contradictory patchwork of ideologies and political motivations (Kepel and Milelli 2008). But it is through the media that it appeals mostly to a loose popular basis: its TV declarations, as well as internet message or video production circulated on DVDs allow the movement to fight a virtual battle with more moderate opponents whose ideology at times is much more coherent than that of Bin Laden's followers.

Both propaganda and actions of al-Qaeda mirror the characteristics of the revolution ushered by contemporary media. In the first place, what matters is more the spectacular form of the message than its content. Second, the virtuality of images means also the loss of authenticity. Propaganda is based on a corpus of written texts but foremost on images shared via the net, satellite TVs and other digital supports. Doctrinal messages tend to be short and straightforward with do-it-yourself techniques (filmed in the countryside, in a cave, or testaments of young 'martyrs', pictures of terrorist attacks, etc.). Such material plays on emotion, fear and voyeurism – as any TV show should.[81] The fluidity and changes within the corpus of virtual pictures makes it impossible to give a name to their authors and therefore to establish their authenticity. Just as important as the 'leaders' of al-Qaeda are the anonymous webmasters or editors of short films circulating the world and copy/pasting ideological texts on a set of images. This notwithstanding, such propaganda, halfway between reality (pictures of operations against NATO troops in Afghanistan) and spectacle, manages to attract new supporters, both militant and non-militant.

Looking again at the terrorist attacks carried out by al-Qaeda, one is also struck by the spectacular form they took. The symbolic and visual dimensions of the attacks of 9/11 eclipse the economic and political ones. Images are central for the propagation of their deeds and with them the logic of virtual reproduction, the use of the metonymy (a synagogue to indicate Israel), of synecdoche (claims in the name of Islam) and of symbols (the Star Spangled Banner to refer to the USA), etc. All of which is perfectly adapted to media that instantly readapt the content on a global scale, but is also consubstantial to them because they could not exist without them: it is through media that these attacks become real in the minds of people.

The second strand of explanation for the surge of political Islam/Islamism has to do with crucial political events in the region, among which we have already mentioned the fact that by the 1950s or 1960s all Middle Eastern countries were independent[82] and were almost masters of their fate. 'Almost' because the context of the Cold War contributed to the creation of praetorian regimes, whose credentials were a combination of military rule with populist nationalist ideologies striving for a forced secularised modernisation (US or Soviet style) (Halliday 2005). Most regimes ('monarchical presidencies', in Owen's [2004] mocking words) were anything but democratic, thus contributing to the radicalisation of the Islamist leaders under forced modernisation plans where little space was left for religion in the political sphere.

But the most important political factor giving indirect support to Islamist ideologies was the 1967 defeat by Israel. The Six-Day War represented a shock defeat and 'a moral blow to Muslim self-confidence' (Owen 2004: 156). Many intellectuals perceived this *naksa* ('setback' in Arabic) as the 'religious victory' of Israel and as a sign for Muslims that they *had* to make religion the central pillar in politics. Among Jews, many also imagined this victory as a religious one. For instance, it is from this moment on that religious groups calling for the creation of Jewish settlements inside the Occupied territories emerged (such as 'Gush Emunim').

81 For an analysis of how the notion of a clash of civilisations functions as a political myth that encapsulates the idea of a society of the spectacle à la Debord, see Bottici and Challand 2010.
82 Except a few spots in the Arabic Peninsula.

Religion thus progressively became the site for the political struggle for imagination. In doing so, it occupied the imaginary space left empty by what I like to call the 'passing of dominant ideologies'. Pan-Arabism failed to produce one Arab kingdom/state during the Great Arab Revolt (1916–18); it was substituted by sub-nationalisms inside newly independent states and also failed to impose a regional alignment free of external domination; it was then replaced by socialist/communist/modernist ideologies. All of these ideologies failed to deliver fruits to the majority of the populations of the Middle East which remained disenfranchised and left out without a say in politics. This popular discontent created a bed for popular opposition and challenge of Islamism from the 1980s onwards (Halliday 2005: 193–228). The Islamic revolution in Iran (1978/79 – a partial vengeance for the US- and UK-supported coup against Mossadegh in 1953), the ('infidel') Soviet invasion of Afghanistan (1979) and the unsettled dispute between Israel and Palestine (the two *intifadas* 1987–1993 and 2000-present day) set further aflame the political imagination of Muslims in the Middle East in search of a local leadership that would not betray their struggle as other Muslim leaders had done so far.

Imagination, to conclude on this point, is central for four reasons. First, Islamism taps into a culturally widespread reservoir of symbols and benefits from the fact that, even in dictatorial regimes, there is absolute monopoly by the states on religious discourses; this provided them with the means for influencing decisively the struggle for people's imagination. Second, the fact that this ideology draws on culturally shared religious repertoires means that it can appear as morally sanctified and presented as morally just (LeVine and Salvatore 2005). Third, this latter element is reinforced by the fact that Islamists appear as a credible and operational alternative to dysfunctional states, especially at the micro level and in remote places, where their network of charities provide food and basic services that no other secular NGOs offer (Challand 2008). By providing basic fundamental services to the most impoverished populations, they nourish the image of a morally sanctified and efficient political alternative: by nourishing the stomach they also provide food for political imagination. Finally, as already mentioned, except for the more recent global jihadi aimed at destroying the 'far enemy', i.e., the USA and the Occident at large (Gerges 2009: 1–15) after a change in the meaning of 'jihad', most Islamist movements have adapted their programmes to the prerequisites of nationalism with its powerful symbolic and imaginary reservoir and are all entrapped in a logic that aims at reproducing the modern states' attributes in their battle against local despots, i.e., the 'near enemy' to rely on Gerges' distinction.[83]

All four reasons converge to make Islam 'a label used to convey mundane social grievances' (Tripp, 1996: 51) thus contributing to transform Islam, the faith, into Islamism, the political ideology that we have tried to describe.

83 See also Abaza and Stauth 1990.

3. The externalisation of religion in a post-foundational setting

The rise of Muslim politics brought about a blurring of the lines between religious and political. Both the ruling regimes of the Middle East that, in order to undercut Islamist opposition (of all kinds), have contributed to its resurgence and to the creation of this political ideology and Islamist themselves have contributed to *externalise* religion, denaturing it and placing it at the level of political ideology.

By *externalisation* of religion, we mean a complex process by which 'religion' (Islam) is increasingly invoked and instrumentalised by lay institutions and secular governing bodies outside of previous places of worship and transmission (mosques, religious schools). Through this instrumentalisation by governing bodies, 'religion' and religious references become increasingly mingled with straightforward political agendas.

Externalisation also serves to denote the fact that Islamist politics is not the prerogative of clerics or religious scholars; it is mostly laypeople who have shouldered the task of (re-)Islamising the *ummah*. The two heads of al-Qaeda, Bin Laden (an entrepreneur) and Al-Zawahiri (a surgeon) are prime illustrations of this transformation of laypeople into religious leaders.[84] Through the transformation of political imagination triggered by the new media, each individual Muslim is ideologically equipped as a potential contender against the representatives of the dominant 'infidel' (*kufr*) regimes (be it the near enemy in the Middle East, or the far enemy [Gerges 2009] in the 'first world').

Examples of this externalisation process include Egypt, where Sadat playing with religious motives was killed by Islamist opponents; Palestine, where the mainstream nationalist party, Fatah, which had always declared its will to create a *secular* state in Palestine, also tried to upgrade its religious profile, introducing in the late 1990s gradual references to the *shari'a* in the project of a Palestinian constitution (Legrain 2001) and has been eventually defeated by the Islamist party Hamas; or Algeria, where the religious identity used as a marker against the former colonial power became a rallying cry for the Islamic opposition in the 1980s and 1990s.

To conclude, Islamism even though it is for many 'an apparent retreat from modernity' or the essence of traditionalism is fundamentally a modern phenomenon (Tripp 1996; Utvik 2003; Zubaida 1993: ix). This is not only due to the fact that the Islamists fight for the control of modern states so that their struggle is unconceivable outside modern states or that they use up-to-date technological

84 Another illustration of this shift is Sayid Qutb (d. 1966) who received a lay education but contributed like no other Islamists to the redeployment of Islam onto a Manichean political vision in which his new definitions of *jihad*, *jahiliya*, or *hakimiyyah* (Haddad 1983: 83–90), far from being accepted by established Muslim clerics, became the new gold standard for Islamist activism.

means to propagate their own views. It is also due to the fact that such a process of externalisation presupposes the experience of the modern image of a secular polity, where politics and religion are completely separated. As we have seen, this is not true anymore (admitting it has ever been the case) and religion has returned to prominence in the political imaginary. This, however, happened *not in the form of its pre-secularisation configuration*, because religion is now contended by all sorts of actors, religious and non-religious alike. In the pre-secularisation setting of Islam, scriptures, interpretation and *ijtihad* (legal reasoning) was the unique domain of religious clerics and not of the laypeople. Moreover, the religious courts coexisted with as much power as proto-state legal courts. With the secularisation drive, there was a clear hierarchy of courts where secular ones had gained the upper hand.[85] Now, in a post-secular condition we are in a totally different setting where 'religion' and its ideological avatar (Islamism) have to be studied under a different analytical prism. In the last part of this work, we will suggest an alternative one, that of the double heteronomy, which accompanied situations of externalisation of religion.

4. Towards a double heteronomy?

One classical tool for the critique of religion has been the category of alienation. Most notably, Feuerbach criticised religion because it 'presents imagined beings as real beings' (Friese 2001: 7197). It is a form of alienation because human beings invented God in their image: they conferred to God, i.e., to an Other (alien) their own essential properties.[86] Religion is, therefore, nothing other than the self-consciousness of man (sic): 'religion, at least the Christian religion, is the expression of how man relates to himself, or more correctly, to his essential being; but he relates to his essential being as to another being' (Feuerbach 1972: 110). By projecting all his essential features onto an Other, human beings also attribute to him their capacity for autonomy: 'Religion is the essential being of man in his infancy' (ibid.: 111).

For Castoriadis, another critic of religion, all monotheistic religions are hostile to the autonomy of the society that sustains them. In his view, in order for a society to be autonomous (and thus not alienated, in Marxian/ Feuerbachian terminology), it needs to have the capacity for auto-institution. Auto-institution and autonomy imply not only the faculty of choosing their own laws (Castoriadis 1986: 518), but also the capacity to *openly* 'call into question their own institution, their representation of the world, their social imaginary significations' (Castoriadis 1997: 17).

Closure and openness are key for Castoriadis' understanding of autonomy (envisaged as a radical project): closure means here the fact that a given society

85 With the exclusion of overtly religious states such as the Islamic Republic of Iran or Saudia Arabia.

86 On religion as a conflicting relation between *ego–alter–Alter*, see Salvatore in this volume.

does not have possibilities to choose the ways and means in which they reflect about themselves. Closure implies heteronomy, i.e., the law of others imposed on this society. By contrast, openness is important not only in terms of choosing its institutional setting but also on an 'informational and cognitive' level (Castoriadis 1986: 513).

Castoriadis sees in monotheistic religion the prime example of closure at the level of language, interpretation of the dogmas and institutions. Religion negates the radical imaginary (it cannot question its origin) and creates its own imaginary, outside society (Castoriadis 1986: 474–477). Religion implies an instituted and heteronomous society, a society that does not recognise itself as its own product because it puts its own origins in an extra-social omnipotent being.

At the foundation of the monotheist religions, 'religion [was] the human enterprise by which a sacred cosmos [was] established. [. . .] Religion is cosmization in a sacred mode' (Berger 1990: 25) and this sacralisation hinders the possibility of questioning not only the origins of scriptures but also the very *origin* of this religious community which is given at once without possible discussion.[87] For instance, the invention of a distinct Christian textual tradition by the founding fathers of the church implies the creation of dogmas, by manipulating texts, and the opposition between true and apocryphal texts. Once the canon is set, it is impossible to re-discuss it. In the best scenario it can be interpreted, but as Castoriadis points out interpretations and commentaries are simply a means for apparently changing things without altering the substance of the text. Similarly the Qur'an is the word of God and cannot be changed or translated like the Table of Laws given to Moses, which cannot even be discussed.

Furthermore, once they had been institutionalised, the three monotheistic religions gave rise to new hierarchies that made the possibility of autonomy even harder. In all this, imagination played a central role: by controlling the means for the interpretations of the Word of God and therefore also of the world, (male) religious hierarchies are in the position of winning from the beginning the struggle for people's imagination.

Castoriadis' discussion of the possibility of an autonomous society in the face of the power of religion is an important step in the critique of religion. This is particularly due to his emphasis on the concept of autonomy/heteronomy. Still, his own critical apparatus, together with earlier critiques of religion in term of alienation, work at best for the monotheistic religions in a pre-modern setting. Today, to set up a critique of religion as a site for the politics of imagination, categories such as those of alienation and heteronomy

87 The issue of the origins is a burning question not only for Islamists (and the belief that an Islamic state ought to be copied on the model of the first four caliphs – the so-called 'Rashidun'). Recent American attempts to outlaw Darwinism from public school is nothing but the same kind of debate.

have only a limited value. In the first place, they are inadequate when used in a post-secularisation setting, because people living in such conditions have had the experience of imagining themselves as secular. In the second place, both Feuerbach and Castoriadis tend to represent the politics of imagination in a one-directional way and do not emphasise enough the *struggle* that actually takes place around it.

Let us illustrate the two points by going back to our discussion of Islamism and the externalisation of religion. Here the problem is not simply that of autonomy: currently Muslims face the danger of a sort of double heteronomy. A simple heteronomy would be the situation described by Castoriadis (or the case of alienation): (wo)mankind put its trust into a supranatural, supra-human being, its fate; religion then decides for them on matters of life and death, without the possibility of questioning the religious laws and the cognitive means to do so. In contrast, in a post-secularisation setting one faces a double heteronomy because this mechanism is externalised onto the sphere of politics and religion becomes instrumentalised by the secular institutions of the modern state. This re-appropriation by secular state institutions and lay politicians is a further form of heteronomy, one that strips religious institutions of the capacity to define and interpret their own religion.[88] Not only have issues of faith, death or life, slipped out of the hands of human beings (after having alienated themselves to religion), but now, with this externalisation process, these issues have increasingly mingled with majority politics and are in another type of hands, namely those of politicians and governing institutions.

There is therefore potentially a double imposition (which, in turn, represents a double heteronomy)[89] of religion on the population at large (religious and secular/atheist alike): to a first imposition of dogmas by religious hierarchies is now added a new imposition of religious logics en bloc by politicians on societies that had before experienced (or at least imagined) themselves as secular. In the first layer, one faces a problem related to *religion* and individual faith, while in the second, the problem is a *political* one since it is a question of ideologies, of claims for truth but also direct relation of power.

In the second place, both Feuerbach's and Castoriadis' critiques of religion are too straightforward. For instance, it would be tempting to frame the externalisation process described in terms of rejection of modernity. This is

88 For example, Bin Laden's call for a global jihad was denounced by one of the most senior Shiite clerics and the late spiritual founder of Hizbollah, Sheykh Mohammed Hussein Fadlallah (d. 2010). See http://news.bbc.co.uk/2/hi/world/middle_east/10501084.stm (accessed 7 July 2010). Fadlallah considered al-Qaeda simply a non-Muslim sect.

89 Olivier Roy in his influential *Failure of Political Islam* also captures the trap of a double heteronomy, although without referring to this notion. See, for example, his quote according to which there are 'happy Muslims' but only 'unhappy Islamists' (198) or when he states, in his concluding sentence, that 'neofundamentalism is seeking its devil in a different god, but does not see the desert within' (Roy 1994: 2003).

very risky, because of inbuilt ethnocentrism which is duplicated in the very discourse and intellectual apparatus of most scholars of modernity. Categories of 'modern' and 'traditional' are very fluid and all depend on the position of the researcher or of the agenda underlying the sociological questioning (Balandier 1981: 115). Moreover, what is easily dubbed as 'traditional(ist)' in the case of Islam can be indeed very modern.[90] We are back to the question of what role the entwinements of social categories ('modernity', 'secularism') with the foundational roles of Others (Islam, savages, Indians, etc.) have played in the shaping of such categories.

Religion is the site for the struggle for people's imagination whose result cannot be established a priori. A more promising approach is therefore to reflect on the general condition in which the ideology of Islamism has emanated and which has made the externalisation of religion possible. What are the keys for Islamist success? How did they win their struggle? A striking element, both in the discourse of many Islamists and of scholars of Islamism, is the representation of the threat of cultural anomie.[91]

In the case of Mawdudi, one of the founding fathers of Islamism, it was the encounter with secularisation that represented a thorough challenge not only to Muslim society but to its theological foundation, thus demanding the elaboration of new concepts. Later on, after the 1967 defeat, Islamism was made possible because of the representation of a state of confusion in the Arab and Muslim world(s), confusion explained by the false adherence to modern secular order. Nowadays, and to illustrate the contribution by governments of Muslim-majority polities to instrumentalise (and therefore externalise) religion, these governments often justify the re-Islamisation of the political sphere in terms of the challenge of globalisation, the imposition of democratisation (when not outright military intervention) by the 'west' in their sphere of action (Béji 2008). In all three cases, the key has been the *representation* of a lack of internal order, a lack of *nomos* that the resort to Islam(ism) should help palliate.

It seems indeed that the externalisation of religion described here happens when influential groups/people manage to project the threat of a cultural anomie in the collective imagination. Note that this does not mean that there is actually a real situation of cultural anomie, but the struggle over people's imagination makes this fact appear as a reality. All this, as we have mentioned before, has been further exacerbated by the new media. One only has to think of the struggle for imagination that takes place when millions of images enter billions of houses around the globe every day.

90 Deeb 2006 on 'an enchanted modern' is a case in point. See also Euben 1999.

91 By anomie, I mean an 'absence, breakdown, confusion, or conflict in the norms of a society' (Scott and Marshall 2005).

5. Conclusion: a lesson for our post-modern Europe?

According to the classical secularisation thesis, in a disenchanted and modern world, religion has been neutralised. The secular regimes existing in most western European countries are the results of long historical battles to keep national churches at bay from politics. The rational-bureaucratic *Amt* should definitely have replaced priesthood.

Still, as many authors have pointed out, the thesis of secularisation as the privatisation of faith is attacked by many (Berger 1999; Casanova 1994). Admitting that there has ever been something like a real secularisation process, we are presently witnessing a worldwide return to religion. And some recent developments about religion in Europe seem to indicate a sort of convergence in terms of the political *problématique* of religions in Europe with that of the Middle East. One of the challenges this return poses is analytical and has to do with the critique of religions.

I argued elsewhere (Challand 2007) that in Europe a post-modern condition has gradually ushered in a legal subjectivity prone to cultural and religious particularisms. This has, in turn, prepared the bed for a return to the 'religious' as one of the most salient features of political identity. This shift can be seen in some decisions by the European Court of Human Rights, which increasingly has to make legally binding decisions regarding religious rights. It has also made decisions that acknowledge that legitimate claims for religious particularisms be recognised officially within Europe (Ringelheim 2006). As a result, European states might feel challenged in their biased version of secularism. The tendency to resort to Christian principles in politics is growing, when one thinks about the debate on the Christian roots of Europe, the religious ethical principles invoked in cases of 'body politics' (abortion, rights over life and death), the French law banning religious symbols, the recently adopted law in Romania about the cultural heritage of religion in the political system and the many intrusions of Pope Ratzinger into the sphere of politics. All of these let us conclude that what we are confronted with now in Europe is a tendency to *re-territorialise* the dominant (Christian) religion with political and legal claims.

Is Europe also facing a process of externalisation of religion? How to conceptualise it? Castoriadis' equation of religion with straightforward heteronomy is at best valid only in a historical perspective, or, indeed, for the foundational and pre-modern moments of religions. In this type of development, the 'essence of religion' was to 'link together the origin of the world to the origin of society, but also to the significance of being and to the being of significance' (Castoriadis 1986: 463). In a post-modern setting, the secular arrangement and modern rationality have put an end to religion's monopoly of explanations about origins, about the institution of society, etc., so that the inherited social imaginaries contain more possibilities than in the past. Darwin is part of this and cannot so easily be eliminated (although some are thinking about it). Today more than ever religion is the site of a *struggle* for people's imagination. And the logic of formally imposing again some religious reasoning into public laws in Europe would be similar to the double heteronomy taking place in parts of the Middle East and described here – a significant setback in the history of modern politics, in our view.

References

Abaza, M. and Stauth, G. 1990, 'Occidental reason, Orientalism, Islamic fundamentalism; a critique', in Albrow, M. and King, E.M. (eds) *Globalization, Knowledge and Society*, London, Sage, pp. 209–230.

Anderson, B. 1983, *Imagined Communities: Reflections on the Origins and Spread of Nationalism*, London, Verso.

Arjomand, S. 2010, 'Islamic resurgence and its aftermath', in *New Cambridge History of Islam*, Cambridge, Cambridge University Press, vol. 6.

Asad, T. 2003, *Formations of the Secular. Christianity, Islam, Modernity*, Stanford, Stanford University Press.

Assmann, J. 2000, *Herrschaft und Heil: politische Theologie in Altaegypten, Israel und Europa*, Munich, C. Hanser.

Ayubi, N. 1991, *Political Islam. Religion and Politics in the Arab World*, London, Routledge.

Balandier, G. 1981, *Sens et puissance. Les dynamiques sociales*, Paris, Quadrige, PUF.

Béji H. 2008, *Nous, décolonisés*, Paris, Arléa.

Benjamin, W. 1986, *Reflections: Essays, Aphorisms, Autobiographical Writing* (trans. E. Jephcott) New York, Schocken Books.

Berger, P.L. 1990, *The Sacred Canopy. Elements of a Sociological Theory of Religion*, New York, Anchor Books.

—— 1999, 'The desecularization of the world: resurgent religion and world politics', Washington, DC, Ethics and Public Policy Center (in coll. W.B. Eerdmans).

Bottici, C. and Challand, B. 2010, *The Myth of the Clash of Civilizations*, London, Routledge.

Bracke, S. and Fadil, N. 2008, *Islam and Secular Modernity under Western Eyes: A Genealogy of a Constitutive Relationship*, Working Paper 2008/05, Robert Schuman Centre, Florence, European University Institute.

Buck-Morss, S. 2003, *Thinking Past Terror. Islamism and Critical Theory on the Left*, London, New York, Verso.

Casanova, J. 1994, *Public Religions in the Modern World*, Chicago, University of Chicago Press.

Castoriadis, C. 1986, *Domaines de l'homme. Les carrefours du labyrinthe*, Paris: Seuil.

—— 1997, *Worlds in Fragments. Writings on Politics, Society, Psychoanalysis, and the Imagination*, Stanford, Stanford University Press.

Challand, B. 2007, 'I paradossi del rapporto tra religione e territorio in un mondo post moderno', in Squarcini, F. (ed.) *Topografie della santità. Terre sante, simbolizzazione religiose dei confini e geografia politica delle religioni*, Firenze, Kykeion, pp. 227– 240.

—— 2008, 'A *Nahda* of charitable organizations? Health service provision and the politics of aid in Palestine', *International Journal of Middle East Studies*, 40 (2): 227–247.

De Vries, H. and Sullivan, L.E. (eds) 2006, *Political Theologies. Public Religions in A Post-Secular World*, New York, Fordham University Press.

Deeb, L. 2006, *An Enchanted Modern. Gender and Public Piety in Shi'i Lebanon*, Princeton, Oxford, Princeton University Press.

Eickelman, D.F. and Piscatori, J. 1996, *Muslim Politics*, Princeton, Princeton University Press.

Esposito, J.L. 2003, *Oxford Dictionary of Islam*, Oxford, Oxford University Press.

Euben, R. 1999, *Enemy in the Mirror. Islamic Fundamentalism and the Limits of Modern Rationalism*, Princeton, Princeton University Press.

Feuerbach, L. 1972, *The Fiery Brook: Selected Writings of Ludwig Feuerbach*, Garden City, NY, Anchor Books.

Filali-Ansary, A. 2002, *L'Islam est-il hostile à la laïcité?*, Arles, Actes Sud.

Friese, H. 2001, 'Imagination: history of the concept', in Smelser, N.J.B. and Paul, B. (eds) *International Encyclopedia of the Social & Behavioral Sciences*, Oxford, New York, Elsevier, pp. 7197–7201.

Gauchet, M. 2005, *La condition historique. Entretiens avec François Azouvi et Sylvain Piron*, Paris, folio essais.

Gerges, F. 2009, *The Far Enemy. Why Jihad Went Global* (2nd edn), New York, Cambridge University Press.

Ghalioun, B., Bisharah, A., Giacaman, G. and Zadani, S.I. 1993, *Hawla al-khiyar al dimuqratii. Dirasaat naqdiyah {On the Democratic Option. Critical Studies}*, Ramallah, MUWATIN (Palestinian Institute for the Study of Democracy).

Haddad, Y. 1983, 'Sayyid Qutb: ideologue of Islamic revival', in Esposito, J. *Voices of Resurgent Islam*, Oxford, Oxford University Press, pp. 67–98.

Halliday, F. 2005, *The Middle East in International Relations: Power, Politics and Ideology*, Cambridge, New York, Cambridge University Press.

Hartog, F. 2005, *Anciens, modernes, sauvages*, Paris, Galaade.

Jones, C. 2003, 'Ideology', in McLean, I.M. (ed.) *The Concise Oxford Dictionary of Politics* (Oxford Reference Online), Oxford, Oxford University Press.

Karam, A. 2004, *Transnational Political Islam. Religion, Ideology and Power*, London, Pluto Press.

Kepel, G. and Milelli, J.-P. (eds) 2008, *Al Qaeda in its Own Words*, Cambridge, MA, Belknap Press.

Laroui, A. 1987, *Islam et modernité*, Paris, La Découverte.

Lefort, C. 1986, *Essais sur le politique: XIXe-XXe siècles*, Paris, Éditions du Seuil.

Legrain, J.-F. 2001, 'Vers une Palestine islamique', *L'Arabisant*, 35: 72–88.

LeVine, M. and Salvatore, A. 2005, *Religion, Social Practice, and Contested Hegemonies. Reconstructing the Public Sphere in Muslim Majority Societies*, New York, Palgrave Macmillan.

Masud, M.K. 2005, 'The construction and deconstruction of secularism as an ideology', *Asian Journal of Social Science*, 33 (3): 363–383.

Owen, R. 2004, *State, Power and Politics in the Making of the Modern Middle East*, London, New York, Routledge.

Pagden, A. (ed.) 2000, *Facing Each Other: The World's Perception of Europe and Europe's Perception of the World*, Aldershot, Ashgate.

Ringelheim, J. 2006, *Diversité culturelle et droits de l'homme: l'émergence de la problématique des minorités dans le droit de la Convention européenne des droits de l'homme*, Brussels, Bruylant.

Roy, O. 1994, *The Failure of Political Islam*, Cambridge, MA, Harvard University Press.

Sadowski Y. 1993, 'The new Orientalism and the democracy debate', *Middle East Report (MERIP)*, July–August: 14–21.

Said, E. 1978, *Orientalism*, London, Routledge.

Scott, J. and Marshall, G. 2005, *A Dictionary of Sociology*, Oxford, Oxford University Press.

Smith, C.D. 1995, 'Secularism', in Esposito, J.L. (ed.) *The Oxford Encyclopedia of the Modern Islamic World*, Oxford, Oxford University Press, pp. 20–30.

Stauth, G. 1993, *Islam und Westlicher Rationalismus. Der Beitrag des Orientalismus zur Entstehung der Soziologie*, Frankfurt, Campus.

Tripp, C. 1996, 'Islam and the secular logic of the state in the Middle East', in Sidahmed, A.S. and Ehteshami, A. (eds) *Islamic Fundamentalism*, Boulder, CO, Westview Press.

Ungureanu, C. 2008, 'The contested relationship between democracy and religion: towards a European dialogical model', *European Journal of Political Theory*, 7 (4): 405–429.

Utvik, B.O. 2003, 'The modernizing force of Islamism', in Esposito, J.L. and Burgat, F. (eds) *Modernizing Islam. Religion in the Public Sphere in Europe and the Middle East*, London, Hurst & Company.

Zubaida, S. 1993, *Islam, the People and the State. Political Ideas and Movements in the Middle-East*, London, I.B. Tauris.

Chapter 9

Modern politics and the historical imaginary

Hayden White

> History does not break down into stories, it breaks down into images.
>
> Walter Benjamin, *On the Concept of History*

We are asked to consider the relation between politics and the imagination, or, to put it more precisely, politics as a struggle for the imagination. In this chapter, I want to consider the extent to which history, considered as both a mode of being in the world and as a kind of knowledge about the world, has been used in that struggle. Let me say at the outset that I regard the study of history or indeed any inquiry into the past as primarily an imaginative enterprise. Bachelard once said that we can study only that which we have first dreamed about. This may or may not be true or may be true of some things and not of others. In any event, insofar as dreaming belongs to the imagination much more than to the rational faculty, Bachelard is telling us something important about the relation between certain kinds of knowledge (or knowledge production) and certain kinds of objects of knowledge.

Historical knowledge or knowledge of history has to do with a domain of existence—the past—which must be imagined before it can become an object of knowledge. For—obviously—one cannot perceive past things directly or invest them immediately as possible objects of rational cognition. They first must be conjured up as *possible* objects of knowledge. Historians conjure up images of possible objects of study by reading both the work of other historians and/or documents relating to a particular time and place where possible "historical" events may have occurred. This means that one must have some general idea of "historicality" by which to identify or distinguish a specifically historical event from other kinds of event or thing.[92]

Not all events of the past are historical in kind. Indeed, most of the events of the past would not qualify as historical at all. Unless, that is, the concept of event is applicable only to the kinds of occurrence that appear to be something

92 See White 2008.

other than "natural." In fact, it is not at all clear that the concept of event has any necessary function in the classification of natural or physical processes. There once was a time when all the things we call events—natural, cultural, supernatural—were thought to be effects of the actions of supernatural beings or forces. Then, when agency was imputed to human beings, natural events consisted of all of those occurrences apprehendible by human beings but not attributable to human causes.

1. Narrative and the politics of history

In the 19th century it was a commonplace widely honored which held that "history was past politics" and that "history" itself—the mode of existence and the consciousness of this mode of existence—came to birth only with the invention of the state (the Greek *polis*) and the apparatus of recordkeeping, discipline, and control needed for the maintenance of the state. This was Hegel's view, at least. But even in the 20th century Arendt and Heidegger held that "history" and "politics" were born on the site (*Stätte*) of the Greek *polis*. Arendt especially came to view history as an alternative to politics, a contemplative domain in which the more activist impulses of politics could be avoided. But Hegel and later Arendt (in *The Human Condition*) added a third component to the history–politics connection, and this was narrative, considered by Hegel to be the discursive mode best suited to the representation of that reality made possible by the discovery of the relationship between history and politics.

Now, the belief that narrative is the discursive form adequate to (indeed, necessary for) the representation of the dynamics of the relationship between politics, on the one side, and history, on the other, reveals something about the imaginary nature of the history–politics nexus. It is no secret that narrative is a mode and a form common, not only to the literary genres of epic, fable, romance, and legend, but also to dream, delusion and myth. In other words, narrative is the mode and the form in which desire, in the genres of the adventure, the quest, and the test or *agon* reaches discourse as wish-fulfillment fantasy. As thus envisaged, narrative is not only a possible container of a more basic substance or meaning, but is a meaning-substance in its own right, what Frank Ankersmit memorably called a "narrative substance," a model, paradigm, or structure of temporal coherence (Ankersmit 1995: 223). Narrative can show how beginnings eventuate in endings consonant with them or, conversely, how an event apprehended as an eruption from the depths of being can be provided with a genealogy that authorized its occurrence early on. The relationship of "before and after" has been recognized as an ontologically significant categoreme since Aristotle and as a ground on which the adequacy of the narrative form to historical process can be presupposed. "Once upon a time" is common to both folklore and historical consciousness.

But every narrative account of anything whatsoever must posit the before and after nexus as a matrix for arranging what would otherwise be only a *series* of events into a *sequence*. Narrativization of a series of real events makes beginnings, middles, and endings out of what would otherwise remain only "one damned thing after another."[93] It endows events with meaning by distributing them into the past–present–future of the general past. The psychological effect of narrative is to dramatize social, cultural, or personal processes by endowing them with the aspect of the dominant meaning-producing systems in a given community or group. In that Greek culture in which "history" was first performed or recited (by Herodotus, even before it was conceptualized), myth, drama, philosophy, and medicine provided different paradigmatic scenarios that could be used to emplot events and identify agents and agencies adequate to the social purposes of historiography.

History is, of course, something quite other than "the past." It presumes a crucial relationship between the past and the present and, more specifically, the notion that every present (including that in which the historian is operating) is at once a fulfillment of a past and the prefiguration (or anticipation) of a future that is latent in it. It is commonly thought that Hegel's notion of the future is teleological, and so it is insofar as Hegel posits an end to history that is both necessary and inevitable. But it is commonly overlooked or, if perceived, not sufficiently stressed, that the end Hegel postulates is more like the end of a story than the end of an argument or a deduction. That is to say, like the end of a story, the end of history is not knowable from within any place in the sequence of events and actions that make up the literal or manifest level of a series of historical occurrences. That history must have an end, Hegel doubted not at all. That we might be able to grasp the *general* nature of this end, he believed for good reasons. That we might be able to discern where and when it would end, he held to be a nonsensical illusion. Narrative was the mode of discourse best suited to the presentation (*Darstellung*) of the "poetry" in "the prose of the world" which was to say, the creativity in the work of destruction carried out at the "slaughter bench" of history.

Hegel originally coined the phrase "die Prosa der Welt" to characterize the Roman state and to distinguish it from its more "poetic"—by which Hegel meant brilliant, idealistic, evanescent, and short lived—Hellenic counterpart, the Athenian *polis*. Rome represented a politics different in kind from that of Hellas by virtue of its practicality, rusticity, literal mindedness, and, above all, success in expanding in space and perduring in time while, unlike China and India, providing a place for the personal lives of individuals and families alongside the public life of assemblies, armies, and rulers. The poet Petrarca

93 "Life is just one damned thing after another" is attributed to the American sage and homespun philosopher, Elbert Hubbard (d. 1915). The phrase has been adapted by a number of thinkers to describe the effect of a merely chronological ordering of historical facts, that is to say, facts without a narrativization.

would later say: "What else then is all history, but the praise of Rome," thereby indicating the appeal of Rome (the *translatio imperii*) to the "imaginary" of every subsequent polity in the west.[94] The political past of Europe, Hegel (1975: 374) maintains, takes its rise not in Greece but in Rome:

> [The] extreme prose of the spirit we find in Etruscan art, which though technically perfect and so far true to nature, has nothing of Greek Ideality and Beauty: we also observe it in the development of Roman Law and the Roman religion.

As thus envisaged, the political imagination of Europe has its object of interest in Rome. The space of the political imagination is infinite in extent, its time endless, and the whole governed by a law that protects both the community and the citizen from an all-devouring *Fatum*.[95]

Rome was the Fate that crushed the gods and all genial life in its hard service, while it was the power that purified the human heart from all speciality. The political past per se is Rome and only Rome because Rome is the secular principle par excellence. Its story provides the plot of every political story that follows afterward, "before" is to the rise of the polity as "after" is to its fall. This pattern of rise and fall is what political history or the history of politics is all about; it is political history's primal scene. This primal scene is sublimated and domesticated by being narrativized, by being made into a story which not only renders what happens on that scene comprehendible but also in the process assigns a value to it.

But how does narrative, which, by common consensus, is only a form of discourse that can be filled with any content, assign a value to that which it contains?

The conventional answer to this question is that the process of narrativization transforms what would otherwise be a series of events into a story, a sequence of events which assigns events different plot functions (for example, beginning, middle, end) but also provides connections between the plot elements so as to produce an explanation (or at least an explanation effect) by the endowment of endings with teleological force (which is rather like saying that the ending of a story explains by being presented as the *telos* latent in the story all along). But narrativization does more than that to a set of events construed as a field of action about which a story can be told. Narrativization dramatizes events, the individuals involved in them, and the kinds of conflict

94 Petraraca quoted in Kolb 1974: 134.

95 Hegel speaks of "the universal *Fatum* of the Roman world" (ibid.: 413) as what must be overcome (*aufgehoben*) in Christianity which, thus understood, is the vision of that liberation from "history" (cf. ibid.: 419) of which St Augustine is the theorist.

that can appear in them. Narrative presupposes a scene (chronotopically organized) in which certain kinds of character can appear, certain kinds of event can happen, certain kinds of act are possible.

Narrativization, moreover, presupposes a limited array of possible scenarios for the emplotment of what can happen in that scene. In the west, there are a limited number of scenarios for the emplotment of sets of events: epic, tragedy, comedy, pastoral, farce, and so on. In other words, narrativization provides a frame for a field of events (real or imaginary or both) which, by means of thematization, sets limits on what can possibly happen in that scene and what can possibly be said and thought about it. By thematization, narrative systematically posits a domain of possibility, on the one hand, and excludes or forecloses certain other possibilities of what can be said about the phenomena being represented, on the other.

Hegel recognized that the professional (or scientific) study of the past must educe more time anxiety and concern (*Sorge*) than it did pride in and satisfaction with human achievement. In fact, it was precisely the scientific study of the past which, because of the image of disconnection and incoherence that it inevitably produced, inspired a kind of horror of it. Thus, in the Introduction to his *Lectures on the Philosophy of History*, Hegel (or his editor) writes that a merely factual account of the events of the past present a picture of fearful aspect because the individuality of historical phenomena does not lend itself to transcendental summation or synthesis. When we cast a glance back over the spectacle of "human passions" which history presents to us, and "observe the consequences of their violence, the unreason that is associated not only with them, but even—rather, we might say *especially*—with *good* intentions and righteous aims; when we see arising from them all the evil, the wickedness, the decline of the most flourishing nations mankind has produced, we can only be filled with grief for all that has come to nothing." Moreover, "since this decline and fall is not the work of mere nature but of the human will, our reflection may well lead us to moral sadness, a revolt of our good spirit (if there is a spirit of goodness in us)" (Hegel 1975: 65).

And this allows us to say, "without rhetorical exaggeration, that a *merely truthful* account of the miseries that have overwhelmed the noblest of nations and polities and the finest exemplars of private virtue forms a most fearful picture and excites emotions of the profoundest and most hopeless sadness, counter-balanced by no consoling outcome" (Hegel 1975: 66).

Hegel is here describing the moral or psychological effect of a merely factual account of the historical past, an account which must, if it be truthful, relate a story of universal ruin and desolation, productive at best of feelings of melancholy. In other words, Hegel regards the simply truthful account of the human past as nugatory. It gives lots of information, the information admits of no more general consideration, and its incoherency is depressing.

The human tendency, Hegel continues, is to "draw back into the vitality of the present, into our aims and interests of the moment" and to "retreat, in short, into the selfishness that stands on the quiet shore and thence enjoys in safety the distant spectacle of wreckage and confusion."[96]

Of course, Hegel does not himself fall into this condition of melancholy. On the contrary, he says, in the face of the image of such universal ruin and abjection, we cannot but ask what end or purpose this spectacle of destruction and ruin inevitably summons up before our minds? And proceeds to lay out his theodicy of history, which purports to demonstrate that this spectacle of unreason and folly secretly, latently, or implicitly figures forth the march of reason in the world and reason's grasping in consciousness of its own possibility and actuality. *It is at this point that Hegel moves from the discourse of the past imaginary to its investment by the symbolic system.* In calling his philosophy of history a *theodicaea*, Hegel openly signals the therapeutic purpose of sublimating the anxieties and care that the products of scientific historiography must arouse by any account of the past in "merely truthful" terms. Because, as Hegel indicates in his distinction among original, pragmatic, and critical historical thinking, scientific history cannot but come to the recognition of its own limitations as an aid to practical reason. "Nobody ever learned anything from the study of history," he says, "except that no one ever learned anything from the study of history." Here Hegel anticipates Foucault when the latter says that, quite apart from that history studied scientifically for which the 19th century is renowned, there was another history, a history of things that resisted coordination with the history of mankind. It is this other history, dominated by the law of entropy, which progressively overtakes and overrides the optimistic version of mankind's heroic production of itself. And it is this other history, which Nietzsche espied on the horizon of Europe's imperium and which authorized his own nihilism, that underwrote the nihilistic politics of the 20th century. Against this other history, which ultimately claimed the authority of Darwin as well as that of Sadi Carnot.

The explicit and self-styled science of history, which contributed to the establishment of the legitimacy of the nation-state, compiled its genealogical line of descent from its origins in the land and the people, and constructed the master narrative of its development over time, this history was accompanied by its metaphysical shadow, which destabilized the very effort to set limits on what could possibly be known about the past by inscribing change, destruction, and entropy into the foundations.

In modernity, of course, politology has taken a somewhat jaundiced view of history. Modern political economy, political science, sociology, and so on were constituted as "sciences" in part in terms of their abandonment of the historicist way of thinking about politics. So in one sense, political philosophy, theory, or speculation can be broken down into two kinds: that which regards history as fundamental to an understanding of politics and the political and

96 Hegel 1986: 34–35.

that which regards history and historiology as irrelevant to an analysis and comprehension of the political per se.

Here Foucault's work may be taken as exemplary of the most advanced thought on this issue. His *Les mots et les choses* culminates in a discussion of the role and function of history among the human and social sciences. First of all, he dismisses the conventional view of a fundamental conflict between the scientific history of the early 19th century and the grand philosophies of history of Hegel, Comte, Marx, Spencer, Spengler, and so on. Foucault insisted that these two enterprises, far from indicating a belief in and reverence for the past, actually manifested a deep anxiety about a present that had become unanchored from every religious and metaphysical foundation and now floated in those "infinite spaces" that had so agonized Pascal. By the end of the18th century, Foucault maintains, it had been discovered that:

> [T]here existed a historicity proper to nature; forms of adaptation to the environment were defined for each broad type of living being, which would make possible a subsequent definition of its evolutionary outline; moreover, it became possible to show that activities as peculiarly human as labor or language contained within themselves a historicity that could not be placed within the great narrative common to things and men.
>
> (Foucault 1970: 367)

And the result of the historization of the cosmos in all its parts was that "the whole lyrical halo that surrounds the consciousness of history [in the early 19th century], the lively curiosity shown for documents or for traces left behind by time—all this is surface expression of the simple fact that man found himself emptied of history," that the "historical scholarship" focused on the hysterical collection of "facts about the past" was a manifestation of an effort to fill up a void that had suddenly opened out before men who had thought it possible to "make history," divine its future, control it and give it direction" (Foucault 1970: 368f.). This new history, this history behind or below or ahead of the manifestly "historical" data served up by scientific historians, is the *antitype* of a historical knowledge that had been meant to show time's and therefore man's fullness of being.

Thus Foucault concludes as follows:

> Obviously, [this] History . . . is not to be understood as the compilation of factual successions or sequences as they may have occurred; it is the fundamental mode of being of empiricities, upon the basis of which they are affirmed, posited, arranged, and distributed in the space of knowledge for the use of such disciplines or sciences as may arise . . . History, as we know, is certainly the most erudite, the most aware, the most conscious, and possibly the most cluttered area of our memory; but it is equally the

> depths from which all beings emerge into their precarious, glittering existence.
>
> (Foucault 1970: 219)

"[T]he emergence of history as both knowledge and the mode of being of empiricity" marks the advent of our modernity. The emergence can be dated: "the outer limits are the years 1775 and 1825" but there are two successive phases in this process of emergence. In the first of these phases, "men's riches, the species of nature, and the words with which languages are peopled, still remain what they were in the Classical age." They are subjected only to a reordering in the mode of temporality. "It is only in the second phase that words, classes [of things], and wealth will acquire a mode of being no longer compatible with that of representation" (ibid.: 221).

This leads Foucault to conclude some 150 pages later in his book:

> History constitutes, therefore, for the human sciences, a favorable environment which is both privileged and dangerous. To each of the sciences it offers a background, which establishes it and provides it with a fixed ground and, as it were, a homeland; it determines the cultural area—the chronological and geographical boundaries—in which that branch of knowledge can be recognized as having validity; but it also surrounds the sciences of man with a frontier that limits them and destroys them from the outset, their claim to validity within the element of universality. It reveals in this way that though man—even before knowing it—has always been subjected to the determinations that can be expressed by psychology, sociology, and the analysis of language, he is not therefore the intemporal object of knowledge which, at least at the level of its rights, must itself be thought of as ageless. Even when they avoid all reference to history, the human sciences (and history may be included among them) never do anything but relate one cultural episode to another (that to which they apply themselves as their object, and that in which their existence, their mode of being, their methods, and their concepts have their roots); they apply themselves to their own synchronology, they relate the cultural episode from which they emerged to itself. Man, therefore, never appears in his positivity and that positivity is not immediately limited by the limitlessness of History.
>
> (ibid.: 371)

Foucault's notion of a doubly articulated historicity provides a kind of equivalent of the psychoanalytic concept of psychic phenomena as possessing a surface-depth structure, not so much in the mode of a (logical) explicit–implicit relationship as, rather, a (tropological) manifest–latent relationship. This provides a way of comprehending how political discourse can invest the "imagination" of the multitude by techniques of "coaction" quite different from those used in traditional rhetorics to construct a secondary content that gives value or quality to what otherwise might appear only as fact or quantity.

Actually, history, historical knowledge, and historiology would seem to be relevant to the comprehension of political structures and processes only in the extent to which political groups and institutions might have an interest in establishing their own identities in *genealogical* terms, were committed to governance in accordance with tradition and precedent, or actually thought that the best way to approach current problems came by way of a comprehension of how peoples in earlier times had dealt with similar or analogous ones. Of course, the public appeal to history for models, examples, ideals, precedents, or alibis and exoneration presumes that knowledge about the past is quasi-scientific or at least is as "secure" as the kind of evidence brought by lawyers before courts of law. The fact that historical knowledge can be considered as "scientific" only in the most tenuous sense of the term or that the authority of legal evidence is commonsensical or conventionalist at best means that any appeal to the past itself must be cast in terms that engage not only the intellect but also other faculties as well, for example, the kind of faculty that is commonly called "the imagination" as well as that of the will and intellect.

2. Beyond imagination: imaginary, censorship, and the process of interpellation

But what could one possibly mean by the term "imagination" at this moment in "history"?

To consider politics in its aspect as participant in a struggle to engage, discipline, control, and educate (the) imagination requires a preliminary if only provisional specification of what we might mean by imagination, what or whose imagination is being invested, and what instruments of control are available at specific times and places in the history of political institutions for the exercise of that control. But put this way, we are immediately confronted by the curious fact that by the term "history" we do not indicate a clear and unambiguous referent. Are we speaking about "the past"? Whose or which past? Are we speaking about a process of development peculiar to certain peoples and geographical areas of the world and not to others, so that others will not be considered to have a history or to exist in history? Are we speaking in the manner of Hegel and Heidegger about a certain mode of being in the world, a mode of existence in which a people or group lives as if it were an agent of its own making, exercising a certain degree of freedom in this operation, and is capable of or fatally compelled to assume responsibility for its own identity? Moreover, it is a troubling fact that "history" or "historical consciousness" or "historical knowledge" has functioned more or less effectively over time as one of the instruments deployed by dominant social groups in the effort to "control the imagination" of the multitude or at least of elites destined to control the multitude—what American ideologues during the Cold War called "winning the hearts and minds" of men. Finally, we must address the troubling fact that the notion of "imagination" is strangely resistant to definitive analysis whether considered (1) as a faculty operating in the service of emotions, the will, or the reason or (2) as a zone or level of what Freud called the "perception-consciousness" system whereon the relation between soma and psyche is negotiated in the process of transforming instinctual impulses into drives (*Triebe*).[97]

In my view, this question was addressed most provocatively in the 1960s and after by Louis Althusser who, in his synthesis of Marxist and Lacanian thinking about ideology, elaborated the concept of "ideological state apparatuses" and focused on the process of "interpellation" as the device by which political regimes transformed individuals into "subjects" by inducing in them an "identity" or "subjectivity" that was not only "submissive" but which, at the same time, produced a sense of pride and self-esteem by the pleasure taken in the awareness of its own self-imposed submissiveness. For Althusser and his group, the question that concerns us regarding the politics of imagination centers on the relation between the notion of legality itself and the notion of what constitutes for the individual a proper identity. Law creates, as St. Paul wrote in "The epistle to the Romans" ("There is no sin before the law"), the conditions under which sin or immorality becomes possible. Where there is no law, there is no sin or crime. Where there is no law, there is neither "normal" nor "proper" human behavior. So it is the law which establishes the condition for distinguishing between the properly human and the non- or un-human. The problem, insofar as politics is engaged in a struggle for the imagination of the individual, is to find a way of inducing the individual to internalize a figure of the law to serve as the simulacrum of that conscience (or inner voice) which disciplines the ego in its efforts to serve the ends of instinctual gratification.

Althusser presents the scene of interpellation as a primal or phantasmatic scene in which the individual is interpellated (addressed and summoned, in the manner of Josef K. in Kafka's *The Trial*) into the juridico-political system, to assume a relation of subordination and self-policing that constantly scans inner impulses for evidence of their possible impropriety. Althusser and his group did not consider the function of historical consciousness–knowledges in

97 Cf. Freud 1915 in which the drive is defined as an instinctual impulse endowed with a possible object cathexis or more precisely a vague image of a possible object of satisfaction. In order, then, to address adequately the question of the relation between politics and the imagination, we must ask what exactly is being invested when politics or politicians or politologists seek to address the subject at the level of or in the zone of the perception-consciousness system called "imagination."

this operation (first, probably, because their idea of history was that of Marxist scientology and, second, because since they thought that historical knowledge was scientific, it had to address itself to consciousness rather than to the unconscious or the *Imaginaire*).

To put the matter in these terms is to question at least implicitly the whole philosophical discourse about the imagination deriving from Kant, who considered imagination as a faculty, which, since it is only pre- or para-rational, constitutes a problem for both pure and practical reason. It is inclined to deviate from its proper function of providing images for consideration by intellect and to degenerate into fantasy, "fancifulness," or playfulness. From the standpoint of an interest in a political investment of the imagination, the imagination must be disciplined on two levels at least, the conscious level at which what Hobbes called "command" operates and the unconscious level where what he called "coaction" (persuasion, or seduction) has to be used.

In the case of Hobbes, when he spoke of coaction as one of the two instruments to be used by the sovereign in the work of compelling assent of the citizenry, he meant—in spite of the dangers they presented to reason and authority—both rhetoric and symbolic language. Here he agreed with Aristotle on the necessity of investing both the body by force or violence and the spirit by techniques of persuasion and seduction. And the famous second half of *Leviathan*, in which the author analyzes the Christian commonwealth, on the one side, and the Kingdom of Satan or the Forces of Darkness, on the other, shows affinities of Freud with Hobbes, insofar as the former, too, grasped the necessity of inverting the psyche of the individual at the level not so much of pre- as rather that of un-conscious desire, anxiety and remorse.

Freud was fascinated by the "politics of imagination," in from *Totem and Taboo* to the late *Beyond the Pleasure Principle*. But it was especially here that he elaborated the relationships obtaining between the wish-fulfillment fantasies (*Wunscherfüllungen*) manifested in dreams and reveries and what he claimed to have discovered of the "phantasmatic" material of the "primal scenes." These concepts, regarding a dimension of the psycho-somatic system at a level below that of pre-consciousness (where memory and recall operate) generates a notion of imagination utterly different from anything conceptualized by Kant and his avatars (including, I think, Castoriadis). The principal difference between most philosophical definitions of the imagination and a psychoanalytical one lies in the tendency of the former to conceive imagination as preintellective, which is to say, preconscious and tending towards irrationality, which means that it must be controlled, educated, disciplined, and regulated by essentially rational and conscious means. Thus, while philosophical thinking has tended to divide imagination into two modes (a priori and constructed, primary and secondary, constructive and reconstructive, passive and active or "radical," and so on), Freud, for example, abandoned the notion of imagination as a mental *faculty* in order to consider it as a zone of transition between consciousness and the unconscious where thinking in images and rebus-like combinations was subjected to the repressive and sublimative operations of the censorship.[98]

Like earlier theorists of the imagination, Freud distinguishes between primary and secondary psychic processes but he extends this difference into what had been considered the voluntative and the rational faculties as well. Where the psychodynamic functions formerly considered to originate in the imagination were now located in a zone of relationship between dynamically unconscious repressed thoughts and images (as the latent content of the dream, for example) and the manifest level of waking consciousness where various kinds of parapraxis betrayed effects of mechanisms very much like those which, in *Die Traumdeutung*, he called *Traumarbeit* or "dreamwork" (the four operations of *Dichtungsarbeit*, *Verschiebungsarbeit*, *Symbolismus* and *sekondäre Bearbeitung*) (Freud 1994: Chapter 6). These operations of condensation, displacement, symbolization, and secondary elaboration or revision, it turns out, correspond to the tropes of neoclassical rhetoric in which they were treated as discursive instruments for the production of figures of both thought and speech that would invest the emotions, giving a certain slant of passionate intensity, at the same time that, on the literal level, the discourse addressed and informed the reason and practical understanding. Indeed, in correlating the tropics of discourse with the mechanisms of the dreamwork, Freud discovers a way of reconceptualizing what might be meant by "a politics of imagination" (Benveniste 1971: 74f.).

This brings us back to Althusser and his Lacan-inspired concept of the transformation of the individual into a subject by interpellation understood as an effect of a simulacrum of the "voice of the father" speaking as or in "the name of the law." Calling the individual into and before the law engages it at the level of primary process thinking and the phantasmata of "primal scenes" of separation anxiety, concern, care (*Sorge*) and wish-fulfillment fantasies of "the fullness of life." Freud gives us a way of understanding not just how what used to be called "imagination" works, but also how it might be manipulated to produce the compliant citizen, the self-policing legal subject.

Freud's substitution of the theory of the drives for the older notion of imagination had the advantage of getting beyond discussions of this "faculty" as being not so much active on one level and passive on another as, rather, operating on the borderline between the psyche and the soma in which the active–passive relation was projected into or onto consciousness in order to account for the split or schizophrenic nature of both will and reason, each in its own way. In *Die Triebe und seine Schicksale* (known in English as "The instincts and their vicissitudes") Freud posits the active–passive relationship along with the axes of the subject–object and the love–hate relationships as modalities of

98 On the shortcomings of the concept of imagination and the passage to the concept of imaginary through psychoanalysis, see also Bottici's contribution to this volume.

the two operations of "reversal" (of love into hate and the reverse) and "turning back upon the self" (of transforming the subject into an object and the reverse) which produce the sado-masochistic and the voyeur–exhibitionist syndromes.

If this kind of topography and dynamics of the psyche appear somewhat antiquated today, it is in part because we are dealing with a politics of the imagination still conceived primarily in terms of "primary modernist" verbal and auditory technologies of interpellation—the technologies of the first industrialism. What has happened since the second technological revolution—the electronic one—is that the technologies of communication have so increased the phatic capacities of the messaging system as to have transcended the conventional exigencies of messaging—conveying information or a command—altogether.[99] Now the imagination can be invested much more completely than anything that the oral oratorical performances could have done, allowing the political machine to invest the subject directly at the level of the phantasmatic, which is to say, primary process consciousness where wish-fulfillment fantasy and anxieties arise in the context of the primal scene(s). Again, as in Kafka's vision of modernity, the state no longer has to argue anything; it merely commands on the assumption that everyone is guilty and is deserving of whatever the state wishes on them. It is implantation of guilt in the consciousness of the citizen that the state is able to effect by its self-presentation as the custodian of the law. "There is no sin before the law," the Apostle teacheth. Neither is there any imagination. Before the law appears, the subject is neither inside nor outside the city, because there is no city before the law.

3. The historical and the politics of imagination

Now we must ask, what is the role of the historical in this more general politics of imagination? Here it is necessary to stress that in posing that question, one is not trying to identify the ways in which the academic study of history has been used to support or to undermine the claims of the modern state to represent the moral or at least legal substance of the nation through "patriotic" or "nationalist" historiography overtly supporting the claims of a certain class or classes to hegemony. As Foucault has pointed out, history or more specifically the work of constructing a specifically "historical past," has "performed a certain number of major functions in western culture: memory, myth, transmission of the Word and of Example, vehicle of tradition, critical awareness of the present, decipherment of humanity's destiny, anticipation of the future, or promise of a return" (Foucault 1970: 367). These functions produced what, following Michael Oakshott's (*On History*) lead, we may call

99 On the novelties brought about by contemporary capitalism, see Bazzicalupo's contribution to this volume.

"the practical past" of western culture, that past which is drawn on by politicians, lawyers, judges, policemen, antiquarians, archeologists, philologists, accountants, educators, and ordinary educated people in the course of their daily affairs any time they feel compelled to advert to what Reinhart Koselleck calls the "space of experience" of their cultural endowment to connect a present world with some aspect of a past one, recent or remote. This practical past is differently configured, differently populated, differently structured, differently shared than is the new "historical past" constructed in the 19th century and after by those disciplinized scholarly communities, located for the most part in the universities, with explicit rules, licensing regulations, review procedures, and so on for the scientific or at least *wissenschaftliches* study of the past.

To be sure, the scientific practice of history has its own "imaginary," with its own "dreams" that manifest the deep psychological levels of consciousness which would seek to invest "the past" as a source of a kind of knowledge that is held to be "desirable in itself" or "a good in itself," a knowledge which has no practical use in or for the present, but the accumulation of which had been conceived to be worth a lifetime spent in cold, drafty, dusty archives that offer small prospect of contact with living beings. Foucault indicated the importance of the distinction between the "practical past" of memory, casual knowledge of the past, intimation of an origin, concern for a heritage, and anxiety of legitimacy, on the one hand, and the interest by professional scholars in "the historical past" which they were concerned to identify, retrieve, and reconstitute on the basis of a scientific study of documents and monuments alone, on the other.

But Foucault, like many other historians of history, identifies this other past as a construction of the discourse of philosophy of history, after the manner of Hegel and Marx (and Darwin), analysts of the concept of history as revealed in professional historical scholarship but which is probed for what it might reveal in the way of history's *meaning*.

Modernist rhetorics differ from traditional counterparts by the terrible power of the technological means used to package sensorially overdetermined messages for delivery to social constituencies. It is these means—represented above all by the kinds of "special effects" met with in contemporary cinema—which, in the disparity they manifest with respect to the verbal and conceptual content of a message, that produces the kind of "sentimental" politics that modern totalitarian regimes have typically favored and deployed. European commentators on American society are characteristically bemused by the rise of fundamentalist religiosity in American politics, seeing it as being at once a paradox for a modern enlightened society and a threat to the rationality of political thought and practice that is thought to be a necessary precondition for the working of democratic political institutions. In my view, however, religiosity is only one of the many forms that fundamentalism can take when the technical means at hand permit the investment of the psyche of the citizen at the level of "imagination" understood as the zone of consciousness at which primal forces such as the pleasure principle and the death drive rage unchecked by any concession to waking rationality or pragmatic concerns about the care and treatment of bodies. Figures such as "the terrorist," "the weapon of mass destruction," "suicide bombers" (and above all, "the female suicide bomber," the wife, grandmother, and girlfriend suicide bomber), "the hijacked jet airplane," the "cell" or "virus" implanted in the inner arteries and veins of "ordinary" (western) society—such figures are given a vivacity and palpability by the techniques of modern media that make the hellfire and brimstone sermons of the pre-electronic preacher pale by comparison.

Indeed, these techniques make of "the preacher" (*iman*, and *ayatollah* also) himself a larger than life player on the political stage. These figures not only directly address the topic of death and destruction, entropy and apocalypse, the end of days, the rapture, and the last things; they also seem to *embody* the messages they circulate. Small wonder that the politician who cannot approach to a similar condition of figural embodiment will have little chance of capturing the heart (or imagination) as well as the mind of the citizen.

Freud's idea of primal scene—the site of psychic consciousness where what was once meant by imagination arises—is the place where bodily anxieties are gathered and the first efforts at their sublimations are attempted. The primal scene is the place where the sleeping ego, deprived of its ego defenses, contrives an imaginary scene, where fantasies of the unknown origin, separation from the body of the mother, loss of the object of possible gratification, mutilation (genital, ocular, and otherwise), loss of identity, and so on are organized into a "scene" on which a drama unfolds of which the subject is at once both (imagined) observer and (imagined) actor. In the dream state and also in reverie, these scenarios play themselves out more or less completely as either anxiety-ridden farces, wish-fulfillment romances, or some phantasmagoria that threatens the dreamer by its failure of plot resolution. These scenes, in Freud's formulation, constitute the bases of what he calls "the dream content" over and against the manifest form of the dream, which he calls "the dream thoughts."

The technique of "coaction" which Althusser dubbed "interpellation" combines address to the individual's (or group's) conscious moral sensibilities and intellectual commitments and at the same time to its unconscious anxieties and wish-fulfillment fantasies. Unlike the military *command* in which the coactive or symbolic element is present as "what goes without saying" or is simply presumed, commands directed from centers of power and authority to civilian or lay individuals intended for subjectivization must engage anxieties of identity and fantasies of fullness activated by the ambiguities and contradictions of a life to be lived as an individual who is *also* a member of a group. This means that the command (masked as a recommendation, suggestion, advisement, or simply appeal) must be cast in such a way as to remind the individual of the law, norm, rule, or protocol in reference to which the desired response on the part of the individual is felt to be *both* necessary or inevitable *and* freely chosen, at one and the same time.

References

Ankersmit, F.R. 1995, 'Statements, texts, and pictures', in Ankersmit, F. and Kellner, H. (eds) *A New Philosophy of History*, London, Reaktion Books.

Benveniste, E. 1971, 'Remarks on the function of language in Freudian theory', in *Problems in General Linguistics*, Coral Gables, FL, University of Miami Press.

Foucault, M. 1970, *The Order of Things: An Archaeology of the Human Sciences*, London, Tavistock Publications.

Freud, S. 1915, 'Instincts and their Vicissitudes' [1915], in Sigmund Freud, *On Metapsychology: The Theory of Psychoanalysis*, Vol. 13 of The Pelican Freud Library, trans under the general editorship of James Strachey (Harmondsworth [U.K.]/ New York: Penguin Books, 1984), pp. 105–38.

—— 1994, *The Interpretation of Deams*, New York, Modern Library.

Hegel, G.W.F. 1975, *Lectures on the Philosophy of World History* (trans. H.B. Nisbet), New York, Cambridge University Press.

—— 1986, *Vorlesungen über die Philosophie der Geschichte*, Frankfurt, Suhrkamp.

Kolb, B.G. 1974, 'Petrarch's prefaces to *de viris illustribus*', *History and Theory*, 13 (2): 159–160.

White, H. 2008, 'The Historical Event', in *Difference: A Journal of Feminist Cultural Studies* (Summer, 2008), Vol. 19, no. 2, pp. 9–34.

Chapter 10

Literature as public reasoning in the political struggles over imagination

Meili Steele

Literature has always been central to philosophical reflection on imagination, but much of that reflection has led to misguided understandings of both terms. In the Introduction to this volume, Chiara Bottici and Benoît Challand help clarify some of these problems in their outline of the two broad lines of investigation of imagination, one through the subjective legacy of Kant and another through the lens of social contexts or imaginaries. My chapter will work through both lines of investigation in order to develop a problematic that makes available literature's relevance to political debate.

I begin by tracing the failure of philosophers in the Kantian line from Habermas to Ricoeur to break the grip of the concept on the understanding of imagination and reason. I then move to the social imaginary as a philosophical problematic that shifts us from a subject who confronts the givenness of the world to the subject who is "thrown," in Heidegger's metaphor, into the practices, social imaginaries, and languages of an historical culture. There are many complex developments from this line, but I will focus on the tension between the transcendental and the historical dimensions of the social imaginary, between a philosophical position about language, subjectivity, etc., and the historical institutions and practices of a particular political community.

Literature can be explored from both perspectives. On the one hand, the literary text can be studied for the ways it contributes to historically effective structures of the imaginary. On the other hand, it can be examined from the philosophical perspective in which it argues through and against the languages of the social imaginary. Bringing these two together will show how to reconcile "the concept of the social imaginary . . . with the free imagination of the individuals" (Bottici, this volume).

My chapter unfolds in four sections. In the first, I will sketch various ways in which philosophers of different types have occluded the social imaginary within political philosophy and literary study. In the second and third sections, I develop the problematic of the social imaginary, while in the fourth section, I do a reconstructive reading of Ralph Ellison's fictional and nonfictional works. In this reading, Ellison's texts take on the questions of language, race, and normativity as a political struggle for people's imaginations, and he engages in this struggle by addressing the discourses of his time in law, sociology, philosophy, and film. In doing this reading, I'm not just interested in the historical imaginaries of 20th-century America, but in Ellison as a philosophical example of how political argument through and with the social imaginary works.

1. The social imaginary and the misunderstandings of the concept

Moral constructivists use procedures, such as Habermas' universal presuppositions of communicative action or Rawls' original position, to separate the production of moral/political concepts from the languages of everyday life.[100] In this way, the principles of rights are protected from the ambiguities of history, language, and interpretation.

Habermas's constructivist device is the idea of the presuppositions of communicative action. In this view, political norms do not "tell actors what they ought to do" (1996: 4) but what presuppositions must inform their dialogues. The theory of communicative action thus reconciles rights and popular sovereignty, reason and will, because "human rights institutionalize the communicative conditions for a reasonable political will-formation" (Habermas 2002: 201). These ideal conditions are then turned into dialogical procedures that embody the norms that assure the legitimacy of the content. Public reasoning about rights thus should be carried out in a normative language that swings free of the semantic context of the imaginary, and these norms are expressed in singular propositions: "Participants must know that this kind of public controversy has to be carried out in the light of publicly acceptable reasons, independently of any philosophy of history or Weltanschauung" (2003: 49).[101] Disagreements, in this view, can be only over the application and best interpretation of "the same constitutional rights and principles" (1998: 225). Habermas purchases universality and consensus about rights by formalizing principles and removing them from the imaginaries that shaped the world and the minds of the actors.

The constructivist mode of isolating moral and political concepts from social imaginaries can also be found in cultural theorists, such as Edward Said. Said takes a social constructivist approach to literature, which aims to show that the object of investigation is not an entity that stands independently of the discourses of investigation but is in fact constituted by them. In such works

100 American constructivists, such as John Rawls and Ronald Dworkin, do not try to separate entirely their political principles from history in the radical way that Habermas does; instead, they tie them to the self-understandings of "democratic traditions" based on the texts of the Founders and the Courts (Rawls 1993: 13–14).

101 Habermas's linguistic philosophy of language works in three theoretical steps, semantics, pragmatics, and background. I offer a systematic critique in Steele 2005b: Chapter 1.

as *Orientalism* and *Culture and Imperialism*, Said takes the languages of texts—whether imperial or resistant—and shows "how all representations are constructed, for what purpose, by whom, and with what components" (1993: 314–315).[102] While Said is certainly offering a powerful critique of liberal imperialism, he makes two liberal moves himself. He objectifies and unmasks the history of culture as an unreliable guide to ethics and politics; he then follows them in an appeal to Kantian cosmopolitan values of moral universalism and justice that can be separated from their damaged historical instantiations that he examined (Salusinszky 1987: 134, 137).[103] Neither Said (social constructivists generally) nor liberals offer a subject of interpretation who reasons through rather than against his/her historico-linguistic embedding in social imaginaries. What moral and social constructivists share is a hostility toward the normative potential of texts.

Conceptual problems also plague philosophers who are sympathetic to literature and narrative, such as Martha Nussbaum and Paul Ricoeur. The mistake that dominates philosophical discussion of literature is the subordination of literature to the philosophical concept as it emerges in both the Kantian and Hegelian traditions so that literature is reduced to supplying sensuous, historical particulars about individuals or their contexts. In other words, they do not integrate language properly into their phenomenologies.[104] In Martha Nussbaum's *Poetic Justice: The Literary Imagination and Public Life*, she attacks the narrow, rule-bound thinking that dominates both the Kantian and utilitarian traditions of moral reasoning. She urges us to draw on literature in order to get a detailed account of what it means to lead a life different from our own (1995: 5). Literature, for Nussbaum, is not a private but a public matter, for she wants us to consider "the literary as a public imagination" (3). Her imagination is one "that will steer judges in their judging, legislators in their legislating, policy makers in measuring the quality of life of people near and far" (3). Nussbaum makes several important moves here. She opens the boundary between literature, everyday speech, law, and philosophy. Literary texts are not sealed off in an aesthetic realm or relegated to the extraordinary. Rather, literature explores and tests the ethical potential in everyday language. Moreover, literary texts do not simply provide examples for philosophical and legal reasoning; rather, the language of literature (and everyday life) is often more perspicuous than the language of philosophy on matters of public

102 Said's analyses stop with the juxtaposition of the stories of colonizer and colonized. See Steele 2005b: Chapter 5 for a detailed discussion of Said.

103 *The Claims of Culture*, Seyla Benhabib, makes precisely the same move (Benhabib 2002: 5, 10).

104 I have discussed all these questions at greater length in Steele 2005b: Chapters 2 and 4. I follow up the Kantian dimension here, but we also see this in neo-Hegelians, such as Robert Pippin, who still retain some version of Hegel's assumption that the sensuous and unreflective insights of art are realized in concepts, the transparent vehicles of reflexive thought. I address Pippin's work in "Moral shapes of time in Henry James."

concern. While I applaud this move to consider literature as public imagination, I reject her understanding of the relationship of citizens to the institutions of meaning—that is, to language, literature, and the court—and their historicity.

For Nussbaum, "public imagination" provides access to an alternative life, a subject to subject conception that is synchronic, individualistic, and phenomenological: literary texts offer a kind of specificity and emotional richness missing from both universalizing normative theory and the social sciences. Nussbaum's ethical framework brackets the problems of historical distance between text and reader, the explanatory concerns of cultural historians, and the interpretive dilemmas posed by the linguistic differences of text and interpreter.[105] For Nussbaum, literature's relationship to history does not require us to consult modern philosophies of history but Aristotle: "Literature focuses on the possible, inviting readers to wonder about themselves" (5). Hence, it is not surprising that she does not see her view as incompatible with that of sensitive Kantians: "My own preferred version of the ethical stance derives from Aristotle, but everything I say here could be accommodated by a Kantianism modified so as to give the emotions a carefully demarcated cognitive role" (xvi). Nussbaum's idealized and dehistoricized approach to literature as a resource for reasoning ignores literature's political ambiguity. Literature is obfuscating as well as clarifying. For instance, as Lara argues in her contribution to this volume, literature has been the means for perpetrating as well as for criticizing gender discrimination throughout history.

Another way in which philosophers misread literature's potential for political argument is through theories of narrative, such as Paul Ricoeur's. His discussion of literature tries to isolate the operation of emplotment from the totality of the literary speech act. Emplotment is not an interpretive act through which the subject dialogues with social imaginaries—other texts, images, etc. Instead, Ricoeur develops his conception of the novel as emplotment by drawing on Aristotle's *Poetics* and on Kant's *Critique of Judgment*: "I cannot overemphasize the kinship between this 'grasping together' power to the configurational act and what Kant says about the operation of judging" (1984–88, I: 66–68). Emplotment "extracts configuration from a succession" in the same way that a reflective judgment "reflects upon the work of thinking at work in the aesthetic judgment of taste and the teleological judgment applied to organic wholes" (66). In a stroke, Ricoeur has reduced the author's engagement with worth and truth of the languages of traditions to a formal aestheticism. Ricoeur does not place the subject in language and narratives so

105 This subject to subject model of imagination can also be found in Arendt's idea of the "imagination going visiting." I develop the failure of Arendt's understanding of imagination and its Kantian roots in the context of her debate with Ellison over desegregation in Little Rock in Steele 2002.

that inchoate narratives are woven into social imaginaries that already inform experience. By looking at narrative as the emplotment of the heterogeneous, Ricoeur blocks out the ways in which emplotment always engages the adequacy and worth of the languages of the emploter, the narrative and symbolic shapes this subject inevitably inhabits. By turning narrative into a merely formal question, Ricoeur abstracts from the historical imaginaries in which they were formed and makes them subjective schematic possibilities in a Kantian sense, blocking other historiographical readings.[106] Thus, Ricoeur wants to keep novelists out of the argument business, limiting them only to emplotment. "Historians are not simply narrators: they give reasons [. . .]. Poets also create plots that are held together by causal skeletons. But these [. . .] are not the subject of a process of argumentation. Poets restrict themselves to producing the story and explaining by narrating [. . .]. [Poets] produce, [historians] argue" (1984–88, I: 186). Not only does this exclude the commentary about the proper understanding of their novelistic worlds offered by such well-known narrators as those of Balzac and Proust, who argue with widespread presuppositions of their cultures, but it ignores the argumentative dimension of narratives that are devoted primarily to "showing" rather than "telling," and it misses the ways that texts argue through parody, alternative thought experiment, and recontextualization. Swift's "narrative" *Gulliver's Travels* argues with Defoe, Locke, and other advocates of modernity by his own counter-thought experiment, which parodies the languages of science, cosmopolitanism, and modern politics. (This is not to say any of them is right, of course.)

2. Literature and the politics of historical imaginaries

The idea of the social imaginary has entered literary and political studies primarily in historical forms, and I will look briefly at three: structuralist, Foucauldian, and hermeneutic. In all cases, they are offered as a critique of the way that atomists and contractarians conceive of the way we understand the constitution of subjectivity in history. Benedict Anderson's study of the transition from premodern empire to modern nations, *Imagined Communities*, is the best-known structuralist account. Anderson's work attends to the mental

106 Ricoeur speaks of change by employing the Husserlian vocabulary of "sedimentation" and "innovation," in which the subject's arguments with historical imaginaries are given no place: "This schematism, in turn, is constituted within a history that has the characteristics of a tradition [. . .]. A tradition is constituted by the interplay of innovation and sedimentation. To sedimentation must be referred the paradigms that constitute the typology of emplotment" (Ricoeur 1984–88, I: 68). "Rule-governed deformation constitutes the axis around which the various changes of paradigm through application are changed. It is this variety of application that confers a history on the productive imagination and that in counterpoint to sedimentation, makes a narrative tradition possible" (1984–88, I: 70).

structures that have been ignored by the history of ideas (e.g., social contract theories) and by functional and causal explanations. Anderson maintains that the novel and the newspaper are not just new aesthetic genres that try to represent realistically the modern world; rather, they are the mental template for the constitution of individual and collective identity that no historical or philosophical account can ignore. The novel and the newspaper took the scientific objectification of the world and the idea of homogeneous, empty time of physics and translated them into an imaginary structure that turned readers into omniscient observers able to hold together unconnected events in the same story space. Author and reader were like God watching them in common space, an organizing form of consciousness that brings people together.[107]

The most powerful influence in literary understanding of imagination, however, has come from Foucault. Nancy Armstrong, for instance, gives a Foucauldian turn to the social imaginary of individualism in *How Novels Think*, examining novelistic structures in a manner such that "writers sought to formulate a kind of subject that had not yet existed in writing" (Armstrong 2005: 3). [108] In works such as *Pamela*, *Robinson Crusoe*, and *Moll Flanders*, we can see characters "perform what Lockeans could only theorize: the possibility that a new form of literacy could provide something on the order of a supplement capable of turning an early modern subject into a self-governing individual" (5).

In *Modern Social Imaginaries*, Charles Taylor introduces the social imaginary as an historiographical problematic that is much broader than literature, a problematic that can articulate the background of modern western institutions in which we are embedded— "the market economy, the public sphere, and the self-governing people" (2004: 2)—in ways that other approaches block out.[109] His definition of the social imaginary incorporates features of the rich Foucauldian account in such a way that complements the transcendental hermeneutic arguments that we find in his earlier work, *Sources of the Self*: "The social imaginary is not a set of ideas; rather, it is what enables, through making sense of, the practices of a society . . .[Thus,] the notion of moral order goes beyond some proposed schedule of norms that ought to govern our mutual relations and/or political life . . . The image of order carries a definition not only of what is right, but of the context in which it makes sense to strive for and hope to realize the right" (Taylor 2004: 2, 8–9). Taylor then argues that "the

107 I will not offer critiques of these historiographical approaches. Anderson's work, for instance, has been subject to a number of important critiques—e.g., that his structuralist grid does not give an adequate portrait of complex cultural variations, of the phenomenology of different subject positions, or of the agency historical subjects.

108 Armstrong can be read as developing this strain of Foucault's thought: "Individuality is neither the real atomistic basis of society [liberal, social contract theory] nor an ideological illusion of liberal economics [Marx], but an effective artifact of a very long and complicated historical process" (Foucault 1977: 194).

109 See Taylor's discussion of "subtraction" theories (both philosophical and sociological) of the transition to modernity (2007: 26–29).

mutation of this view of moral order into our social imaginary is the coming to be of certain social forms" (2). Taylor proposes a new historiographical problematic that brings into view the complex changes in western institutions, languages, and practices that have gone into the present institutional imaginary that we now take for granted. While all these historiographical perspectives open new ways of understanding, none answers the question of how we think of imaginaries in the context of individual freedom and action from a first- or second-person angle.

3. The philosophical articulation of the social imaginary

When we shift to the philosophical perspective of what it means to speak and act through the problematic of the imaginary, we are asking different questions than the historian is. Instead of looking for the ways literary works have structured our implicit and explicit imaginaries, we are looking for the ways that individual works engage the assumptions and connections among the conceptual packages and social practices (see also Lara, in this volume, for the role of feminist critique as disclosive imagination). The particularity of the argument through and against other imaginaries rather than the work's structural similarity to others is at stake. To explore this dimension of literature, I will connect the imaginary to philosophy of language, specifically linguistic holism as it emerges in Taylor's work. Taylor is important for me here because he, like Castoriadis (1987), argues for the logical priority of the imaginary in a way that discredits from the ground up the philosophies discussed in the first section, that draws on the historical studies of the second section, and that opens the way for a new understanding of literature in political argument. However, he himself does not develop this dimension, limiting his discussion of literature to historical possibilities. I will look quickly at his critique of political constructivism, address the limits of his literary discussion and then draw on Mikhail Bakhtin and Anthony Cascardi to fill out my portrait of literature and the social imaginary.

In the first section of Taylor's *Sources of the Self*, and in many other places in his work, Taylor develops a transcendental argument for "what it is to be in the world as a knowing agent" (Taylor 2003: 159). These arguments do not look at the historical effectiveness of the legacies of Locke and Kant, as he does in *Modern Social Imaginaries*; instead, they level a transcendental criticism at their problematics, at those of their contemporary reincarnations, such as Habermas and Rawls.[110]

110 For instance, Taylor says, "Locke tried to maintain that even the ideas in our minds which have general import are themselves particulars. The deep muddle has its source in the entire 'building block' theory of thinking" (1989: 167). I discuss Taylor's work in a comprehensive manner in Steele 2005b: Chapter 3.

While both moral and social constructivists presuppose that we can step outside our social imaginaries or "evaluative frameworks," to use Taylor's term from *Sources*, we should think of these imaginaries as logically prior to choice, reflection, and concept formation. They make the world and thought possible. Rather than searching for universalized moral rules that can swing free of life forms, we reason by seeking "to articulate a framework [. . .], to try to spell out what is it that we presuppose when we make a judgment that a certain form of life is truly worthwhile, or place our dignity in a certain achievement" (1989: 26). In his view, Habermas, like Rawls, is surreptitiously appealing to the good and hence misdescribing his claims: "We have to draw on the sense of the good that we have in order to decide what are adequate principles of justice" since the good "gives the point of the rules which define the right" (89).

Any singular statement of a political position depends on large-scale assumptions about language, subjectivity, historical particulars. The articulation of background provides an historical dimension to political debate that is completely missing from Habermas's conception of background, as the innocuous inarticulate medium of what "is intuitively known, unproblematic [and] unanalyzable" (Habermas 1987: 298). This means that the task of rationality cannot be divided, in Habermasian fashion, between the theoretical account of the rules of speaking, on the one hand, and the normative account of morality, on the other. Such an account simply evaporates public imagination into shared meaning.[111]

Social imaginaries must be understood holistically rather than in terms of collections of building blocks. Taylor's articulations interrogate this space, seeking "to transfer what has sunk to the level of an organizing principle for present practices and hence beyond examination into a view for which there can be reasons either for or against" (Taylor 1984: 28). Hence, Taylor wants to begin reasoning by reopening the assumptions of modernity and displaying the complex, conflicted historical inheritance that lies behind current usage. This means learning to reason historically about how we came to be who we are today by "undo[ing] forgetting" (Taylor 1984: 28). Such a project is interpretive because the self-understandings and changes of the past cannot just be described and explained but evaluated. Such evaluations can take various forms, from "escaping from given social forms"—we could call this the Foucauldian response—to the recovery of lost practices—we could call this the hermeneutic dimension (1984: 39). Background for Taylor is the ambiguous

111 Taylor distinguishes three levels of articulation. The first concerns the "explicit doctrine about society, the divine or the cosmos." The second is "the symbolic," which is found in art and ritual and close to what historians call "mentalités," and the third is "embodied understanding," or "habitus" (1999: 167). See also Castoriadis 1987, especially 165–220.

historical/cultural medium through which we live but that we can never stand over, against, or take as given.[112]

The articulation of background is crucial for overcoming what Bottici calls "the reification of context" (Bottici, this volume), such as we find in the pragmatism of Richard Rorty's alternative linguistic holism. Rorty aims to show how epistemological and moral claims cannot stand free of our "form of life," but in doing so he dissolves language and social imaginaries into a self-conscious ethnocentrism about our tools (Taylor 2003: 158–159). My idea of the social imaginary and literature does not fold us back into our forms of life but opens their internal dynamics by articulating their histories, putting them in new contexts. Acknowledging our inescapable embeddedness in imaginary backgrounds is an invitation to engaging these backgrounds in political contexts, not to advocating our cultural particularity. Arguing through articulation means rejecting the familiar oscillation between factual assertion and normative assessment since this move depends on the absolute boundary between the subject and the object of judgment. Literature can be an important resource for bringing out the ways that moral concepts, images, and situations are woven together in different sites of the social imaginary.

However, Taylor himself encourages some of this communitarian misreading by his avoidance of many of the political problems of modernity—racism, genocide, etc., never appear—and by his focus on the "pervasive bewitchment" of stepping outside evaluative frameworks and the "loss of meaning." The imaginary is more of an historical background than it is a resource for arguments about current political debates. From my point of view, this lacuna in Taylor is part of a larger problem in his treatment of the literature, particularly his excessive reliance on Heidegger and Gadamer in his critique of the "subjectivization of aesthetics." While I certainly agree with the Gadamerian critique of Kant, Taylor does not go far enough beyond Heidegger's and Gadamer's very narrow treatment of literature. Taylor, like them, focuses almost exclusively on poetry and avoids the genre that engages most comprehensively the discourses of modernity, the novel.

An alternative reading of the relationship of philosophy and literature to those we have discussed so far is proposed by Mikhail Bakhtin and Anthony Cascardi. For them, modern literature, particularly, the distinctively modern genre, the novel, provides modes of thematizing the social imaginary in ways that are missing from philosophy and social science. Cascardi's work

112 Taylor thus joins thinkers who use the "political" in opposition to politics to designate an investigation of the background conditions—both historical and philosophical—that underpin but remain unrecognized by our current understanding of "politics." Chantal Mouffe (2005), for instance, says, "We could . . . say that politics refers to the 'ontic' level while 'the political' has to do with the 'ontological' one. This means that the ontic has to do with the manifold practices of conventional politics, while the ontological concerns the very way in which society is instituted" (9).

brings this philosophical dimension out very well: "By virtue of its form, the novel stands in opposition to any genre, including philosophy, that is built on the premise that there ought to be only one privileged way of speaking the truth" (Cascardi 2009: 164). Thus, the novel can open up the "insights that philosophy regards as achieved . . . and articulates those things that philosophy tends to leave largely unspoken" (167). In *Don Quixote*, we see the emergence of the novel's relationship to modernity not as the structural translation of a scientific grid (Anderson), but as an awareness of the interplay and historicity of various discourses in and outside literature through which we struggle to understand ourselves. This literary mode of inhabiting the imaginary does not strive to wriggle free from its grip in order to establish normative foundations, empirical truth, or the logic of its patterns of signification; rather, literature seeks to articulate, juxtapose, deflate, and elevate various kinds of significance, so that a form of life opens up its various folds through constant debate.

Bakhtin pursues the novel's particular linguistic reflexivity, the way it incorporates and reworks the registers and multiplicity of a culture's languages. Criticizing traditional poetics for its focus on the formal or stylistic unity of a work, Bakhtin asks us to see that "what is realized in the novel is the process of coming to know one's own language as it is perceived in someone else's language, coming to know one's own conceptual horizon in someone else's conceptual horizon (1981: 365). The novel is not concerned with the transcription of speech but with what he calls, "the image of language," which "reveals not only the reality of a given language but also, as it were its potential, its ideal limits" (Bakhtin 1981: 356). The novel orchestrates and engages all the languages of the imaginary—literary, political, sociological, philosophical, etc.—while shifting among third-, second-, and first-person stances.[113]

Although neither Cascardi nor Bakhtin is concerned directly with politics, I will put their suggestions to work in my reading of the novel's capacity to make nuanced political claims through social imaginaries that are unavailable through models of public reason. The social imaginary becomes a space of critique and autonomy, not a communitarian bunker.

4. Literature as political argument through the imaginary: the example of Ralph Ellison

We can get an example of how a literary argument through the social imaginary might work by reconstructing the texts of Ralph Ellison—i.e., putting them in the vocabulary of the imaginary. I will begin by contrasting Ellison's argument with the reasoning of the Supreme Court's two forms of reasoning

113 Bakhtin's philosophy of language and the novel is far too rich and complex for me to develop here. I have developed my own ideas (2005a) in 'Ontologie linguistique et dialogue politique chez Bakhtine'.

about race, antidiscrimination, and antidomination, and then look at his engagement with broader political arguments.[114] In the antidiscrimination reading, which is the dominant paradigm in the American legal tradition and public culture, *Brown v. Board of Education* (1954) represents the principle that the law should be colorblind.[115] The metaphor of blindness captures nicely western modernity's misguided urge to achieve normative clarity by blocking out the historical background that makes such thought experiments intelligible (see also Lentin's contribution in this volume).

By contrast, the antisubordination thesis argues that the *Plessy v. Ferguson* doctrine of "separate but equal" was part of a larger pattern of racial subordination, a pattern that the antidiscrimination thesis systematically occludes. Hence, the moral/political point of the antidomination argument is, in Owen Fiss's words, "that certain social practices . . . should be condemned not because of any unfairness in the transaction . . . but rather because such practices create or perpetuate the subordination of the group of which the individual excluded or rejected is a member" (Fiss 2004: 3–4). Antisubordination readings look beyond the intentions and self-understandings of the law to its effects—e.g., damage to black school children in *Brown*. Antisubordination theorists claim that looking through the single lens of classification helps, as Jack Balkin says, "to freeze the cumulative black disadvantages in place" (Balkin 2001: 13). Thus, "it encourages people to explain persistent black inequality as the result of private choices, cultural differences, or black inferiority rather than at least partially as the result of facially neutral legal policies that help preserve social stratification" (13). [116] Although the antisubordination approach has initiated important changes in society—e.g., desegregation, affirmative action—this perspective does not address directly the normative and referential languages of self-understanding through which much of the subordination takes place.[117]

For Ellison, the crucial impediment to the realization of human rights and popular sovereignty at his time is the deliberative medium through which a society articulates itself. Ellison rejects trying to step outside the imaginary in order to establish independent facts and norms. Instead, he criticizes the separation of referentiality and normativity simultaneously from within the imaginary, drawing on multiple discourses and disciplines.

114 The Supreme Court is the privileged site of public reason in American political philosophy and popular consciousness. As Rawls says, "To check whether we are following public reason we might ask: how would our argument strike us presented in the form of a Supreme Court opinion" (1993: 254).

115 Robert Post says, "The image of the orchestra audition distills the logic of American antidiscrimination law" (2001: 19).

116 For an excellent survey of the two legal approaches to race, see Siegel 2003–4.

117 For my purposes here, I will ignore the ways *Brown* was connected to Cold War politics. There was pressure on the Court by other agencies of government to get rid of embarrassing racial practices that undermined America's image. For a general discussion of the U.S. Cold War cultural campaign, see David Monod. For the connection to *Brown*, see Balkin 2001.

I will begin with his critical review of the Swedish sociologist Gunnar Myrdal's *American Dilemma*, a review that attacks the complicity between normativity and social science in occluding oppressive imaginaries. Myrdal's work was cited by Chief Justice Earl Warren in *Brown* to document the damage that school segregation did to African American children. The antisubordination thesis, as articulated by *Brown* at the time, and the anticlassification thesis both assumed that African American culture had been so damaged by racism that it was only a prison house of internalized oppression, while the dominant culture had emerged unscathed. For Ellison, neither white nor black culture could be affirmed in an unqualified way. Both were severely damaged and needed to be critically worked through: "What is needed in our country is not an exchange of pathologies but a change in the basis of society. This is a job which both Negroes and whites must perform together" (1995: 340). No thought experiment of blindness can provide satisfactory critical distance and no collection of data can document the damage done to all Americans. Both depend on a language that can ask questions, understand historical imaginaries in a perspicuous way, a language that, in Ellison's view, was not available. While Myrdal's sociological study brings out many significant features of the American racial landscape, Ellison objected to his assumptions that "Negroes [were] simply the creation of white men" and that "Negro culture and personality [were] the product of a 'social pathology'" (1995: 339). Ellison acknowledges that "Negro" culture has some undesirable features, but he insists that "there is much of great value and richness, which because it has been secreted by living, has made their lives more meaningful" (1995: 340). African Americans have thus "helped to create themselves out of what they found around them" (339). Moreover, this culture is not in the narrow service of identity politics, for "in Negro culture there is much of value for America as a whole" (340).

Myrdal's misreading led him to assume that "it is to the advantage of American Negroes as a group to become assimilated into American culture, to acquire the traits held in esteem by the dominant white Americans" (1995: 339). Antisubordination remedies, such as integration or affirmative action, do not address these questions directly. Legal reasoning does not have the resources to address the deep, historically layered racial formations of the American imaginary and political conflict.

On the contrary, Ellison sees the need to widen the sphere of political argument beyond the horizon of the courts and beyond the demands for formal equality and inclusion. The most important terrain of political conflict for him was the social imaginary. The battle was not just to expose racism but to provide new resources for sustaining public life for all Americans and the two dimensions are directly related.

He insists that the complex ways that race is woven into the existing imaginaries of both black and white Americans requires a genealogical treatment that unpacks these histories: "This unwillingness to resolve the conflict in keeping with his democratic ideals has compelled the American, figuratively, to force the Negro down in the deeper level of his consciousness, into the inner world, where reason and madness mingle with hope and memory and endlessly give birth to nightmare and to dream; down into the province of the psychiatrist and the artists, from whence spring the lunatic's fancy and his work of art" (1995: 149). One of the effects of this inarticulate conflict is the unacknowledged presence of race in every facet of what white culture understands as "white" (1995: 149).

These features of the imaginary have been argued into place not just by legal and historical texts and practices but also by popular arts such as film, which access the unconscious symbolic complexities of the imaginary. Ellison was aware of the argumentative power of film, and he analyzed some of this in his discussion of D.W. Griffith's *Birth of a Nation* (1915): "Griffith's genius captured the enormous myth making potential of the film form almost from the beginning" (1995: 304).[118] This film is not simply a narrative account of the nation. It is a *Bildungsroman* of the nation and white male subjectivity. We are not just told a story with names and dates, causes and effects, but given an education about how we should understand ourselves as citizens. The real subject of the film is the spectator who views the action through the eyes of white male subjectivity. This citizen is educated and empowered through this reading of American history. He is the kind of subject who writes the majority opinion in *Plessy v. Ferguson* (1896), which established the infamous "separate but equal" doctrine that *Brown* overturned. At the same time, the film develops black stereotypes and makes them part of an argument for Jim Crow (the name for the social, legal, and political culture that subordinated blacks): "The anti-Negro images of Hollywood films were (and are) acceptable because of the existence throughout the United States of an audience obsessed with an inner psychological need to view Negroes as less than men. Thus psychologically and ethically, these negative images constitute justifications for all these acts, legal, emotional, economic and political which we label Jim Crow. The anti-Negro image is thus a ritual object of which Hollywood is not the creator but the manipulator. Its roles have been that of justifying the widely held myth of Negro inhumanness and inferiority by offering entertaining rituals through which that myth could be reaffirmed" (1995: 305).[119] Criticizing the naturalized reality of *Birth of a Nation* through appeals to principle could not

118 Griffith's film incorporated quotations from Woodrow Wilson's *History of the American People* and the film was screened in the White House during Wilson's presidency. The NAACP, the National Association for the Advancement of Colored People, protested the film's distribution, but was unsuccessful. *Birth of a Nation* was the highest grossing film of its day.

119 Ellison wrote of *Birth of a Nation*: "The propagation of subhuman images of Negroes became financially and dramatically profitable. The Negro as a scapegoat could be sold as entertainment, could even be exported. If the film became the main manipulation of the American dream, for Negroes that dream contained a strong dose of such stuff as nightmares are made of" (1995: 304).

do the critical work that Ellison wanted. To thematize and counter these powerful imaginaries and myths requires more than a principle of antidiscrimination or subordination; it requires a new language that can reveal the American nightmare and prepare for new imaginaries, not one more invocation of universal presuppositions or a reconstructed definition of political concepts.[120]

This collective inarticulacy was not just limited to such obvious forms of racism. Ellison contested similar misreadings by thinkers from the left as well, such as the well-known literary Irving Howe and the African American novelist and essayist Richard Wright. The details of the debate are not so important, but Ellison's thematization of the social imaginary and his understanding of the novel as a mode of argument are. The novel provides ways to take on the dominant configurations of the social imaginary of his time—whether they emerged in fiction, history, political discourse, newspaper columns, films, etc. The unit of argument cannot be the empirical or normative proposition but the vocabularies of the social imaginary: "All novels of a given historical moment form an argument over the nature of reality and are, to an extent, criticisms of each other" (1995: 165). Hence, for Ellison, "art is social action itself" (1995: 91). Ellison addresses directly language's political ambiguity and its ontological power to imprison and empower: "If the word has the potency to revive and make us free, it has also the power to blind, imprison, and destroy . . . The essence of the word is its ambivalence" (1995: 81). The novel moves beyond any facile claim about the social construction of race and identity in order to argue with its historical predecessors and their languages for the superiority of its way of understanding our imaginaries that are common to law, literature, philosophy, and history.

The Prologue to *Invisible Man* announces the text's challenges to the received public languages. In the opening scene, the narrating subject of the present—that is, the subject who has already been through the entire story that is about to be told—confronts the reader with an allegory of recognition. In this fable, the protagonist attacks someone who does not see him. This allegory initiates a drama of recognition, not just within the work but between text and reader, a warning that readers will simply repeat the misrecognition, commit a hermeneutic mugging of the text, if they are not prepared to give up the assumption of a shared linguistic world, which means giving up their self-understanding and going through a linguistic apprenticeship. Getting to the point where he could write the Prologue has required transformation and loss for the narrator and the reader should expect a similar wrenching.

The *Invisible Man* takes the entire novel to learn that he is "an invisible man" (1981: 5). Ellison brings out many of the dominant patterns of the

120 See Chiara Bottici's *A Philosophy of Political Myth*, which argues that myth is a perennial feature of the social imaginary that is continuously reworked in different times and places in the search for significance (Bottici 2007).

languages of his time—e.g., the discourse that urged acceptance of the status quo (the writer and educator Booker T. Washington), the discourse of black nationalist (Marcus Garvey), and the American Communist Party—and then has his protagonist inhabit and work through them, not just for himself but for the reader. Ellison describes the way he first evokes and then transforms these patterns: "I could not violate the reader's sense of reality, his sense of the way things were done, at least on the surface. My task would be to give him the surface and then try to take him into the internalities, take him below the level of racial structuring" (1995: 532). In the famous Battle Royal scene, in which a naked white women is paraded before black fighters, Ellison starts his staging of the myths of black sexuality, particularly the myth of the black rapist of white women that we find depicted in such works as Griffith's *Birth of a Nation*. Elllison did not seek to represent historical events or people but to draw out the structures of the imaginary that make available the world of reference: "I didn't want to describe an existing Socialist or Communist or Marxist political group, primarily because it would have allowed the reader to escape confronting certain political patterns, patterns which still exist" (1995: 538). The past cannot be simply put behind us "because it is within us. But we *do* modify the past as we live our own lives" (1995: 413). Ellison does not just expose negative languages; rather, he exercises his autonomy by combining genealogical and hermeneutical strategies to bring out the imaginaries in which we are embedded and to offer a new language for addressing the present. Ellison attends to the resources of various literary and social traditions, such as myths, African American folktales and modernist techniques of writing (e.g., his use of ritual drawn from T.S. Eliot). Ellison portrays language as an ambiguous protean medium that connects and isolates us, that shapes us in ways that open and foreclose the possibilities in the world.[121]

Ellison agrees with Habermas that human rights depend on popular sovereignty; however, instead of connecting them formally, Ellison reworks and theorizes the medium of deliberation. In the Introduction to *Invisible Man*, he announces his concern with the conditions of self-governance, conditions that cannot be thematized only in the liberal language of rights: "[D]uring the early, more optimistic days of this republic it was assumed that each citizen could (and should prepare to become) President. For democracy was considered not only a collection of individuals . . . but a collectivity of politically astute citizens who, by virtue of our vaunted system of universal education and our freedom of opportunity, would be prepared to govern" (1981: xxi). But if, as Habermas says, "popular sovereignty . . . resides in 'subjectless' forms of

121 This is what the subject-to-subject model of imagination of both Nussbaum and Hannah Arendt leaves out. During the desegregation struggles in Little Rock, Arendt thought the existing public language was in good enough shape for her to imagine what African Americans were thinking. See Steele 2002 for a critique of Arendt's philosophy of imagination.

communication and discourse circulating through forums and legislative bodies" (1996: 136), we need to understand the powers and constraints of these forms with a richer problematic than regulative ideals, one that addresses the capacity to imagine the relationship of individual to popular sovereignty.

Ellison's texts illustrate how the social imaginary is a rich interdisciplinary site for grasping political self-understanding and debate, whether one comes from a philosophical, sociological, or literary point of view. My development of the problematic of the social imaginary focused on overcoming the division in contemporary research on politics and the imagination noted by Bottici and Challand in the Introduction between two broad conceptions of the imagination—that is, as a faculty of the subject and as social context. While Ellison's texts can be read as part of an historical story about the shapes of the American imaginary during a particular period, they can also be read as one way of realizing the potential of the philosophical claim that the social imaginary is the inescapable, logically prior, terrain of argument that has been occluded by philosophy and social science. My reading of Ellison's fictional and nonfictional works shows some of the ways that political argument can draw on the broad canvas of the social imaginary to make its claims, but there are many more.

References

Anderson, B. 1991, *Imagined Communities: Reflections on the Origin and Spread of Nationalism*, London, Verso.

Armstrong, N. 2005, *How Novels Think: The Limits of Individualism from 1719–1900*, New York, Columbia University Press.

Bakhtin, M. 1981, *The Dialogic Imagination* (trans. C. Emerson and M. Holquist), Austin, University of Texas Press.

Balkin, J. 2001, *What Brown Should Have Said*, New York, New York University Press.

Benhabib, S. 2002, *The Claims of Culture*, Princeton, Princeton University Press.

Bottici, C. 2007, *A Philosophy of Political Myth*, Cambridge, Cambridge University Press.

Cascardi, A. 2009, 'The novel', in *Oxford Handbook of Philosophy and Literature*, Oxford, Oxford University Press.

Castoriadis, C. 1987, *The Imaginary Institution of Society* (trans. K. Blamey), Cambridge, MA, MIT Press.

Ellison, R. 1981, *Invisible Man*, New York, Vintage.

—— 1995, *The Collected Essays of Ralph Ellison*, New York, Modern Library.

Fiss, O. 2004, 'Another equality', *Issues in Legal Scholarship*, Article 20, http://www/.bepress.com/ils/1552/art20.

Foucault, M. 1977, *Discipline and Punish* (trans. A. Sheridan), New York, Vintage.

Habermas, J. 1987, *The Philosophical Discourse of Modernity* (trans. F. Lawrence), Cambridge, MA, MIT Press.

—— 1996, *Between Facts and Norms: Contributions to a Discourse Theory of Law and Democracy* (trans. W. Rehg), Cambridge, MA, MIT Press.

—— 1998, *The inclusion of the other: studies in political theory*, Cambridge, MA, MIT Press.
—— 2002, 'On legitimation through human rights', *Global Justice and Transnational Politics*, Cambridge, MA, MIT Press.
—— 2003, *Truth and Justification* (trans. B. Fultner), Cambridge, MA, MIT Press.
Meister, R. 1999, *Human Rights in Political Transitions: Gettysburg to Bosnia*, New York, Zone Books.
Monod, D. 2003, '"He is a cripple an' needs my love": Porgy and Bess as Cold War propaganda', in Scott-Smith, G. and Krabbendam, H. (eds) *The Cultural Cold War in Western Europe, 1945–1960*, London, Frank Cass.
Mouffe, C. 2005, *On the Political*, New York, Routledge.
Nussbaum, M. 1995, *Poetic Justice: The Literary Imagination and Public Life*, Boston, MA, Beacon Press.
Post, R. 2001, *Prejudicial Appearances*, Durham, NC, Duke University Press.
Rawls, J. 1993, *Political Liberalism*, New York, Columbia University Press.
Ricoeur, P. 1984–88, *Time and Narrative*, 3 vols. (trans. K. Blamey and D. Pellauer), Chicago, University of Chicago Press.
Said, E. 1978, *Orientalism*, New York, Pantheon.
—— 1993, *Culture and Imperialism*, New York, Knopf.
Salusinszky, I. 1987, 'Interview with Edward Said', in *Criticism in Society*, New York, Methuen, pp. 122–149.
Siegel, R. 2003–4, 'Equality talk: antisubordination and anticlassification values in constitutional struggle over Brown', *Harvard Law Review*, 117: 1470–1547.
Steele, M. 2002, 'Ellison versus Arendt on Little Rock: the role of language in political judgment', *Constellations: A Journal of Critical and Democratic Theory*, 9: 184–206.
—— 2005a, 'Ontologie linguistique et dialogue politique chez Bakhtine', in Thomson, C. and Collinot, A. (eds) *Bakhtine et la pensée dialogique*, London, ON, Mestengo Press: pp. 23–31.
—— 2005b, *Hiding from History: Politics and Public Imagination*, Ithaca, NY, Cornell University Press.
—— forthcoming, 'Moral shapes of time in Henry James', *Analecta Husserliana*.
Taylor, C. 1984, 'Philosophy and its history', in Rorty, R., Schneewind, J.B. and Skinner, Q. (eds) *Philosophy in History*, Cambridge, Cambridge University Press.
—— 1989, *Sources of the Self*, Cambridge, Harvard University Press.
—— 1999, 'Two Theories of Modernity', *Public Culture* 11(1): 153–74.
—— 2003, 'Rorty and Philosophy', in Guigon, C. and Hiley, D.R. (eds) *Richard Rorty*, Cambridge, Cambridge University Press.
—— 2004, *Modern Social Imaginaries*, Durham, NC, Duke University Press.
—— 2007, *A Secular Age*, Cambridge, Harvard University Press.

Chapter 11

Feminist imagination

The aesthetic role of critique and representation

María Pía Lara

The importance of the category of imagination is closely tied up with the conceptual development of the aesthetic discipline in the 18th century. Kant (1987) was the first author who situated this category at the center of his aesthetic theory in his *Critique of Judgment* (1987). He related such a category to its cognitive powers, although he did not think they were related to truth's validity. The aesthetic produced its own validity. Kant's concept of imagination gave account of the active operations which take place in the free play of understanding and sensibility. The concept of imagination differed from past versions because Kant did not regard it as a passive operation—a mimetic imagination—but as an active, productive imagination. With Kant's concept of imagination the category ceased to be conceptualized as a mirror projecting reflections of some external reality. Instead, imagination was seen as central to all knowledge and as a creative capacity. This kind of knowledge, Kant thought, was neither entirely subjective nor objective. It was a shared knowledge and the result of common sense (*sensus communis*).[122] The following development of this category taken by Hannah Arendt (1982) only enhanced Kant's original intuitions. As Mary Warnock claims "the mystery of how on earth we communicate with each other has been solved. For the world as it appears is genuinely common to us all, though grasped and understood by each" (1994: 14). We humans share the identical cognitive faculties of imagination and understanding projected on our capacity to communicate our judgments and on sharing our common sense (intersubjectivity). Thanks to the relevance of Arendt's intervention in rescuing Kant's original contribution to the concept of imagination, we now think about this concept as involving a Copernican revolution.[123] How did this revolution happen? It took some time—I wish to argue—to configure the new scenario where such a concept

122 For an eloquent development of the concept of *sensus communis* and of the role of imagination, see Ferrara 2008.

123 Key to these later developments on the concept of imagination are the works of Heidegger (1929: 140–149), Ricoeur (1969, 1978: 199–200, 1984, 1986: 215–216), Kearny (1994, 1998), Makkreel (1990), Ferrara (2008), and Lara (2007).

would play a significant role in providing the tools for the feminist revolution. To trace back some of the important historical developments that led to this conceptual transformation will be the subject of this chapter.

The concept of imagination in philosophy has always been regarded with suspicion or even rejections because of its relation to the concept of truth. Indeed, Kant and Arendt were two great exceptions in favor of considering imagination as an important category for knowledge. Romanticism made the category of imagination central for aesthetics and it remained as such until postmodernism tried to get rid of this romantic vision of imagination. Postmodern thinkers criticized the dichotomy involved when thinking about imagination as fiction versus knowledge and truth, or imagination and representation versus an original and a copy. With the emergence of numerous efforts led first by structuralists, post-structuralists, and deconstructionism, the philosophical category of imagination appeared to be dissolving into the plural and anonymous play of language. The thematization about imagination transferred into a discussion about the "imaginary" (Lacan). Such a concept carried a connotation of an impersonal—not subjective—entity. The so-called "humanist imagination" was replaced by notions of imitation where our understanding of the world was seen as preconditioned by plural performances and simulacra. Postmodern philosophers denied the very idea of an origin in a work of art (key to our understanding of imagination as a creative tool). Deprived from the earlier conception given by its aesthetic use, the category of imagination finally collapsed. Postmoderns argued that since there are no pre-existing truths of any kind, we are limited to finding the imitation as an imitation and this *ad infinitum* sequence denies any origin beyond itself. The paradoxical nature of this move against imagination is that with the social imaginary there was a curious return of the notion of mimesis (copy). At the same time, new theories about the social imaginary were developed by social scientists such as Benedict Anderson (1983) and Cornelius Castoriadis (1998). Their concerns with the social imaginary were built around notions of institutions and societies and how their identities were products first of the spaces of the imagined communities. They also reflected a new phenomenon: new social movements began using and developing a new conception of the powers of imagination. It was this version of imagination as powerful that led to the changes and transformations of contemporary societies after 1968. I wish to claim that along with the awoken self-awareness of an emergent global civil society, the new ways of understanding the social imaginary also shaped the most interesting revolution of the century: feminism.

In *Moral Textures* (1998), I focused on how feminist theories and contributions to the public literary sphere elaborated a concept of moral subjects by using the powerful tools of imagination. Feminists transformed our notions of moral identities with novel creations of expressive identities (such as self-fashioning and self-disclosure). My argument here will be to show how all the imaginative strategies used by feminism depended on the transformation of the concept of imagination tied up with an historical effort to imagine itself as the first global social movement. I trace the starting point of this process with the conceptual crisis that 1968 brought to the public discussion, which was followed by decades of transformations that led finally to a conceptual revolution. In other words, this conceptual crisis gave place to a new form of revolution: with the use of an aesthetic critique, which disclosed new communicative spaces of the social, the claims of women began to be expressed in terms of redefining the whole scenario of justice. In order to be able to trace back to the moment of conceptual change about the notion of imagination and the role that such a concept played in the aesthetic critique, I will focus first on three different historical stages at which certain narratives gave rather different accounts about how this happened (the social transformations that took place). In the second part of the chapter, I describe how the normative notion of the social imaginary and of imagination coined first by social theorists and then used by feminist interventions allowed for the transformation of the concept of social revolution—in the public sphere—through diverse techniques: (a) through a reinterpretation showing how political theories failed via omission or avoidance to include women as equals despite their claims of justice and equality, the two normative principles that were the core of modernity and of enlightenment; (b) through a discussion of how social practices and habits were parts of the established institutions of society that were designed by men (their designs were clearly targeted at confining women to the private sphere); (c) through immanent critique (social and political) which allowed those theorists of feminism to finally create new vocabularies of justice. I call this last stage *disclosive* because it entailed the new conceptual tools needed for a concept of agency and of empowerment. I call this process, therefore, the use of disclosive imagination.

1. Three narratives of the crisis and revolution

I wish to argue that contrary to the postmodern philosophers who argued about the death of the concept of imagination, 1968 and the decades that followed were periods not only of crisis, but also of deep transformations. They produced a major change in our vocabulary of social critique and justice. Indeed, the use of key concepts for social critique is one indicator of a major social transformation enacted after the historical events of 1968. I focus on three different narratives conceptualizing the paradigmatic changes that took place after 1968, which allow me to present the novel ways in which an aesthetic critique transformed our notions of social critique and justice. They were done through the use of the social imaginary, which helped reshape the ways in which humans conceived of themselves.

In the first narrative, developed by Luc Boltanski, the period was conceptualized as a crisis; in the second, developed by, among others, several Mexican writers, changes were conceptualized as revolutionary societal transformations;

and in the third, the feminist narrative developed by Nancy Fraser, the period is considered not as a rigid date of societal transformations, but rather, as a dynamic process of changes involving tensions, but also, important social transformations that led to a change in our notion about the meaning of justice (the different realms of justice). In my view, this third narrative—the feminist—discloses the paradigmatic moment of change that led to questioning the previous paradigm of justice, and replaced certain categories with others which illuminated the new social dimensions of justice involved in its critical scope. I will argue that this was done by how social movements and the different feminist theoretical interventions—coming from different positions—began to use the aesthetic category of public imagination (related to the social imaginary) and connected their concrete goals of transforming the spaces of social critique and of representation.

2. The crisis narrative

The first narrative, developed by Luc Boltanski, envisions the years preceding 1968 as a scene in which the role of critique was displayed in two different ways: One was the aesthetic critique inspired by artists and their notions of change and transformation.[124] It was inspired by questions related to social life that had not been included in a Marxist critique such as questions about the good life (happiness), the relations between autonomy and authenticity, and the inspiration of art as a locus of new ways of self-expression. The other kind of critique, *social* critique, was nurtured by different claims coming from labor conditions developed mainly by the left against capitalism. According to Boltanski, the goal of aesthetic critique targeted capitalism for "engendering a society of mass production and mass consumption"; it also put a special emphasis on the need to question the bourgeois form of life and to nurture the spontaneity of "individual creativity" based on the ideal of authenticity. As such, this kind of critique tended weakly toward the aim of "equality" and placed the accent on the creative quality of actions, happenings, and the politics of performance (Boltanski 2002: 6–7). The other kind of critique, the social, targeted different problems of capitalism and modernity.[125] This critique, according to Boltanski, got a specific reaction from capitalists' institutions in absorbing the claims from such a critique in order to revitalize capitalism.[126]

124 See Boltanski 2002.

125 Boltanski argues that "the years of 1965–1975 are marked by a very sharp rise in the level of critique against capitalism, culminating in 1968 and the following years. These critiques threatened capitalism with a significant crisis because they were "targeted at almost all of the established tests upon which the legitimacy of the social order was based" (2002: 8, 9).

126 Boltanksi argues that "one of the results of this redeployment is to have caused the balance between salaries and profits, which in the 1970s had shifted in favor of the employees, to

The success of the aesthetic critique in illuminating new social spaces and the absorption of the social critique by capitalism had the paradoxical result of depriving the role of the social critique from its edge against capitalistic forms of exploitation, and it displaced its main focus previously grouped around the production of material goods, and turned the attention to questions about the identity of human beings and their reproduction. This narrative claims that if the social critique failed to produce a new conceptual revolution, it was because of the way the aesthetic critique helped overshadow the quest for equality and placed its emphasis on identity and kinship relations without the further aim of radically transforming the relations of economic oppression coming from capitalism. The changes produced by the aesthetic critique caused a cultural revolution, but the social critique lost its focus against capitalism.

Boltanski's narrative gives the role of the aesthetic critique negative lenses, and his criticism against the social spaces opened by this kind of critique does not consider the innovative perspective of the social revolution promoted by feminist theories and social movements. Instead, Boltanski and Chiapello argue in *Le nouvel esprit du capitalisme* that the aesthetic critique based on the philosophical ideal of authenticity led to a new way to connect desire to consumerism.[127] Boltanksi develops a critique of how this ideal was taken also by capitalism in order to make it function as processes where fashioning identities would appeal to techniques of desire reified in terms of consumerism.[128] Features of how the authentic self evolves from being a locus of desire to being a consumer agent on the market makes this notion appear also as tainted by capitalist strategies. According to Boltanski's narrative, in the second half of the 1960s and the 1970s, the subject of authenticity underwent critical examination by postmodern thinkers such as Deleuze and Derrida. Their critical target was the ideals of authenticity coming from the aesthetic critique. They developed a critique against the concept of authenticity as stimulating social prejudices against popular classes (the masses, according to Bourdieu), against the metaphysics of presence (the metaphysical ideals of truth, according to Derrida), and against the concept of representation (the critical denial of an original versus the copy, according to Deleuze). These criticisms were targeted against the previous notion of a mimetic imagination

be tipped in a direction beneficial to capital. However, this was at the expense of a growth in inequality, job security and the impoverishment of significant groups among wage-earners" (2002: 11).

127 They consider Heidegger and Sartre as the two main figures who proposed the notion of authenticity as "the cure" for Heidegger and the "responsibility" in the case of Sartre, and they also include some members of the Frankfurt School such as Adorno, Horkheimer, and Marcuse as using similar notions related to authenticity, despite their criticism of Heidegger's philosophy (Boltanski and Chiapello 1999: 554).

128 The question of reification has been taken now by Axel Honneth (2007) in one of his most recent works.

(seen as an external mirror). Yet, their criticism of mimesis is really an inversion since they thematized the idea of art as a self-parody (Kearny 1998: 255). The result is that everything turned out to be a construction, a code, a spectacle and a simulacrum where there was no place for any kind of authority or notions of validity (Boltanski and Chiapello 1999: 576). Postmodern suspicions about the concept of imagination replaced it with a notion of the imaginary. Indeed, as Richard Kearny argues "the Romantic theory of imagination as a quasi-divine expression of some transcendental subject, the creation of new meaning out of nothing, is replaced by a postmodern concept of parody. The idea of an original imagination is revealed to be no more than an 'effect' of the endless *intertextuality* of language itself" (Kearny 1998: 182). Thus, Boltanski concludes, the aesthetic critique reached a paradoxical perspective with the postmoderns because their criticism threatened the critical validity of their own perspective due to the fact that for them everything was spectacle and simulacrum, and there was no exterior reference; neither was there any notion of truth or authenticity.

Since Boltanski's revision of the different roles of the aesthetic critique is very negative, his own perspective about what changed in the social dimension pays little attention to feminism. Thus, Boltanski's notion of the meaning of revolution is narrow, and impedes us from seeing what was novel about feminism when their social perspective was enriched by an aesthetic critique, and in how their novel use of the role of social imaginary was used to open the spaces of social critique. We will see that this is precisely what the second kind of critique highlights, albeit feminism is still absent from it.

3. The second narrative of social transformation

The second narrative is a mixture of how the Mexican writers—Carlos Fuentes (1968), Carlos Monsiváis (1971), and Jorge Volpi (1998)—approached the narration of the events of 1968 as an historical moment of revolution because of the aesthetic critique. The original and peculiar way in which this transformation took place was the means by which the aesthetic and cultural expressions appropriated the tools and categories of politics because politics needed the spaces and objects of the aesthetic realm to produce a new kind of critique. Indeed, for these writers, 1968 provided the first radical critique of modern art and of modern politics by establishing links between them. This was done by transforming the meaning of social imagination to supply the space for critique of the social and political powers.[129]

129 Indeed, the concept of modernity has been closely associated with the evolution of the aesthetic realm as a philosophical discipline that provided new categories associated with individuals' self-perceptions—such as autonomy, authenticity, subjectivity, identity, etc. The category of aesthetic subjectivity and the creation of categories associated with the new system of aesthetics became the tools with which to think about the historical and

The origin of this aesthetic revolution goes back to Marcel Duchamp. It was he who introduced the ready-made object which catalyzed an awareness of art as a system dominated by language and context, with meanings determined by consensus and use, rather than by qualities inherent in a handmade object. This initiative can be called the "Duchamp effect,"[130] and it deals with a notion of imagination as being disclosive because it is tied up with how language makes realities appear through the coining of concepts. The emergence of conceptualism illustrates how processes of "dematerialization" allowed one to redefine objects as carriers of meaning. In countries with repressive political regimes such as Mexico and other Latin American countries, dematerialization broke the stranglehold of the state in relation to the display of art. "Idea art" was easier to slip by the censors. As deployed by mainstream artists, institutional critique was derived from analysis of the conditions of capitalism and the problematic status of material goods (Huyssen 1990: 246). The struggles against authoritarian regimes galvanized much of the conceptualists' works in Latin America. Latin American conceptualists often aspired to address and mobilize the entire civil society. Artists became political activists and conceptual art became associated with political projects. Thus, dematerialization became a tool to approach art making and the emergence of an aesthetic critique—embodied in the poetical ways in which the aesthetic critique filtered the critical social claims from Mexican civil society. Soon, they became the tools and the subject of the students' revolt against the authoritarian regime in Mexico.

The student revolts already happening during May of 1968 in Paris inspired the Mexican students' movement. The common thread was the goal against authoritarianism and the rigid structures of capitalist societies. Much of what Boltanksi mentioned in his story is explored in the narratives of these writers, but their views are positive with regards to how the global claim against capitalism and authoritarianism took hold in the Mexican students' contribution to the Mexican social imaginary. The French poetic phrases

philosophical moment that we now call modernity. Modern art became the expression of this radical conception of change and acceleration investing the transformation of works of art as expressions of the new age—an avant garde—that led to the revolutionary movements in which the aesthetic expressions exploded. The peak of those changing movements that aspired to transform our conceptions of art and our perceptions could be exemplified with the so-called emergence of conceptualism. An important part of this process refers to the substance of how art had reached a point where it needed to leave behind traditional ways of understanding the work of art, the role of the spectators, and the realm of the public sphere. The beginning of this rupture can be traced to when Marcel Duchamp made his "ready-made" pieces.

130 Andreas Huyssen argues that "the revival of Marcel Duchamp as godfather of 1960s' postmodernism is no historical accident' because "the major goal of the historical European avant-garde (Dada, early surrealism, the postrevolutionary Russian avant garde) was to undermine, attack and transform the bourgeois institution of art and its ideology rather than only change artistic and literary modes of representation" (1990: 244).

that fed the social imaginary taken by the students' critiques against their authoritarian states opened a field of critique by removing old ideals, customs, and ways of seeing the world in the nascent conception of a society as a civic community against the state (Steele 2005: 410).[131] They used their disclosive–critical capacities to open up the space of the social imaginary and they invented new expressions of radical critique about social life. Fuentes, for example, reproduced the graffiti painted on the walls of the UNAM (the biggest university in Mexico City) and claimed that these efforts were the true poetry of liberation. Here are some examples offered by the writer which he found in the graffiti written in the walls of the campus: "I order the state of permanent happiness" (Faculty of Political Sciences), "Being free in 1968 means to participate" (Political Science), "The infinite has no accents" (Medicine), "Men are not stupid or intelligent, they are free or not" (Medicine); the most well known is "Behind the cobblestones there is the beach" (Sorbonne). Other imaginative examples in French campuses were "All power abuses, absolute power absolutely abuses" (Nanterre), "Our hope can only come from those who have no hope" (Political Science), "Don't take the elevator, take the power," "Be realistic, demand the impossible" (Fuentes 1968). The use of language to convey social criticism through the critical effect of the semantic shock produced by those phrases that reinvent a new meaning is what creates new ways of seeing the world. For the students, the issue was to redefine freedom and justice. However, the students' movement was still immersed in the Marxists' conceptual vocabulary, and thus, they saw the claims of women as secondary to the aim of an economic revolution (Cohen and Frazier 2004: 591–623).

It is true that the use of these poetic claims is also well embedded in Romanticism and on ideas about authenticity that led to what Boltanski's narrative has already highlighted. But it is also true that the shocking effects of metaphors that are used to displace the meaning into something altogether different became a way to enact a social critique by means of an aesthetic expression, which helped change Mexican society despite the failure to enact a social revolution. In 1968 Mexico was an authoritarian regime (governed by one party—the PRI) that would remain in power for more than 60 years. There was no real public sphere, freedom of speech, or any space for social critique. The initial demands from the students were aimed at the democratization of public institutions, the defense and respect for the constitution, and a clear demand for the enactment of rights. The narrative of these writers claimed that

131 Indeed, as Steele has argued, by "'public imagination' I mean not only the explicit linguistic concepts of a culture but also the images, plots, symbols, and background practices through which citizens imagine their lives. This social imaginary includes normative languages and assumptions about personhood, history, language, rights, etc." (Steele 2005: 410). See also his contribution to this volume.

the students' revolt became a renewal of a utopian imagination. The greatest claim—"all the powers to imagination"—opened the space of the social imaginary. It was a protest directed against conventions and institutions that appeared firmly and unchangeable established, against rules and regulations that had been established during decades and which were often met by tight control from the state. As such, capturing the historical moment via these narratives highlights the normative dimension of this kind of critique (the aspiring goals of change and transformation).

One of the most interesting elements about the ways in which the social imaginary came to fill the spaces of collective imagination was in how the students' movements embodied the first global movement. I wish to highlight that this embodiment could not have been possible without the existence of cinema, novels, the influential presence of authors, philosophers, and social scientists, who played the role of very public figures around the students' movements (Jean-Luc Goddard, Jean Paul Sartre, Simone de Beauvoir, etc.).

Although Volpi is critical about the real changes that occurred during 1968, he accepts that many of the changes that took place in the decades afterwards crystallized in the so-called *social* imaginary and occupied an important place in the transformation of Mexico as a democratic country. In my view, however, it was also the kind of provocation and spectacle—inspired by Dadaists' movements—that allowed the students revolt to enact a public spectacle which awoke Mexican civil society. The rigidity of habits and costumes, the meaning of political participation, and the capacity to demand many social and political rights that had been denied by the authoritarian state were until then unquestioned. Once 1968 unleashed the social critique, the goals of transforming the society remained latent in the minds of Mexican civil society. Dreaming about the impossible clarified how the effect of social critique had a big impact triggered by an aesthetic critique. As a process of critical self-examination, it contributed to the collapse of the authoritarian Mexican state.[132]

4. The feminist narrative of social revolution

This was a contested time. The use of imagination generated very different products. Feminism underwent a big change when theorists stopped re-interpreting modern liberal theories and their problematic views about women, and began by changing their focus of interest to the ways in which women are represented in the social imaginary, the culture, the novels, and the impact

132 Indeed, as Volpi recalls, "it is undeniable that between 1976 and 1994 there are two historical events that revived the spirit of 1968. The earthquake of 1985 provoked a generalized social reaction not seen before except during the student revolt in 1968; in front of the passivity, the uncontrolled and sloppiness of the Mexican government, Mexican civil society reacted by organizing themselves to cope with the challenge of the magnitude of the tragedy" (1998: 424).

that such narratives had in making apparent the male ideology underneath. The question of representation began to appear as the most relevant theoretical problem. Women refused to categorize themselves with essentialist features. Recall Huyssen's conclusion about the influence that art, movies, and fiction had in stimulating new critical works. This shift in focus was also influenced by postmodern theories and their recovery of the category of social imagination.

In order to trace how social imaginary became the conceptual scenario of feminism, we need to go back to Castoriadis' work. As Bottici has argued in her contribution included in this collection, Castoriadis was one of the first theorists to focus on the concept of the social imaginary by defining it as an institution. He claimed that "the institution of society" is filled with "a magma of social imaginary significations" which "institute the world" (Castoriadis 1998: 359). The way people imagine themselves and the way in which they draw significations are both tied up with an historical horizon in which language and meaning are intertwined. Needless to say that in the different concepts about the social imaginary there were changing notions coming from that magma of significations. Therefore, not only is the space of the imaginary historically situated but it also projects a normative agenda. This is the reason why, years later, Taylor added this normative part as an explicit definition of the social imaginary initially given by Castoriadis. Taylor argues that what he means by this is "something broader and deeper than the intellectual schemes people may entertain when they think about social reality in a disengaged mode." Indeed, "the way people imagine their social existence, how they fit together with others, how things go on between them and their fellows, the expectations that are normally met, and the deeper normative notions and images that underlie these expectations" (Taylor 2004: 23) configure the whole space of the social imaginary.

Paul Ricoeur developed the connection between the concept of disclosive imagination and social imaginary. In his influential book, *Time and Narrative* (1984), he focusses on how narrative imagination and the reader's reception of the text are connected in how we reshape ourselves in what we read. For Ricoeur, the act of reading became a laboratory of self-creations, the ways in which we shape ourselves. Plots are not only found in literature, but they are also part and parcel of how we invest ourselves into collective stories and histories, they exercise a formative influence in our modes of behavior in society through the social imaginary. As you can see, this view recovers well what the Mexican authors had already highlighted about the way in which 1968's profusion of culture and the media reshaped the normative agenda of young people.

It is through the use of those spaces of critique and representation that feminism entered a so-called cultural turn. The effects of this shift in emphasis became apparent when feminists linked representation to action and performance. Language was at the center of their research because it was filled with unknown power and power came to be the key category linked to action.

Thus far, I have mentioned the role of literature as a part of the aesthetic critique that helped build the critical stance for feminism and its conceptual connection to postmodern theories about the social imaginary. Literature, however, played its own distinct role in the cultural reconfiguration of language and the subject.[133] First, narratives were important because they codified a social order to legitimate the oppression of women. This is the main concern of feminists such as Teresa de Lauretis[134] and Sherry B. Ortner. The latter, for example, argues:

> I once spent time analyzing Grimm's *Fairy Tales*, with an interest in seeing the ways in which female agency was constructed differently from male agency, the ways in which heroines were different from heroes. I suppose I expected to find usual binaries: passive/active, weak/strong, timorous/brave, etc. What I had not quite expected to see was a recognition in the tales that female characters had to be *made* passive, weak, timorous, that is, a recognition that agency in girls had to be *unmade*. Most of Grimm's heroines are in the mode of what the folklorist Propp (1968) calls "victim heroes"; although they are protagonists, the action of the story is moved along by virtue of bad things happening to them, rather than their initiating actions in the case of the majority of male heroes. Thus non-agency, passivity, is to some extent built into most of them from the outset. Yet in many cases these victim heroines take the roles of active agency in the early parts of the story. Though their initial misfortunes may have happened to them through outside agency, they sometimes seize the action and carry it along themselves, becoming—briefly—heroines in the active questing sense usually reserved for male heroes.
>
> (Ortner 1996: 9)

Both de Lauretis and Ortner focus on the structure of narratives in order to deconstruct the concept of identity and our ways of representing women. As

133 To be fair, it was Julia Kristeva who connected the concept of the social imaginary to a hermeneutic approach. For her the imaginary is connected to psychoanalytic hermeneutics. See Kristeva 1987. This shift in emphasis is well captured by Kearny 1998: 186.

134 Teresa de Lauretis explains that "in a splendidly erudite and fascinating essay, 'Oedipus in the Light of Folklore' written in the years before the *Morphology* (1928) and 'The Historical Roots of the Fairy Tale', Propp combines the synchronic or 'morphological' study and motifs with their diachronic or historical transformations, which are due, he argues, to the close relationship between a society's folklore production and its modes of material production. However, he cautions, plots do not directly 'reflect' a given social order, but rather emerge out of conflict, the contradictions, of different social orders as they succeed or replace one another; the difficult coexistence of different orders of historical reality in the long period of transition from one to the other is precisely what is manifested in the tensions of plots and in the transformations or dispersion of motifs and plot types" (de Lauretis 1984: 113).

many contemporary feminists rightly understood, the complexity involved in the cultural codes of stories connected to male structures lies in how they (men) developed the concept and practices of the plot. Critical theories by Mikhail Bahktin, Vladimir Propp, and Tzvetan Todorov give full account of how this happens. Feminists used them in order to pursue different ways to theorize and construct feminist theories about representation and cultural critique. The significance of the meaning of the structure of the plot revealed how men saw their actions through narrative devices (the beginning, the development of a conflict, and the end as the resolution). Plots have been the cultural sources of *meaning* since the times of Greek literature. These earlier efforts by feminists grasped that the politics of representation could be understood also as political practices. Thus, many of them agreed that even though there is no place outside cultural codes that constitute the semiosis of those representational configurations, they needed a critical way to examine them. Faced with the challenges placed by the postmodern critique of the concept of imagination as lacking any validity, these theories needed to relate themselves to the products of literature that had already taken off from subject's representations based on the male's forms of plots. A key example about how literature had started to present some complex ways to understand subjectivity, language, and the role of the psyche can be found in Virginia Woolf's novels, more particularly, in *Mrs. Dalloway*, *Orlando*, and *The Waves*. *Orlando* is the story of a person whose gender changes according to different historical moments. Woolf offers us no linear plot of a hero such as Achilles. Orlando is undefinable because she is both a woman and a man, depending on the different historical moments. *Mrs. Dalloway* is a woman whose internal voice connects with different spaces and historical situations—an interior monologue—in one single day. *The Waves* is one of the first works of fiction to develop the formal consequences for the literary presentation of unbounded subjectivity. As Gabrielle Schwab argues, "it abandons the narrative structure of the novel in favor of an interior dialogue, a dialogue based on a new form of abstract and recurrent poetic images that does not unfold within characters but between them as *forms of unconscious dialogical interaction*" (Schwab 1994: 19; emphasis mine). Thus, with Woolf's texts we find already new configurations of poetic language heading toward new forms of expressing literary subjectivity and the poetic power of language.

The interesting feedback between literature and the aesthetic critique becomes apparent when one begins to understand that the critical efforts by feminist theorists (many of them were related themselves to postmodern theories)—following the two decades after 1968—concentrated on conceptualizing a radical reconfiguration of the notion of subjectivity. The issue was not the historical emphasis of the ways in which subjectivity was related to other concerns. Rather, by thematizing language and subjectivity, one could locate agency and power in a better way. Thus, the problem of the subject became highly politicized. In this way, feminists influenced mainly by Foucault's ideas on questions about representation extended their critique to this notion. They concluded that "this process with an *episteme was marked by the end of {the notion of} representation*" (Schwab 1994: 3). The following efforts were aimed at finding new and possibly fruitful notions about the concept of action as performance.

Faced with challenges placed by the postmodern critique of the concept of imagination as lacking any validity, feminist theories targeted conceptions of the subject, the moral agent, and the essentialist view of gender and sexuality. The most illustrative example of this radical shift was taken by Judith Butler who conceived social subjects as sites of performance and resignification. She argued that the gender parody of drag could be used as a potentially powerful political strategy to explore the fluidity of identities.[135] She developed her imaginative deconstruction of the meaning of gender and sex. As she argued in *Gender Trouble*, "although the gender meanings which are taken up in these parodic styles are clearly part of hegemonic, misogynist culture, they are nevertheless denaturalized and mobilized through their parodic recontextualization. As imitations which effectively displace the meaning of the original, they imitate the myth of *originality* itself" (Butler 1990: 188; emphasis mine). Butler then conceived social subjects as sites of resignification. Much of her subsequent work is developed by using the tools of the postmodern theory of the social imaginary (Althusser, Foucault, Kristeva, Lacan) to explore the hidden and imperceptible spaces (the psyche) where social subjects become subjected. She connected her critique to psychoanalysis in order to explore the paradoxes of subjection. At the same time, the disclosive dimension of the deconstruction of gender as a normative subjection technique was being questioned by the separation of sex and heterosexuality. Butler's particular way of defining her notion of critique is developed as a site of resistance. It involved a whole reconsideration about the meaning of agency. This is the reason she concentrates her best efforts not in defining identities as fixed but towards the exploration of the unknown (with tools of a psychoanalytic kind). She "explores the complicated relationships between will, desire, and power" (Allen 2008: 73). For example, in *Gender Trouble*, Butler examined drag in order to clarify the imitative structure of gender and its contingent or culturally determined nature (Butler 1990: 338). She concluded that the gender parody of drag could be used as a potentially powerful political strategy to explore the fluidity of identities. Butler develops the most accomplished connection to Foucault with her thematization of power.[136] For her, the task of feminists is to explore political genealogies of gender ontologies in order to expose the contingent acts that create the appearance of natural necessity. With this turn, she closes

135 Even though it was Julia Kristeva who first connected psyschoanalysis to the social imaginary, the interesting twist that Butler enables is to explore ways in which individual agents are subjected through normative definitions of the self.

136 For an analysis of feminism and Foucault, see McNay 1992. And for a very stimulating examination of Butler's ideas in relation to Foucault, see Allen 2008.

the foundational conception of politics and starts using critical reflection by thematizing subjection and resistance to test its limits, albeit with the same kind of complexities that Boltanski had already dealt with in his criticism of the postmodern aesthetic critique.

We can now move to Nancy Fraser's role as an example of the feminist narrative. I choose Fraser because she embodies a position that critically recovers the different positions of feminism and her aim is to go beyond the cultural turn. I find a striking resemblance between her account and the critique elaborated earlier by Luc Boltanski. They share some similarities in their criticism about what happened after the 1960s' revolutions—an historical time when feminist theories lost sight of the economic dimension of social justice. Both claimed that this was due to much of what happened during the 1970s and the 1980s in relation to claims about difference and about identity politics. The big difference between these two narratives is that Fraser is not concerned with recovering the conceptual vocabulary of Marx (classes, modes of production, etc.). Rather, her aim is to bring back the Marxist concern about the notion of equality into a new formulation. In order to do so, she coins a normative concept—"parity of participation"—which is a concept that presupposes imagining human beings as capable of interacting with each other with equal standing. Participatory parity means that redistribution is a much needed measure in order to allow material resources to assure independence and voice to all participants. Second, the focus on institutional patterns of cultural value are seen as most relevant since we need to see how transformations are needed in our cultural paths and how we represent one another so that we can assure all participants an equal opportunity to achieve social esteem. Thus, parity of participation is a category that comes as a result of historical reflexivity, a process which has allowed the possibility of envisioning new ways in which to define justice. Fraser also offers us a core intuition about agency with three different features: independence, self-esteem, and empowerment. The result of her theory ends up redesigning key connections between the categories of equality and moral worthiness.

Fraser is also the best example of disclosive imagination because she is not only concerned with economic reforms or the representation of gender in the social imaginary. Rather, her newly coined concepts disclose previously unseen spaces of justice: in the economical, in the institutional practices of status, and in the political dimension of political *representation* (*who should participate and why*).

In order to understand how this happened, we need to go back to Fraser's earlier critique of Habermas' (1995) concept of one single public versus the state. The public sphere appeared in Habermas' historical reconstruction as a "space" which arose "in the broader strata of the bourgeoisie as an expansion and at the same time completion of the intimate sphere" (1995: 50). Habermas argued that "the bourgeois public sphere may be conceived above all as the sphere of private people [who] come together as a public" (1995: 27). Fraser criticized Habermas' definition of a "public" as a singular entity because such a notion was used by liberal theories as "an ideological notion that functioned to legitimate an emergent form of class (and race) rule" (1997: 76). Fraser understood correctly that the public sphere and the idea of one public were both vehicles of historical transformations produced by the political domination of a *male, white public*. Thus, in her criticism the Marxist element of power (as domination) was thematized as the locus of how one stratum of society rules the rest by using normative notions that are universal only on formal basis. Her way of making this criticism extended its scope by highlighting the features of this masculine bourgeois notion of the public sphere (Habermas 1995). The first feature critically examines the notion of representation because the assumption that it is possible for interlocutors in a public sphere to bracket *status differentials* to deliberate "*as if they were social equals*" (Fraser 1997: 76), when in reality they were not, is at the center of the problem of inequality. Fraser showed how this situation cannot be overcome by focussing on formal exclusions but by showing how the liberal model of the bourgeois public sphere requires the "bracketing [of] *inequalities of status*" (1997: 77). This critical concern was already pointing to the need for a transformation of a concept of representation for the actors in the public sphere. This was the reason that led Fraser to conclude that actors could not participate as equals because "*social inequalities were not eliminated but only bracketed*" (1997: 77; emphasis mine). This critique about how to bring back the concern for equality will dominate her work until she finally coined the normative principle of "parity of participation."[137] This principle is meant to provide the possibility of an active way to solve the problems of inequality as we will see in her expanded view of justice.

Against Axel Honneth's enlarged conception of recognition, she claims that a vision about justice where one category is supposed to provide all the tools and references to overcome the ills of society is never enough. Instead, Fraser argues, we need to enlarge our understanding of justice to be three dimensional. We need to envision how the spaces of economic redistribution along with the dimension of misrecognition and the lack of political representation are parts of an enlarged paradigm of justice (Fraser and Honneth 2003: 36).

Thus, at the heart of Fraser's analysis is the concern to focus on institutional patterns and institutional spaces in need of being reconceptualized within the social imaginary. Precisely because of her concern with the different levels of justice related to practices and institutions, Fraser needed to add a third dimension of justice: the political now conceived as a critical normative question about what political representation means for whom and why.[138]

137 Her definition of this concept is the following: "According to this norm, justice requires social arrangements that permit all (adults) members of society to interact with one another as peers" (Fraser and Honneth 2003: 36).

138 She is dealing here with political exclusions and marginalization. This political dimension considers the problem of the frame: "For every issue, they should ask: who precisely are the relevant subjects of justice?" (Fraser and Honneth 2003: 87).

Fraser understands that claims of recognition are situated in the social imaginary as parts of the larger scenario of the institutions of society. Although the neo-Hegelians such as Axel Honneth (1995) and Charles Taylor (1994) had contributed to the debate about justice and the good life with their recovery of the category of recognition, it was Fraser's criticisms leveled against both authors that centered the key critical issues about this category on an institutional basis. Contrary to what Honneth and Taylor argued, recognition for her becomes part of the problem of justice because she understands that when subjects are mistreated—either by ways of being portrayed or by the prejudices expressed in our ways of being represented—we need to address the problem as *institutional* mechanisms of *misrecognition*. In order to do this we need to focus on the relation between the social imaginary and the institutions that shape social and political identities and their social and political *practices*. If Habermas dealt with the public sphere and the literary practices that contributed to define the new social subjects, Fraser pointed at the ways in which those literary works, codes, plots and images institutionalize patterns of domination. Thus, we need to deal with how institutional forms of misrecognition and normative claims about representation should interpenetrate our critical analysis. This is the reason why she realized that there was a need to reconfigure the limits and frontiers of the political by reformulating the question about who can become a subject of justice, that is, by addressing the question about the *fairness* of the frame. Fraser thus elaborated a map where frames and borders could be thematized as normative meta-questions concerning the fairness of the frame. With Fraser's new paradigm, the concept of representation stopped being used only as a mirror effect of social exclusions, and turned out to be a reflexive stance, a critical, creative device. It became a normative site where disclosing the expansion of the spaces of justice were possible by creating a new vocabulary of justice.

Thus, Fraser's narrative expands the meaning of social and theoretical tensions in order to explore the paradigm of justice. Here is an example of how she maps the feminist imagination:

> It originated, in other words, as a part of a broad effort to transform an economist political imaginary that had narrowed political attention to problems of class distribution. In this first (the new social movements) phase, feminists sought to burst open the *imaginary*. Exposing a broad range of forms of male dominance, they propounded an *expanded view of the political as encompassing 'the personal'* [notice here how the disclosive sentence was raised as a critique]. Later, however, as the utopian energies of the New Left declined, feminism's anti-economistic insights were resignified and selectively incorporated into an emerging *new political imaginary* that foregrounded cultural issues [observe the resemblance with Boltanski's views and her original intuitions]. Effectively captured by this culturalist imaginary, *feminism reinvented itself* as politics of recognition. In this second

> phase, accordingly, feminism became preoccupied with culture and was drawn into the orbit of identity politics. Although it was not often noticed at the time, feminism's identity politics phase coincided with a broader historical development, the fraying of nationally based social democracy under pressure of global neoliberalism. Under these conditions, a culture-centered politics of recognition could not succeed.
>
> (Fraser 2005: 296)

Her critique of the *dangerous liaison* between feminism with neoliberalism made her push her efforts further than simply making a critique of the previous historical stages of feminism. In her view, feminism needs to push forward into becoming an exemplar of a new social theory about emancipation.

In a following article, Fraser (2008) called "abnormal justice" the stage that led to the conceptual crisis of how to define justice as a new enlarged paradigm. This term highlights the tensions of the historical period through the effects caused by the changes in our recent past vocabularies. The concept of the imaginary that she uses is also disclosive in the sense that her criticism understands the links created by the different questions regarding the processes of socialization and individuation through institutional means and practices. Even though she partially acknowledges the role of an aesthetic critique, Fraser uses the notion of a social imaginary by drawing on how the conceptual spaces of justice can enlarge the meaning of inequalities when new social dimensions are disclosed by normative claims. One example of this disclosive use of the concept of imagination in Fraser's analysis is her feminist frame about the problem of misrecognition related to status. When addressing the problem as such, a development of a concept of public imagination is needed, since we need it to make us aware of how the question of status representation involves images, narratives, institutional portrayals of ourselves that feed our social imaginary.

5. Conclusion

Thus, the connection of the mapping of new spaces, along with the development of a concept of a social imaginary as a part of the space for critique is what provides us with a better understanding of how feminism enacted a radical revolution. It involved a huge process of development of theories that led to a change in the conceptual vocabulary. It took a critical effort to assess how concepts about class and production could not give full account of the inequalities existing between men and women. It also needed to develop different concepts that define social institutions and their ways of oppression (the family and the state). The question of how Marx envisaged the "superstructure" could not give the full account of how the complexity of social institutions (including the market) is also involved in non-causal ways to the social and the political spheres. Feminists first needed to contextualize their critique in terms of the roles they occupied as social agents (representation), and how they were reflected in terms of institutional practices and in the social *imaginary*. *Only in this perspective* could social actors visualize the kinds of inequality involved in the relations between men and women. Even if identities are conceived as culturally and socially constructed, they can be questioned critically precisely in terms of forms of domination and by clarifying the normative places subjects should occupy in our practices. Transformations can occur only when there are possibilities of offering new institutional normative designs and in a category that highlights equality as an institutional right (parity of participation). Fraser's critique allows us to think in terms of the measures needed in order to transform our previous notions of justice by focusing on social institutions and its practices. Understood in this way, we can see how Fraser's account becomes one good example of the feminist revolution enacted by means of the expansion of the scope of justice.

References

Allen, A. 2008, *The Politics of Ourselves. Power, Autonomy, and Gender in Contemporary Critical Theory*, New York, Columbia University Press.

Anderson, B.R. 1983, *Imagined Communities: Reflections on the origin and spread of nationalism*, London, Verso.

Arendt, H. 1982, *Lectures on Kant's Political Philosophy*, Chicago, University of Chicago Press.

Boltanski, L. 2002, 'The left after May 1968 and the longing for total revolution', *Thesis Eleven*, 69: 1–20.

Boltanski, L. and Chiapello, E. 1999, *Le nouvel esprit du capitalisme*, Paris, Gallimard.

Butler, J. 1990, *Gender Trouble: Feminism and the Subversion of Identity*, New York, London, Routledge.

Castoriadis, C. 1998, *The Imaginary Institution of Society*, Cambridge, MA, MIT Press.

Cohen, D. and Frazier, L.J. 2004, 'México 68: hacia una definición del espacio del movimiento. La Masculinidad heroica en la cárcel y las "mujeres" en las calles', *Estudios Sociológicos*, XXII (66): 591–623.

de Lauretis, T. 1984, *Alice Doesn't. Feminist Semiotics Cinema*, Bloomington, IN, Indiana University Press.

Ferrara, A. 2008, *The Force of the Example. Explorations in the Paradigm of Judgment*, New York, Columbia University Press.

Fraser, N. 1997, *Justice Interruptus. Critical Reflections on the 'Post-Socialist' Condition*, New York, London, Routledge.

—— 2005, 'Mapping the feminist imagination: from redistribution to recognition to representation', *Constellations*, 12 (3): 295–307.

—— 2008, 'Abnormal justice', *Critical Inquiry*, 34 (3): 393–422.

Fraser, N. and Honneth, A. 2003, *Redistribution or Recognition. A Political-Philosophical Exchange*, London, New York, Verso.

Fraser, N. and Nicholson, L. 1990, 'Social criticism without philosophy: an encounter between feminism and postmodernism', in Nicholson, L.J. (ed.) *Feminist and Postmodernism*, New York, London, Routledge.

Fuentes, C. 1968, *París: la revolución de mayo*, Mexico City, Era.

Habermas, J. 1995, *The Structural Transformation of the Public Sphere. An Inquiry into a Category of Bourgeois Society*, Cambridge, MA, MIT Press.
Heidegger, M. 1929, *Kant and the Problem of Metaphysics*, Bloomington, IN, Indiana University Press.
Honneth, A. 1995, *The Struggle for Recognition: The Moral Grammar of Social Justice*, Cambridge, MA, MIT Press.
—— 2007, *Reificación. Un estudio en la teoría del reconocimiento*, Buenos Aires, Katz.
Huyssen, A. 1990, 'Mapping the postmodern', in Nicholson, L.J. (ed.) *Feminist and Postmodernism*, New York, London, Routledge.
Kant, I. 1987, *Critique of Judgment*, Indianapolis, Cambridge, Hackett Publishing Company.
Kearny, R. 1994, *The Wake of Imagination*, New York, London, Routledge.
—— 1998, *Poetics of Imagining. Modern and Post-Modern*, New York, Fordham University Press.
Lara, M.P. 2007, *Narrating evil: a postmetaphysical theory of reflective judgment*, New York, Columbia University Press.
—— 1998, *Moral textures: Feminist narratives in the public sphere*, Berkeley, University of California Press.
Kristeva, J. 1987, *Soleil noir: depression et mélancolie*, Paris: Gallimard.
Makkreel, R.A. 1990, *Imagination and Interpretation in Kant. The Hermeneutical Import of the Critique of Judgment*, Chicago, London, University of Chicago Press.
McNay, L. 1992, *Foucault and Feminism*, Boston, MA, Northeastern University Press.
Monsiváis, C. 1971, *Días de guardar*, Mexico City, Era.
Ortner, S.B. 1996, *Making Gender. The Politics of Erotic Culture*, Boston, MA, Beacon Press.
Propp, V. 1968, *Morphology of the Folktale*, Austin, University of Texas Press.
Ricoeur, P. 1969, *Le Conflit des interpretations*, Paris, Seuil.
—— 1978, *The Rule of Metaphor*, London, Routledge.
—— 1984, *Time and Narrative. Vol. III*, Chicago, University of Chicago Press.
—— 1986, *Du texte à l'action*, Paris, Seuil.
Schwab, G. 1994, *Subjects without Selves. Transitional Texts in Modern Fiction*, Cambridge, MA, Harvard University Press.
Steele, M. 2005, 'Hiding from history: Habermas' elision of public imagination', *Constellations*, 12 (3): 409–436.
Taylor, C. 1994, 'The politics of recognition', in Gutman, A. (ed.) *Multiculturalism: Examining the Politics of Recognition*, Princeton, NJ, Princeton University Press.
—— 2004, *Modern Social Imaginaries*, Durham, NC, London, Duke University Press.
Volpi, J. 1998, *La imaginación al poder. Una historia intelectual de 1968*, Mexico City, Era.
Warnock, M. 1994, *Imagination and Time*, Cambridge, Blackwell.

Chapter 12

Visual studies and global imagination

Susan Buck-Morss

1. Introduction

Whatever the stated goals of visual studies, its effect is the production of new knowledge and its first challenge is to be aware of this.[139] According to one well-established, critical tradition, this means questioning the conditions of its own production. Why is visual studies a hot spot of interest at this time? Whose interests are being served? In analyzing the technologies of cultural production and reproduction, can visual studies affect their use? Is this inquiry merely a response to the new realities of global culture, or is it producing that culture, and if the latter, can it do so critically? These questions are not academic. They are concerned unavoidably with the larger world, and with the inevitable connection between knowledge and power that shapes that world in general and fundamentally political ways.

I will be very bold. Visual studies can provide the opportunity to engage in a transformation of thought on a general level. Indeed, the very elusiveness of visual studies gives this endeavor the epistemological resiliency necessary to confront a present transformation in existing structures of knowledge, one that is being played out in institutional venues throughout the globe, and discussed in other parts of this volume.

Western scientific and cultural hegemony was the intellectual reality of the first 500 years of globalization, lasting from the beginning of European colonial expansion to the end of the Soviet modernizing project. It will not remain hegemonic in the next millennium. Our era of globalization, in which communication rather than coinage is the medium of exchange, presses

139 This chapter, published in a slightly shorter form in *Papers of Surrealism* (2004: 2), was originally the transcript of a lecture given during a trip to the United Kingdom as the 2004 Visiting Scholar at the AHRB Research Centre for Studies of Surrealism and its Legacies. It was delivered at the universities of Manchester and Essex as well as the Tate Modern, London (June 3, 2004). The eponymous lecture was accompanied by a series of pictures and sculptures illustrating Susan Buck-Morss' talk. The webcast of the lecture and following questions can be seen at http://channel.tate.org.uk/media/26613605001 (accessed July 2010).

technologically toward transforming the social relations of knowledge production and dissemination (see Bazzicalupo's contribution in this volume for a discussion). We are at a cusp. Visual studies exists within this transitional space as a promise and a possibility, capable of intervening decisively to promote the democratic nature of that transformation. Nothing less is at stake for knowledge. Transdisciplinary rather than a separate discipline, visual studies enters a field of negotiation for the move away from western hegemony towards the construction of a globally democratic public sphere.

The global transformation of culture that catches us in its midst is not automatically progressive. The technological possibilities of the new media are embedded in global relations that are wildly unequal in regard to production capacities and distributive effects. Their development is skewed by economic and military interests that have nothing to do with culture in a global, human sense. But there are forces now in play that point to the vulnerability of present structures of power. Images circle the globe today in de-centered patterns that allow unprecedented access, sliding almost without friction past language barriers and national frontiers. This basic fact, as self-evident as it is profound, guarantees the democratic *potential* of image production and distribution – in contrast to the existing situation.

Globalization has given birth to images of planetary peace, global justice, and sustainable economic development that its present configuration cannot deliver. These goals are furthered not by rejecting the processes of globalization, but by reorienting them. Reorientation becomes the revolution of our time.

2. Reorientation: the history of art

I do not wish to overstate the role that critical intellectual practices can play on a global scale. Academics are participants in these global processes, nothing more, but also nothing less. Reorientation means precisely to be aware of this participatory status, which can mean in our case, not to narrow our vision to academic politics as if all that were at stake in the advent of visual studies were funding decisions and departmental hiring. And yet the debate over these very parochial concerns is where to begin, because reorientation occurs vis-à-vis particular positions, not some abstract universal. "Think global: act local," as the slogan has it, and in this context, the widely held view that visual studies is a recent offshoot of art history deserves our scrutiny. What does reorientation entail in the local sense of one academic discipline, the history of art, which has become central to discussions of visual studies? There is no facile or single answer to this question because this discipline, as a microcosm of the general situation, finds itself in a contradictory position: On the one hand, the history of art as traditionally practiced is most vulnerable to the challenge of visual studies. On the other, as the most authoritative domain for the modern study of the visual, it can lay strong claim to be its legitimate home. How did the situation of this one academic locality arise?

The history of art has in the past been content as a small discipline, approaching the development of, specifically, *western* art (indeed, it has treated art and western art as nearly synonymous). It adhered to an established canon of artists and works, only slowly allowing new names to enter sainthood. Within American universities, its greatest impact was the survey course that it traditionally offered undergraduates, who learned from large lectures and dual slide projectors what counts as art, and why. This is "art appreciation," and has been a staple of higher education, producing future generations of museum goers. At the same time, and against all modest pretensions, art history was unabashedly elitist in its presumptions of connoisseurship. With growing alarm, it defended the boundary that separates culture, indeed, civilization itself, from the barbarous kitsch of an increasingly invasive culture industry.

The attack came from within, however, from the artists themselves, who brought the Trojan horse of commodity culture into the hallowed grounds of the museum. Andy Warhol's Brillo Boxes were a defining moment, an invasion of the museum by commercial design causing, as Arthur Danto famously expressed it, nothing less lethal than the "end of art" (Danto 1984). Yet since that pronouncement (four decades ago) the production of art has not only increased, it has exploded, establishing its own global orbit as the "artworld."

Although we now accept it as commonplace, the artworld is, in fact, a historically unique phenomenon. Its precondition was the transformation of art patronage and art purchases that occurred with the new global economy. The world trade in art intensified in the 1970s and 1980s as part of a general financial revolution, along with hedgefunds, international mortgages, and secondary financial instruments of all kinds. The explosion of the art market caused a reconfiguration of the history of art: the western canon (which now included the art of a modernism-grown-obsolete) became only one of the founding traditions of contemporary art that for its part, with the aid of corporate patronage, expanded globally along an ever-increasing circuit of biennials and international exhibitions.

Whereas in Warhol's art and pop art generally, corporate images provided the content for art interventions, now corporations are art's entrepreneurial promoters. Their logos appear as the sponsors of art events, the enablers of art and, indeed, high culture generally. Within the confines of the artworld, everything is allowed, but with the message: THIS FREEDOM IS BROUGHT TO YOU BY THE CORPORATIONS. Corporate executives have become a new generation of art collectors (advertising and PR giant Charles Saatchi, for example), connecting the business class directly to the class of art connoisseurs. But unlike their predecessors (William S. Paley of CBS-TV, for example, whose beautiful collection of small oil paintings was intensely personal), the taste of the new art moguls is special, particularly in regard to size. Corporate patronage encourages Big Art—art that precisely cannot be privately housed and exhibited. Note that size is a formal characteristic that has nothing to do with art's content. With Big Art, the authenticity of the original assumes its aura on the basis of sublime proportions.

There is something remarkable about this shift in the position of big business from being the visible content of pop art to being the invisible producer of global exhibitions, from *being* the scene to being *behind* the scenes: the profits that result from the advertising and packaging of products (value added to commodities produced by cheap labor globally) now gives financial support to the high culture of a new, global economic class.

But before concluding that globalization is the problem, we need to recognize the global artworld as itself a contradictory space—suggesting again that reorientation rather than rejection is the best political strategy. On the one hand, globalization transforms art patronage into corporate financing of blockbuster shows and turns the art market into a financial instrument for currency hedging. On the other, its cavernous size allows ample opportunities for alternative art, myriad forms of cultural resistance. Moreover, the global artworld's inclusion of the vibrant, new work of non-western artists is quickly overwhelming the traditional story of art as a western narrative. Non-western artists are denied the luxury of imagining art as an isolated and protected realm. Reflection on the larger visual culture, the collective representations of which frame their art, is difficult, if not impossible to avoid. Even if the artworld's financial motives for the inclusion of these new artists have been less than laudable—the establishment of market niches for culture produced by the exotic "other"—the results have been so transformative that the history of art as an inner historical phenomenon can no longer contain it. Western art history, once deeply implicated in the history of western colonialism, has, in turn, become threatened, in danger of colonization by the global power that visual culture has become.

3. The crisis of art history

It is noteworthy that while departments of literature have also felt the onslaught of the new, global visual culture, they appear to be less threatened. Film studies, for example, can be absorbed within traditional literary categories of narrative, plot, and authorial style. Movie genres replicate the narrative forms of written fiction: comedy, mystery, science fiction, melodrama, historical drama, and the like. Shakespeare as playwright and Shakespeare's plays as cinema can be fruitfully compared. The critical methods of literature when applied to films not only work, they tend to reaffirm literature's superiority. The techniques of filmmaking tend to get less attention than cinema's narrative and textual qualities, which are culled as virgin territory for theories designed in other university venues: psychoanalysis, semiotics, queer theory, feminism, post-colonialism—with the unfortunate consequence that the visual is often repressed in the process of its analysis, blanketed over by thick, opaque layers of theoretical text so that, visually, only a few film stills or video clips remain.

If the discipline of the history of art is more profoundly affected, it is because unlike literary studies, it cannot avoid direct discussion of the visual. Visuality is the point of crisis at which the history of art and the study of visual culture necessarily collide. To be sure, imagery (symbol, allegory, metaphor, and the like) plays a dominant role in literature. Language is full of images, and there is no way within literary studies that an analytical distinction between image and word can be sustained. But the image that is visibly perceptible is distinct. In it, the word participates as itself an image, as calligraphy or as print material (in collage, for example), the meaning of which is tied to its visibility, and cannot be reduced to semantic content.

It was the advent of photography that allowed an experience of the image in its pure form, separate from both literary texts and works of art. Of utmost significance is the fact that the visual experience provided by the photograph is of an image collectively perceived. Unlike the inner experiences of a mental image, dream image or hallucination, this image is not the product of individual consciousness. Photographs were first conceived as a "film" off the surface of objects. (Painting retreated from mimetic realism and moved into visual modalities where the camera could not follow.) Now, the history of art as a discipline became indebted to the new technology of photography in ways largely unrecognized within the discipline's own foundational stories, and without parallel in literary studies' relationship to cinema.

In Europe's early modern era, art appreciation depended on visiting the sites; the grand tour of the ancient art and architecture of Italy and Greece was the classic example. Later the national museums brought the masterpieces to urban capitals and lent to them accessibility beyond the aristocratic class, while art classes of national academies took place in the galleries themselves.

I do not know when coffee-table books of art first became common and inexpensive enough to grace the homes of the middle classes. Books of plates of art masterpieces are much older, dependent on reproduction technologies of early printing. But since the end of the 19th century, art history as a university discipline has relied on the technology of the slide projector, displaying images of masterpieces from those small, squares of film mounted in frames, called "transparencies," that enabled the transportation of art masterpieces to educational settings far apart from the original artworks' museum home.

It is in the moment of the digitalization of art slide collections that we are made aware of the extent to which the history of art has been mediated by the photographic image, allowing art to be shown as slides. Transparencies do strange things to the art original: they destroy the sense of material presence, of course. But they also flatten brushstroke texture, they play tricks on the luminescence of the original, and, most strikingly, they distort scale. All images shown in the art history lecture hall (and also in the coffee-table art book) are the same relative size, dependent, not on the size of the object (salon paintings and gothic cathedrals are equivalents) but on the size of the book page, or on the focal distance between projector and screen.

What I am getting at is that the history of art has long been a visual study of images as well as—and often more than—a study of present art objects. Hence the challenge of visual studies is that it exposes the history of art as having been visual studies all along.

4. The mysteries of the image

Visual studies, for which the image is of central concern, begins with a dilemma. It can be expressed in the juxtaposition of two modern judgments of the image. The first is by Julia Kristeva from an interview in *Parallax*: "[I]mages are the new opium of the people" (Kristeva 2003: 22). The second is by Walter Benjamin from his 1928 essay on surrealism: "Only images in the mind motivate the will" (Benjamin 1999). Are images the inhibitor or are they the enabler of human agency? Can these two, apparently contradictory, claims be reconciled?

When Marx declared religion as the opium of the masses, he did not merely dismiss it, but took religion seriously as an alienated form of collective social desire. Likewise, Kristeva acknowledges that images do provide "a temporary relief" from "the extinction of psychic space"; but she warns that insofar as they are substitutes for psychic representations, they are themselves a symptom of the problem, which she sees as the decline of psychic imagination in this "planetary age" (Kristeva 2003: 21–2).

Benjamin's optimism is not irreconcilable with Kristeva's critique, if what she sees as our endangered "psychic representations" are his surrealist-inspired "images in the mind." But there is no easy equivalence in these two approaches—her psychic representations are individual and internal; his images are collective and social. What is at issue is the philosophical status of the image *tout court*, leading us to the mysteries of the image. What is it? Where is it located? If non-mental images are a film off of objects, how does this record of the world become a psychic representation, an "image in the mind"? What is the relation of non-mental images to mental ones, to causality, to reality, to sociality?

The *political* question is this: How can individual, psychic representations have social and political effect if *not* through the sharing of images, and how can these be shared if not through precisely that image culture that threatens to overwhelm our individual imaginations that, Kristeva claims, need protection from it?

Let us consider more closely the mysteries of the image, which photography and cinema bring into sharp relief. If we can name anything as an object specific to visual studies, it is the image. It is a medium for the transmission material reality. But it would be wrong to conclude that we should conflate visual studies with media studies, as if only the form of transmission matters. An image is tied to the content that it transmits. The traditional artwork is tied to content too, of course, but with this difference: The artwork is produced through the active intervention of a subject, the artist, who may be working realistically to render an object as an imitation of nature, or romantically to express an inner feeling, or abstractly to express the pure visual experience itself. But the artwork in all these cases represents, whereas the image gives evidence. The meaning of the artwork is the intention of the artist; the meaning of the image is the intentionality of the world.

If the world as picture (Heidegger's phrase) fits reality into a frame and gives it meaning in that way, the world as image takes intentionality from the object, as its material, indexical trace. The image is taken; the artwork is made. When I speak of evidence here I mean it in a phenomenological rather than legal sense—not juridical proof, but closer to Husserl's description of the *schlagender Evidenz* ("striking evidence") of sensory intuition. (Husserl and Bergson, philosophers of the era of photography and early cinema, have become central to discussions of visual studies.) The fact that photographic evidence is regularly manipulated and can often lie, the fact that we "see" what we are culturally and ideologically predisposed to see, is not the point. False evidence is no less *evident* than true evidence (the term refers to visibility, the ability to be seen at all). An image—its evidence—is apparent; its adequacy is a function of that which appears, regardless of whether this is an accurate reflection of reality. An image takes a film off the face of the world and shows it as meaningful (this is what I am describing as objective intentionality), but this apparent meaning is separate from what the world may be in reality, or what we, with our own prejudices, may insist is its significance.

Note that in the case of a slide transparency of a painting, the evidence provided is of the artwork itself. Leaving the romantic idea of artist-as-image-creator behind, the image-as-evidence that records the intentionality of the object points to the priority of the material world. Of course, it takes artistic vision to produce a scene from which a filmic image can be taken. But the scene itself is composed of objects (in Luis Buñuel and Salvadore Dali's *Un chien andalou*, a dead donkey's head on a grand piano). The distinction between subjective and objective intentionality is not necessarily the same as that between art and photography: In "arty" photographs, subjective intention dominates, whereas artists have produced "paintings" in which the intentionality of the object is recorded (as in Picasso's collage). Is a collage art, or is it reality? Is a film reality, or is it art? Many of the early 20th-century artists and filmmakers experimented in ways that cast doubt on the difference.

Walter Benjamin's brilliant essay "The work of art in the age of its technological reproduction" (the second variant, now available in English in Benjamin 2002: vol. III) is a milestone in realizing the implications of this transformation of the significance of the image, now understood not merely as representing the real, but as producing a new reality, a sur-reality: the image in its pure form. The visual image as a film off of objects is recognized as having its own status, along with its own material presence. What I find important for our own historical moment is that Benjamin in his theorizing was inspired less by philosophers and art critics than by the practices of artists themselves—the Bolshevik avant garde and surrealists most intensely. This theorizing of the image world out of artistic practice, instead of fitting art practices into preexisting theoretical frames is, I want to claim, the approach that we need to take today.

Consider the surrealist project, *Un chien andalou*, the short silent film shot by Luis Buñuel and Salvador Dali in 1928, at the dawn of the first sound film—hence the most mature, the twilight stage of silent film—and the same year Benjamin wrote his essay on surrealism. It in fact shows us a world consisting, as he wrote, "one hundred percent" of images (Benjamin 2002: vol. II, 217), film taken off objects as evidence of material reality. These images are not internal and psychic, but non-mental and collectively visible in social space. The objects in the images are real enough, but they do not represent reality. Visible space is legible, but incredible. The same is true of time. The film's sequence jumps forward and falls backward ("once upon a time"; "eight years later"; "sixteen years before"; "in the spring").[140]

The point is that the viewer quickly gives up trying to see the film as the representation of characters, or actions, or a place. Fetish objects: a necktie, a severed hand, a locked box, a dead donkey on a grand piano, ants crawling on an open palm—these images appear to us as full of meaning, while at the same time unmotivated by any subjective intent. Their meaningfulness, their intentionality is objective, not subjective. The filmed objects, while fully perceptible in an everyday way, appear estranged from the everyday. They are the day's residues of dreams, but without the memory of the dreamer who could decipher them.

Benjamin compared surrealist thinking to the philosophical realism of medieval illumination, as "profane illumination." Not as representations of something else but as themselves, these images enter the mind, and leave a trace there. But how can such images provide a *political* orientation? The answer to this question, central to visual studies, implies a *reorientation of aesthetics*.

5. Aesthetics I, II, III . . .

I teach a graduate seminar in aesthetics—not in the art history department, but as political theory. The course concerns itself with the intersection of aesthetics and politics in western critical theory. I have found it helpful conceptually to separate three strands of modern aesthetics (the word means literally the "science of the sensible") because they have different origins, different premises, and different historical trajectories. I call them, plainly enough: Aesthetics I, Aesthetics II, and Aesthetics III (there could be more).

140 For stills of the film, see http://www.kyushu-ns.ac.jp/~allan/Documents/societyincinema-03.htm at *Un Chien Andalou* (accessed 14 July 2010).

All these develop out of western modernity, where empirical experience is the basis of knowledge, and where aesthetics therefore takes on a heightened significance, because in lieu of religious revelation, sensory experience is called on to yield the meaning of life; it is the source of value and existential truth. Western aesthetics has, however, taken very different forms, or better put, it has assumed different *orientations*. Note that these are not stages successively overcome, but related perspectives that have developed parallel to each other, if at different historical speeds and intensities, and all of them exist today.

Aesthetics I is concerned fundamentally with art. It finds a philosophical *Urtext* in Kant's third critique, the *Critique of Judgment*, which became significant in the Romantic era to both artists and political theorists, and has remained a seminal text. The influential art critic Clement Greenberg privileged Kant's self-critical method, justifying the development of modern art, culminating in abstract expressionism, as a working out of Kantian logic: the content of non-representational, or abstract art was visual experience itself in pure form. Moreover, he connected this art (produced by individuals, appreciated by the cognoscenti) with the culture of democracy, at the same time condemning as kitsch both commercial art and political propaganda.

Aesthetics I has outgrown Greenberg's grand narrative. It now includes philosophies of art from Hegel to Derrida. It has expanded creatively to encompass non-western art and new media art, and it addresses the visual cultural context of artworks in a multidisciplinary way. Aesthetics I can be seen to encompass the most progressive methods and approaches of departments of art history that have embraced a certain meaning of visual studies, one for which art, however broadly defined, remains the central object of investigation.

Aesthetics II is the often gloomy brother. It is grounded in the Hegelian distinction between truth or essence (*Wesen*), which is accessible only through concepts, and appearance (*Schein*), which is available to sensory perception. While truth appears, it does so in illusory form—so much the worse for the image. For Hegel, art is logically and historically superseded by philosophy. The legacy of Hegel is to be suspicious of the senses, because they cannot grasp, as does the concept, the supersensible whole. Evidence of the world transmitted by the image is thus necessarily deceiving. Reification is a key concept here: The truth of the object lies behind its appearance. This is Marx's lament: commodities are fetishes worshipped by modern man, preventing knowledge of the true nature of class society.

Thinkers such as Georg Simmel, Sigfried Kracauer, and Georg Lukács elaborated the further Marxian insight that the instrument of perception, the human sensorium, changes with the experience of modernity. The urban metropolis, the factory, the bourgeois interior, the department store—these sensory environments shape perception and determine the degree to which it can lead to knowledge. Aesthetics, no longer equated with art as it was for Hegel, becomes corporeal, or sensory cognition, criticized in its modern form as having the effect, rather, of *an*aesthetics.[141] Aesthetics II infuses traditions of critical sociology, practiced today by social theorists and geographers. The abundant literature criticizing the culture industry belongs here as well.

Postcolonial theory joins the tradition of Aesthetics II when it exposes the ethnographic imaginary of the "primitive" as distorting perceptions that have their origins in western modernity. "The world as staged," Timothy Mitchell has called it, placed on exhibition by the west as the representation of its own superiority. In Mitchell's postcolonial critique, the need, again, is to see past the staged appearance of reality to the mechanisms of colonial control that underlie it. Aesthetics II embraces visual studies through the path of visual culture—cultural studies is the link between its critical theoretical heritage and its empirical, socio-political concerns.

Aesthetics III is more sanguine about the image, approaching it as a key, rather than a hindrance to understanding. Like powerful binoculars, the image intensifies experience, illuminating realities that otherwise go unnoticed. Benjamin spoke of "unconscious optics," discovering in surrealism the "long-sought after image space" for a world of "actualities" and action. He was referring not just to photography and cinema, but to the experience of the city that opens up to the flâneur, and that finds expression as well in Baudelaire's poetry, Bolshevik constructivism and photomontage. Images, no longer subservient to the text as its illustration, are free to act directly on the mind. The collectively accessible assemblage of images is the antithesis of the cult of artistic genius that expresses a private world of meaning. With the affirmative orientation of Aesthetics III, one risks falling victim to the illusions of the society as spectacle, but the risk is worth the promise of illumination.

The image is the *medium* for Aesthetics I. It is the *problem* for Aesthetics II. In discussions of visual studies, Aesthetics III has received far less attention. What are the implications of an orientation of aesthetics that looks to the image for *inspiration*?

Aesthetics III does not search for what lies behind the image. The truth of objects is precisely the surface they present to be captured on film. As Deleuze writes, cinema helps him to think philosophically—and Deleuze is a theorist of visual studies oriented toward the image itself. The political implications of Aesthetics III are suggested by the singularity of the image, its ability to name itself, to propose its own caption, rather than fitting within preexisting frames of meaning. Images, while collectively shared, escape the generalization of the concept, so that we need to come to them to decipher their meaning. In short, we need to see them.

But how, if not by submission to a text, does the image have political effect? Can the radical freedom discovered by the surrealists enable the politicization

141 This was the argument in my article, "Aesthetics and anaesthetics: Walter Benjamin's artwork essay reconsidered" (Buck-Morss 1992).

of the image world without turning it into propaganda? And how are we to relate the image's political effect to its knowledge effect? Can images be disciplined (as an object of visual studies) and still be "free"? Moreover, can this discussion be brought back to the claim made at the outset of this essay that visual studies can contribute to the democratization of culture in the context of the new globalization? Again, let us take the discipline of art history as our point of departure.

6. Discipline

Otto Pächt describes the method of the art historian, for whom "there is always something disquieting about the isolated work of art":

> In art history it is possible . . . to take an art object that has knocked around the world, nameless and masterless, and to issue a relatively precise birth certificate for it . . . Errors and misjudgments quite often occur, but this does not seriously compromise the value of the techniques employed . . . In principle the equation holds good: to see a thing rightly is to date and ascribe it rightly.
>
> (Pächt 1999: 61–62)

But the fact about images is that they do float in isolation, moving in and out of contexts, freed from their origin and the history of their provenance. The superficiality of the image, its transferability, its accessibility—all of these qualities render the issue of provenance ambiguous, if not irrelevant. An image is stumbled on, found without being lost. Arguably most at home when it "knocks around the world," an image is promiscuous by nature.

If visual studies is viewed simply as an extension of art history, then its task would seem to be to apprehend these images and return them to their rightful owners. By the same token, if visual studies is to live up to its democratic *political* potential, this is the point where the methods of these knowledge pursuits may need to go separate ways. In doing so visual studies will take its lead, not from the discipline of art history, but from the contemporary practices of the many artists, globally, who have made the wandering image the very content of their work.

A discipline (as Foucault argued) produces its object as an effect, telling the subject what questions it can ask of the object, and how; and telling the object what about it is meaningful to study (defining the object in ways that make it accessible to the questions posed to it). The confining aspect of a discipline is evident to any student who specializes in one or another of them. The world is not divided into the pie slices that are created by the disciplines, as it is the same world studied in all cases; rather, the way it looks back at the viewer changes as disciplinary boundaries are crossed.

Unlike the other disciplines, an orientation of visual studies that has the image as its object is not a pie slice, not a delineated sector of the world, but a film off of the world's surface. The surface of the image is itself the boundary that allows a certain idea of visual studies to emerge. The image surface immediately sends out two lines of force, one toward the viewer, and one toward (any aspect of) the world. Both lines move away from the surface, so that the image boundary appears to disappear. Objects are in the image, not in their entirety, but as an intentionality, a face turned toward the perceiver. Lines of perception moving across the surface of multiple images traverse the world in infinite direction and variation. Cutting through space rather than occupying it as an object with extensions, image lines are rhizomic connections—transversalities rather than totalities. These image-lines produce the world-as-image that in our era of globalization is the form of collective cognition (image form replaces the commodity form).

7. Possession and the means of production

Nothing gives a stronger sense of the promiscuity of the image, as opposed to the legitimate birth of the artwork, than dragging and clicking from a Google image search onto your computer's desktop—"subject to copyright," to be sure, but no less available for the taking. What do you possess? Given the minimal labor of moving a computer mouse, no *labor* value is added to the image by its procurement. Moreover, without the metadata necessary to interpret the image according to the intention of the artist (or photographer, or cinematographer) the formatting palette on your computer will never get it right. By the standards of the art object, to be sure, the digital copy is irrevocably impoverished and degraded. But if this matters, and should matter, for the discipline of the history of art, for another understanding of visual studies it does not. Benjamin applauded Baudelaire who, when confronted with the loss of aura of the artwork, was content to let it go. The reproducibility of the image is infinite (with digital technology it is instantaneous), and quantity changes the quality, allowing for the reappropriation of the components out of which our image world is formed. The image disconnects from the idea of being a reproduction of an authentic original, and becomes something else.

Separated from its source, disposable, dragged to the trash at any moment, what is its value? And to whom does this value rightfully belong? A computer session is not a day on the beach. To see the value of the image in terms of information, standard in discussions of digital processing, is also misleading, just as referral to a computer menu does not mean that you get something tasty to consume. A computer is a tool.

Unlike the machines of the Industrial Revolution, however, this tool can be personalized: users may be multiple, but they are discreet; access demands a private password. Still, under present conditions, even if you own a PC, it is not quite the same as owning the means of production. The relation is more like outsourcing. For if the work of travel agents, bank tellers, sales clerks and checkout workers is presently being exported (from the USA to India, for example), the ultimate savings of labor costs is when consumers do the work themselves.

The word cybernetics (ancient Greek for the helmsman who orients a ship) was chosen to refer to the capacity of the machine to mimic human thought, although much of the present work demanded by computers is mindless. It demands attention and accuracy, insisting on "autocorrect," hence an inhuman freedom from error, which is another way of saying that it allows only strictly programmed responses.

The so-called information generated in the information age in fact consists largely of instructions, whereby computer users replace service workers by performing tasks that were previously part of production. But if they try to use the computers imaginatively, innovatively, in ways that produce value for *them*, they are just steps away from violation of copyright. They are dangerous as pirates or hackers—net criminals, all.

But in regard to this new means of production, the danger must be tolerated by the global capitalist system. Indeed, the system benefits from the expansion of computer technology worldwide (expansion is not synonymous with equitable distribution). In order for profits to be made, the means of production—computers—need to be put into people's hands. In the process, they learn to appropriate the internet for personal (and political) use, which unlike appropriations of pens and paper from an office supply room, entails taking from sources that are inexhaustible—including music, DVDs, and images of every kind.

Granted, there are setup costs that may be ongoing, but digital archives, Web pages, and data banks are socialized resources almost by definition. Pirates and hackers, unlike the wreckers of old, do not throw a wrench in production, they accelerate it—to a point that escapes the private property relations that undergird the copyright system. This trend seems inevitable. The more anti-piracy legislation and the shriller the rhetoric on its behalf, the greater the indication that the global computer system cannot sustain—and cannot be sustained by—the old bourgeois notions of commodity exchange, whereby the world and its wealth are divided and controlled by exclusive proprietors.

Against the model of Bill Gates, whose software copyrights bring in revenues larger than that of many nations and whose idea of redistribution is limited to personal philanthropy, a socialist ethic appears to evolve naturally from the free, productive use of computer power. Cyberspace is open by definition; private access is to a public good. It is plausible that sharing the inexhaustible resources of the computer will lead to a consciousness that exhaustible resources, too, are collective values that belong in the public trust. If the global monopolies of the culture industry stand to lose against the socializing tendencies inherent in the new technology, they should yield to their own sacred laws of the market and close down business. The music will be better for it.

But if music and movies are still entertainment, hence ruled to a certain degree by commodity logic even without infinite copyright income, the case of the image is different. The force of the image occurs when it is dislodged from context. It does not belong to the commodity form, even if it is found—stumbled across—in that form, as it is so powerfully in advertisements.

Images are used to think, which is why attribution seems irrelevant. Their creation is already the promise of infinite accessibility. They are not a piece of land. They are a mediating term between things and thought, between the mental and the non-mental. They allow the connection. To drag and click an image is to appropriate it, not as someone else's product, but as an object of one's own sensory experience. You take it, the way you take a photograph of a monument, or a friend, or a landscape. The image is frozen perception. It provides the armature for ideas. Images, no longer viewed as copies of a privately owned original, move into public space as their own reality, where their assembly is an act of the production of meaning. Collectively perceived, collectively exchanged, they are the building blocks of culture. Collectors of images like Aby Warburg recognized this when in his ongoing work *Mnemosyne Atlas*, an archive of social memory, he placed images of ancient Greek figures-in-motion next to newspaper photos of women golfers because the folds of drapery of their dress were the same. Walter Benjamin wrote in 1932 that Warburg's library was "the hallmark of the new spirit of research" because it "filled the marginal areas of historical study with fresh life" (Benjamin 1972: vol. III, 374).[142]

These image archives resemble the older print archive that we know as the dictionary. Dictionaries, like data banks, have copyrights, but it would be absurd to claim that their publishers or compilers own the words listed in them. If I copy someone's words, it is plagiarism. If I use the same words for different thoughts, it is not. Indeed, the power of the word-in-use, and what we value in a writer or poet, is the ability to infuse old words with new life. The same holds, or should hold, for images. Of course, a proprietary relationship to the word is exactly what is claimed by trademarks—I cannot type the word Xerox or Apple without the autocorrect software capitalizing it to indicate possession. But the moral concept that functions legitimately here is accountability rather than property. Trademarks not only have a marketing function; they hold the producer responsible to the public who can be deceived by falsely naming. As the importance of private property wanes, that of public accountability will need to intensify.

Images, then, are not art copies and they do not replace the art experience. As tools of thought, their value-producing potential demands their creative use. Both in their original form and in what is made of them, this value

142 Gerhard Richter's *Atlas* (583 panels) is a similar collection, and provided the image material for his 1995 paintings.

requires, rightly, that we acknowledge those artists, or others who made them—they deserve our credit (the word means faith, trust, approval, honor), not our cash.

Imagine you are searching online some of the famous pictures taken by Walker Evans in 1936 (with a Google search "walker evans hale county") and you find instead one of Sherrie Levine's reprints of Evans' original pictures. Whose property is this? Is it Sherrie Levine's from "After Walker Evans," her series of photographs published in the early 1980s? Or is it Walker Evans'? Might it not as well be the property of the person whose face is depicted? Or is it my property, as I think, and ask you to think with me, about the image? If I post my private photo on the web, is it public? Can I own a copyright on it, or does it have no value? Who decides? Let us come back to our image search. I was looking in vain for Sherry Levine's photograph, until I realized that it would be posted under Walker Evans. His photograph, taken with government funds as part of the FSA project of 1930s, is "owned" by the US Library of Congress (and therefore by me as a tax-paying, US citizen?). Who is accountable for this image? Whom do I credit, if not the website from which I dragged it into a slide presentation?

8. The sur-face of the image

We have argued that the image does not represent an object. Rather, objects are in the image, not in their entirety but as an image trace, at one unique instant when the objects are caught, taken, apprehended. They show a face, a sur-face. We have said that this surface of images is a boundary that shifts a certain idea of visual studies away from the discipline of art history—a boundary that itself becomes the object of critical reflection. We can develop this idea of the image sur-face, describing its implications.

Even when they are accessed as streaming video, images are frozen perceptions. They can be manipulated, but the result is still a new image, a new perception. Once a perception is fixed, its meaning is set in motion. Manipulation occurs on the surface of an image, not its source. Only if we are concerned with the image as representation of an object are we deceived, or the object maligned.

The one-time-only, unique nature of this perceptual moment captured in the image contrasts sharply with its infinite reproduceability. An image is shared. As with a word, this sharing is the precondition for its value.

Images are the archive of collective memory. The 20th century distinguishes itself from all previous centuries because it has left a photographic trace. What is seen only once and recorded, can be perceived any time and by all. History becomes the shared singularity of an event.

The complaint that images are taken out of context (cultural context, artistic intention, previous contexts of any sort) is not valid. To struggle to bind them again to their source is not only impossible (as it actually produces a new meaning); it is to miss what is powerful about them, their capacity to generate meaning, and not merely to transmit it.

The image establishes a specific relationship between the singular and the universal. An image can be taken off any object—landscape, human face, artwork, sewer, molecule, growing plant, a ghost, or an unidentified flying object. In an image, one particular face of a person, place or thing is fixed as a surface and set loose, set in motion around the world, whereas the person, place, or thing cannot itself move in this multiplying and speedy fashion.

Images are sent as postcards, satellite transmitted, photocopied, digitalized, downloaded, and dragged. They find their viewers. We can observe people around the globe observing the same images (a news photo, a movie, the documentation of a catastrophe). The political consequences are not automatically progressive.

Meaning will not stick to the image. It will depend on its deployment, not its source. Hermeneutics shifts its orientation away from historical or cultural or authorial/artistic intent, and toward the image event, the constantly moving perception. Understanding relies on empathy that mimics the look of the image. A new kind of global community becomes possible—and also a new kind of hate. People are in contact as a collective of viewers who do not know one another, cannot speak to one another, do not understand one another's contexts. Mimesis can be ridicule as well as admiration, stereotype rather than empathic identification.

9. Conclusion(s)

Here are three variants of a conclusion to this essay (there could be more).

9.1 The Bubble Problem (Aesthetics II meets Aesthetics III)

In the global image world those in power produce a narrative code. The close fit between image and code within the narrative bubble engenders the collective autism of television news. Meanings are not negotiated; they are imposed. We know the meaning of an event before we see it. We cannot see except in this blinded way.

Escape from the bubble is not to "reality," but to another image realm. The promiscuity of the image allows for leaks. Images flow outside the bubble into an aesthetic field not contained by the official narration of power. The image that refuses to stay put in the context of this narration is disruptive (see also Lara's power of the feminist "disclosive imagination" elsewhere in this volume). We have no more startling example of this than the image event of the Abu-Ghraib prison. With digital and video cameras, 1800 images were produced, capable of instant, global circulation on the internet. The images of US soldiers, both men and women, humiliating and abusing Iraqi prisoners were described by members of the Bush administration as "radioactive," and in fact their leak did not merely disrupt the official narrative, it caused a meltdown, exploding the myth of the US preemptive war as a moral struggle of good against evil. After all attempts at censorship and control, all the embedded journalism that characterized the war itself, this image event, produced unwittingly by a few individuals acting under orders, exploded the entire fantasy, simply blew it apart. Its effect was no less deadly to the US war effort than a guerrilla attack on an oil pipeline or an army transport. In destroying the Bush regime's credibility and undermining its legitimacy, it was arguably more destructive.

State terror is viscerally present in these photographs. As a film taken off the bodies of the prisoners and the perpetrators, terror continues to exist in these images. They do not represent terror; they are terrifying. The terror multiplies precisely because meaning will not stick to these images. (What in some circumstances allows for playfulness here multiplies the terror.) As they circulate, these images do harm. They must be made public to expose the dangerous despotism of the Bush regime. But their publication, in fact, delivers on the intended threat of the torturers: not just families and neighbors, but the whole world sees these beautiful young men humiliated, their bodies defamed. By viewing them, we complete the torture and fulfill the terror against them.

9.2 Art on the surface (Aesthetics III meets Aesthetics I)

The image world is the surface of globalization. It is our shared world. Impoverished, dim, superficial, this image surface is all we have of shared experience. Otherwise we do not share a world. The task is not to get behind the image surface but to stretch it, enrich it, give it definition, give it time. A new culture opens here on the line. We have to build that culture. We can follow the lead of creative practitioners who are already deploying themselves on the image surface in art, cinema and new media—the great experimental laboratories of the image. Their work gives back to us the sensory perception of a world that has been covered over by official narratives and anaesthetized within the bubble. They lead the way for visual studies as an aesthetics, a critical science of the sensible, that does not reject the image world but inhabits it and works for its reorientation.

Exemplary of such transformation of the image surface is the work by Joana Hadjithomas and Khalil Joreige, Lebanese artists whose *Wonder Beirut* tells the fictional "Story of a pyromaniac photographer" who produces postcards for the Ministry of Tourism until the 1976 Civil War in Lebanon destroys his studio. He rescues the negatives. He begins to damage them, burning them, and "making them correspond to his shattered reality." The artists' work gives evidence of this fictional account as a series of images that transform postcard clichés (Aesthetics II!) into a moving documentation of the psychological experience of urban warfare. One of their images is the cover of *Thinking Past Terror: Islamism and Critical Theory on the Left* (Buck-Morss 2003; see Figure 12.1).

Figure 12.1 Book cover of *Thinking Past Terror: Islam and Critical Theory* (London, Verso, 2003), with a detail from Joana Hadjithomas and Khalil Joreige, *Wonder Beirut, Novel of a Pyromaniac Photographer*, 1998–2002. (Reproduced with permission.)

Consider also the video/performance piece by Elias Khoury and Rabih Mroué, *Three Posters* (2000), created after a video cassette fell into their hands, a tape made by a Lebanese resistance fighter in August 1985, hours before he carried out his suicide attack against the occupying Israeli army (see Figure 12.2). What draws the artists' attention is the fact that this video is a series of takes, done three times before the camera: "I am the martyred comrade Jamal Satti." Announcing his own being-dead, "his words betray him, hesitating and stumbling between his lips. His gaze is unable to focus, it wavers and gets

Figure 12.2 Video still from Elias Khoury and Rabih Mroué, *Three Posters*, 2000. (Reproduced with artists' permission.)

lost." The artists intersperse the three takes with performers playing Satti, the Communist politician who acts behind him, a performer as himself. The event becomes a laboratory for the analysis of the video image, exploratory, testing, slowing down the politics of spectacle, the time between life and death, and allowing the full play of repetitions to reveal "a desire for the deferral of death, in these depressing lands where the desire to live is considered a shameful betrayal of the State, of the Nation-State, of the Father-Motherland" (Mroué 2002: 117).

9.3 A global public sphere? (Aesthetics I, II and III as a place of politics)

On February 15, 2003, an internet-organized global demonstration took place to protest the imminent US preemptive invasion of Iraq. Several hundred cities took part in this collective performance, producing a planetary wave of solidarity that moved with the sun from east to west. Evidence of this image event was collected on the website www.punchdown.org/rvb/F15. It created an archive of over 200 images showing the global desire for peace. It can be downloaded by anyone, anywhere—and it is free for the taking (although the publisher does not want to print it here).

Finally, these questions: Scholars have argued that the architecture of cathedrals, temples, and mosques creates a sense of the community of believers through the ritual practices of everyday life. Benedict Anderson has claimed that the mass readership of newspapers and novels creates an imagined community of the nation. *What kind of community can we hope for from a global dissemination of images, and how can our work help to create it?*

References

Benjamin, W. 1972, *Gesammelte Schriften*, Band III, Frankfurt, Suhrkamp.

—— 1999, 'Surrealism: the last snapshot of the European intelligentsia', in *Selected Writings, II* (trans. R. Livingstone et al.), Cambridge, MA, London, Belknap Press, pp. 76–100.

—— 2002, 'The work of art in the age of its reproducibility', in *Selected Writings, III* (trans. E. Jephcott et al.), Cambridge, MA, London, Belknap Press Harvard University Press, pp. 101–133.

Buck-Morss, S. 1992, 'Aesthetics and anaesthetics: Walter Benjamin's artwork essay reconsidered', *October*, 62 (Fall): 3–41.

—— 2003, *Thinking Past Terror. Islamism and Critical Theory on the Left*, London, New York, Verso.

Danto, A. 1984, 'The end of art', in Berel, L. (ed.) *The Death of Art*, New York, Haven.

Kristeva, J. 2003, 'The future of a defeat: Julia Kristeva interviewed by Arnauld Spire', *Parallax*, 9 (2, April–June).

Mroué, R. 2002, 'The fabrication of truth', in Chakar, T. et al. (eds) *Tamáss 1: Contemporary Arab Representations*, Beirut, Lebanon, Rotterdam, de Witte and Fundacio Antoni Tapies.

Pächt, O. 1999, *The Practice of Art History: Reflection on Method* (trans. D. Britt), London, Harvey Miller.

Index

Page numbers in **bold** represent figures.